Paul D. Allison

SURVIVAL ANALYSIS USING THE SAS® SYSTEM

A PRACTICAL GUIDE

The correct bibliographic citation for this manual is as follows: Allison, Paul D., *Survival Analysis Using the SAS® System: A Practical Guide*, Cary, NC: SAS Institute Inc., 1995. 292 pp.

Survival Analysis Using the SAS® System: A Practical Guide

ACKNOWLEDGMENTS

Many people provided useful comments on earlier versions of this book. I particularly want to thank Nicholas Christakis, Theodore Venet, and the participants in my 1994 and 1995 summer workshops on survival analysis. For permission to use data, I am indebted to Nicolas van de Walle, Henry Bienen, Kenneth Lenihan, and Scott Long. Stephen Lagakos helped me clarify some of the ideas in Chapter 6. I am especially grateful to the reviewers who discovered several errors and made numerous suggestions for improvements: Bruce Turnbull, Michael Phelan, Donna Neuberg, Ying So, Michael Stockstill, Gordon Johnston, and Annette Sanders. I take full responsibility, of course, for any errors that remain. My editor, Judy Whatley, was unfailingly efficient, helpful, and pleasant.

CONTENTS

ACKNOWLEDGMENTS **iii**

Chapter 1 Introduction   1

p. **1** *What is Survival Analysis?*

p. **2** *What is Survival Data?*

p. **4** *Why Use Survival Analysis?*

p. **5** *Approaches to Survival Analysis*

p. **6** *What You Need to Know*

p. **7** *Computing Notes*

Chapter 2 Basic Concepts of Survival Analysis   9

p. **9** *Introduction*

p. **9** *Censoring*

p. **14** *Describing Survival Distributions*

p. **17** *Interpretations of the Hazard Function*

p. **19** *Some Simple Hazard Models*

p. **22** *The Origin of Time*

p. **25** *Data Structure*

Chapter 3 Estimating and Comparing Survival Curves with PROC LIFETEST   29

p. **29** *Introduction*

p. **30** *The Kaplan-Meir Method*

p. **36** *Testing for Differences in Survivor Functions*

p. **41** *The Life-Table Method*

p. **49** *Life Tables from Grouped Data*

p. **52** *Testing for the Effects of Covariates*

p. **56** *Log Survival and Smoothed Hazard Plots*

p. **59** *Conclusion*

Chapter 4 Estimating Parametric Regression Models with PROC LIFEREG   61

p. 61 *Introduction*

p. 62 *The Accelerated Failure Time Model*

p. 66 *Alternative Distributions*

p. 78 *Categorical Variables and the CLASS Statement*

p. 79 *Maximum Likelihood Estimation*

p. 85 *Hypothesis Tests*

p. 88 *Goodness-of-Fit Tests with the Likelihood-Ratio Statistic*

p. 91 *Graphical Methods for Evaluating Model Fit*

p. 97 *Left Censoring and Interval Censoring*

p.101 *Generating Predictions and Hazard Functions*

p.104 *The Piecewise Exponential Model*

p.109 *Conclusion*

Chapter 5 Estimating Cox Regression Models with PROC PHREG   111

p.111 *Introduction*

p.113 *The Proportional Hazards Model*

p.114 *Partial Likelihood*

p.127 *Tied Data*

p.138 *Time-Dependent Covariates*

p.154 *Cox Models with Nonproportional Hazards*

p.155 *Interactions with Time as Time-Dependent Covariates*

p.158 *Nonproportionality via Stratification*

p.161 *Left Truncation and Late Entry into the Risk Set*

p.165 *Estimating Survivor Functions*

p.173 *Residuals and Influence Statistics*

p.181 *Testing Linear Hypotheses with the TEST Statement*

p.183 *Conclusion*

Chapter 6 Competing Risks   185

p.185 *Introduction*

p.186 *Type-Specific Hazards*

p.189 *Time in Power for Leaders of Countries: Example*

p.190 *Estimates and Tests without Covariates*

p.195 *Covariate Effects via Cox Models*

p.200 *Accelerated Failure Time Models*

p.206 *An Alternative Approach to Multiple Event Types*

p.208 *Conclusion*

Chapter 7 Analysis of Tied or Discrete Data with the LOGISTIC, PROBIT, and GENMOD Procedures   211

p.211 *Introduction*
p.212 *The Logit Model for Discrete Time*
p.216 *The Complementary Log-Log Model for Continuous-Time Processes*
p.219 *Data with Time-Dependent Covariates*
p.223 *Issues and Extensions*
p.231 *Conclusion*

Chapter 8 Heterogeneity, Repeated Events, and Other Topics   233

p.233 *Introduction*
p.233 *Unobserved Heterogeneity*
p.236 *Repeated Events*
p.247 *Generalized R^2*
p.249 *Sensitivity Analysis for Informative Censoring*

Chapter 9 A Guide for the Perplexed   253

p.253 *How to Choose a Method*
p.256 *Conclusion*

Appendix 1 Macro Programs   259

p.259 *Introduction*
p.259 *The SMOOTH Macro*
p.261 *The LIFEHAZ Macro*
p.263 *The PREDICT Macro*
p.264 *The WLW Macro*

Appendix 2 Data Sets   **269**

p.269   *Introduction*

p.269   *The MYEL Data Set: Myelomatosis Patients*

p.270   *The RECID Data Set: Arrest Times for Released Prisoners*

p.271   *The STAN Data Set: Stanford Heart Transplant Patients*

p.272   *The BREAST Data Set: Survival Data for Breast Cancer Patients*

p.272   *The JOBDUR Data Set: Durations of Jobs*

p.272   *The ALCO Data Set: Survival of Cirrhosis Patients*

p.273   *The LEADERS Data Set: Time in Power for Leaders of Countries*

p.274   *The RANK Data Set: Promotions in Rank for Biochemists*

p.275   *The JOBMULT Data Set: Repeated Job Changes*

References   **277**

Index   **283**

CHAPTER 1
Introduction

p. **1** *What is Survival Analysis?*

p. **2** *What is Survival Data?*

p. **4** *Why Use Survival Analysis?*

p. **5** *Approaches to Survival Analysis*

p. **6** *What You Need to Know*

p. **7** *Computing Notes*

WHAT IS SURVIVAL ANALYSIS?

Survival analysis is a class of statistical methods for studying the occurrence and timing of events. These methods are most often applied to the study of deaths. In fact, they were originally designed for that purpose, which explains the name survival analysis. That name is somewhat unfortunate, however, because it encourages a highly restricted view of the potential applications of these methods. Survival analysis is extremely useful for studying many different kinds of events in both the social and natural sciences, including the onset of disease, equipment failures, earthquakes, automobile accidents, stock market crashes, revolutions, job terminations, births, marriages, divorces, promotions, retirements, and arrests. Because these methods have been adapted—and sometimes independently discovered—by researchers in several different fields, they also go by several different names: event history analysis (sociology), reliability analysis (engineering), failure time analysis (engineering), duration analysis (economics), and transition analysis (economics). These different names don't imply any real difference in techniques, although different disciplines may emphasize slightly different approaches. Since survival analysis is the name that is most widely used and recognized, it is the name I use here.

This book is about doing survival analysis with the SAS System. I have also written an introduction to survival analysis that is not oriented toward a specific statistical package (Allison 1984), but I prefer the approach taken here. To learn any kind of statistical analysis, you need to see how it's actually performed in some detail. And to do that, you must use a particular computer program. But which one? Although I have performed survival analysis with many different statistical packages, SAS is the one I currently use for both research and teaching. One reason is its wide availability and portability—I can be reasonably confident that my students will have access to SAS wherever they go or whatever machine they use. More important, I am convinced that SAS currently has the most comprehensive set of full-featured procedures for doing survival analysis. When I compare SAS with any of its competitors in this area, I invariably find some crucial capability that SAS has but that the other package does not. When you factor in SAS's extremely powerful tools for data management and manipulation, the choice is clear. On the other hand, no statistical package can do everything, and some methods of survival analysis are not available in SAS. I occasionally mention such methods, but the predominant emphasis in this book is on those things that SAS can actually do.

I don't intend to explain every feature of the SAS procedures discussed in this book. Instead, I focus on those features that are most widely used, most *potentially* useful, or most likely to cause problems and confusion. You should always consult the official documentation in the *SAS/STAT User's Guide, Version 6, Fourth Edition, Volume 1* and *Volume 2* or in the appropriate technical report.

WHAT IS SURVIVAL DATA?

Survival analysis was designed for longitudinal data on the occurrence of events. But what is an event? Biostatisticians haven't written much about this question because they have been overwhelmingly concerned with deaths. When you consider other kinds of events, however, it's important to clarify what is an event and what is not. I define an *event* as a qualitative change that can be situated in time. By a *qualitative change*, I mean a transition from one discrete state to another. A marriage, for example, is a transition from the state of being unmarried to the state of being married. A promotion consists of the transition from a job at one level to a job at a higher level. An arrest can be thought of as a transition from, say, two previous arrests to three previous arrests.

To apply survival analysis, you need to know more than just who is married and who is not married. You need to know *when* the change occurred. That is, you should be able to situate the event in time. Ideally, the transitions occur virtually instantaneously, and you know the exact times at which they occur. Some transitions may take a little time, however, and the exact time of onset may be unknown or ambiguous. If the event of interest is a political revolution, for example, you may know only the year in which it began. That's all right so long as the interval in which the event occurs is short relative to the overall duration of the observation.

You can even treat changes in *quantitative* variables as events if the change is large and sudden compared to the usual variation over time. A fever, for example, is a sudden, sustained elevation in body temperature. A stock market crash could be defined as any single-day loss of more than 20 percent in the market index. Some researchers also define events as occurring when a quantitative variable crosses a threshold. For example, a person is said to have fallen into poverty when income goes below some designated level. This practice may not be unreasonable when the threshold is an intrinsic feature of the phenomenon itself or when the threshold is legally mandated. But I have reservations about the application of survival methods when the threshold is arbitrarily set by the researcher. Ideally, statistical models should reflect the process generating the observations. It's hard to see how such arbitrary thresholds can accurately represent the phenomenon under investigation.

For survival analysis, the best observation plan is prospective. You begin observing a set of individuals at some well-defined point in time, and you follow them for some substantial period of time, recording the times at which the events of interest occur. It's not necessary that every individual experience the event. For some applications, you may also want to distinguish different kinds of events. If the events are deaths, for example, you might record the cause of death. Unlike deaths, events like arrests, accidents, or promotions are repeatable; that is, they may occur two or more times to the same individual. While it is definitely desirable to observe and record multiple occurrences of the same event, you need specialized methods of survival analysis to handle these data appropriately.

You can perform survival analysis when the data consist *only* of the times of events, but a common aim of survival analysis is to estimate causal or predictive models in which the risk of an event depends on covariates. If this is the goal, the data set must obviously contain measurements of the covariates. Some of these covariates, like race and sex, may be constant over time. Others, like income, marital status, or blood pressure, may vary with time. For time-varying covariates, the data set should include as much detail as possible on their temporal variation.

Survival analysis is frequently used with *retrospective* data in which people are asked to recall the dates of events like marriages, child births, promotions, etc. There is nothing intrinsically wrong with this as long as you recognize the potential limitations. For one thing, people may make substantial errors in recalling the times of events, and they may forget some events entirely. They may also have difficulty providing accurate information on time-dependent covariates. A more subtle problem is that the sample of people who are actually interviewed may be a biased subsample of those who may have been at risk of the event. For example, people who have died or moved away will not be included. Nevertheless, although prospective data are certainly preferable, much can be learned from retrospective data.

WHY USE SURVIVAL ANALYSIS?

Survival data have two common features that are difficult to handle with conventional statistical methods: *censoring* and *time-dependent covariates* (sometimes called time-varying explanatory variables). Consider the following example, which illustrates both these problems. A sample of 432 inmates released from Maryland state prisons was followed for one year after release (Rossi et al. 1980). The event of interest was the first arrest. The aim was to determine how the occurrence and timing of arrests depended on several covariates (predictor variables). Some of these covariates (like race, age at release, and number of previous convictions) remained constant over the one-year interval. Others (like marital status and employment status) could change at any time during the follow-up period.

How do you analyze such data using conventional methods? One possibility is to perform a logit (logistic regression) analysis with a dichotomous dependent variable: arrested or not arrested. But this analysis ignores information on the timing of arrests. It's natural to suppose that people who are arrested one week after release have, on average, a higher propensity to be arrested than those who are not arrested until the 52nd week. At the least, ignoring that information should reduce the precision of the estimates.

One solution to this problem is to make the dependent variable the length of time between release and first arrest and then estimate a conventional linear regression model. But what do you do with the persons who were not arrested during the one-year follow-up? Such cases are referred to as *censored*. A couple of obvious ad-hoc methods exist for dealing with censored cases, but neither method works well. One method is to discard the censored cases. That method might work well if the proportion of censored cases is small. In our recidivism example, however, fully 75 percent of the cases were not arrested during the first year after release. That's a lot of data to discard, and it has been shown that large biases may result. Alternatively, you could set the time of arrest at one year for all those who were not arrested. That's clearly an underestimate, however, and some of those ex-convicts may *never* be arrested. Again, large biases may occur.

Whichever method you use, it's not at all clear how a time-dependent variable like employment status can be appropriately incorporated into either the logit model for the occurrence of arrests or the linear model for the timing of arrests. The data set contains information on whether each person was working full time during each of the 52 weeks of follow-up. You could, I suppose, estimate a model with 52 indicator (dummy) variables for employment status. Aside from the computational awkwardness and statistical inefficiency of such a procedure, there is a more fundamental problem that all the employment indicators for weeks *after* an arrest might be *consequences* of the arrest rather than causes. In particular, someone who is jailed after an arrest is not likely to be working full time in subsequent weeks. In short, conventional methods don't offer much hope for dealing with either censoring or time-dependent covariates.

By contrast, all methods of survival analysis allow for censoring, and many also allow for time-dependent covariates. In the case of censoring, the trick is to devise a procedure that combines the information in the censored and uncensored cases in a way that produces consistent estimates of the parameters of interest. You can easily accomplish this by the method of maximum likelihood or its close cousin, partial likelihood. Time-dependent covariates can also be incorporated with these likelihood-based methods. Later chapters explain how you can usefully apply these methods to the recidivism data.

APPROACHES TO SURVIVAL ANALYSIS

One of the confusing things about survival analysis is that there are so many different methods: life tables, Kaplan-Meier estimators, exponential regression, log-normal regression, proportional hazards regression, competing risks models, and discrete-time methods, to name only a few. Sometimes these methods are complementary. Life tables have a very different purpose than regression models, for example, and discrete-time methods are designed for a different kind of data than continuous-time methods. On the other hand, it frequently happens that two or more methods may seem attractive for a given application, and the researcher may be hard pressed to find a good reason for choosing one over another. How do you choose between a log-normal regression model (estimated with the LIFEREG procedure) and a proportional hazards model (estimated with the PHREG procedure)? Even in the case of discrete-time versus continuous-time methods, there is often considerable uncertainty as to whether time is best treated as continuous or discrete. One of the aims of this book is to help you make intelligent decisions about which method is most suitable for your particular application. SAS/STAT software contains six procedures that can be used for survival analysis. Here's an overview of what they do:

LIFETEST	is primarily designed for univariate analysis of the timing of events. It produces life tables and graphs of survival curves (also called survivor functions). Using several methods, this procedure tests whether survival curves are the same in two or more groups. PROC LIFETEST also tests for associations between event times and time-constant covariates, but it does not produce estimates of parameters.
LIFEREG	estimates regression models with censored, continuous-time data under several alternative distributional assumptions. PROC LIFEREG allows for several varieties of censoring, but it does not allow for time-dependent covariates.
PHREG	uses Cox's partial likelihood method to estimate regression models with censored data. The model is somewhat less restrictive than the models in PROC LIFEREG, and the estimation method allows for time-dependent covariates. PROC PHREG handles both continuous-time and discrete-time data.
LOGISTIC AND PROBIT	are designed for general problems in categorical data analysis, but they are effective and flexible in estimating survival models for discrete-time data with time-dependent covariates.
GENMOD	estimates the same discrete-time survival models as LOGISTIC and PROBIT. The procedure is also good for estimating the piecewise exponential model (described in Chapter 4).

Although not discussed in official documentation, all of these procedures can be used to estimate *competing risks* models that allow for multiple kinds of events, as described in Chapter 6, "Competing Risks." Only PROC PHREG has special capabilities for handling *repeated* events like arrests or hospitalizations. See Chapter 8 for more details.

WHAT YOU NEED TO KNOW

I have written this book for the person who wants to analyze survival data using SAS, but who knows little or nothing about survival analysis. The book should also be useful if you are already knowledgeable about survival analysis and simply want to know how to do it with SAS.

I assume that you have a good deal of practical experience with ordinary least-squares regression analysis and that you are reasonably familiar with the assumptions of the linear model. There is little point in trying to estimate and interpret regression models for survival data if you don't understand ordinary linear regression analysis.

You do not need to know matrix algebra, although I sometimes use the vector notation $\boldsymbol{\beta}\mathbf{x} = \beta_1 x_1 + \beta_2 x_2 + \ldots + \beta_k x_k$ to simplify the presentation of regression models. A basic knowledge of limits, derivatives, and definite integrals is helpful in following the discussion of hazard functions, but you can get by without those tools. Familiarity with standard properties of logarithms and exponentials is essential, however. Chapters 4 and 5 each contain a more technical section that you can skip without loss of continuity. (I note this at the beginning of the section). Naturally, the more experience you have with SAS/STAT and the SAS DATA step, the easier it will be to follow the discussion of SAS statements. On the other hand, the syntax for most of the models considered here is rather simple and intuitive, so don't be intimidated if you are a SAS neophyte.

COMPUTING NOTES

Most of the examples in this book were executed on a FastData 486 machine running at 33 MHz with 8 MB of memory. I initially used Release 6.04 SAS software running under the DOS operating system, but I later switched to Release 6.08 under the Windows operating system. The examples requiring Release 6.10 were run on a Power Macintosh 7100/80 with 16 MB of memory using a preproduction release of SAS. Occasionally, I report comparisons of computing times for different procedures, options, sample sizes, and program code. These comparisons should only be taken as rough illustrations, however, since computing time is heavily dependent on the software and hardware configuration.

8

CHAPTER **2**
Basic Concepts of Survival Analysis

p. 9 *Introduction*

p. 9 *Censoring*

p. 14 *Describing Survival Distributions*

p. 17 *Interpretations of the Hazard Function*

p. 19 *Some Simple Hazard Models*

p. 22 *The Origin of Time*

p. 25 *Data Structure*

INTRODUCTION

In this chapter, I discuss several topics that are common to many different methods of survival analysis:

- censoring, a nearly universal feature of survival data.
- common ways of representing the probability distribution of event times, especially the survivor function and the hazard function.
- choice of origin in the measurement of time, a tricky but important issue that is rarely discussed in the literature on survival analysis.
- basic data structure required for most computer programs that perform survival analysis.

CENSORING

Not all survival data contain censored observations, and censoring may occur in applications other than survival analysis. Nevertheless, because censored survival data are so common and because censoring requires special treatment, it is this topic more than anything else that unifies the many approaches to survival analysis.

Censoring comes in many forms and occurs for many different reasons. The most basic distinction is between *left censoring* and *right censoring.* An observation on a variable *T* is right censored if all you know about *T* is that it is greater than some value *c*. In survival analysis, *T* is typically the time of occurrence for some event, and cases are right censored because observation is terminated before the event occurs. Thus, if T is a person's age at death (in years), you may know only that $T > 50$, in which case, the person's death time is right censored at age 50. This notion of censoring is not restricted to event times. If you know only that a person's income is greater than \$75,000 per year, that income is right censored at \$75,000.

Symmetrically, left censoring occurs when all you know about an observation on a variable T is that it is *less* than some value. Again, you can apply this notion to any sort of variable, not just an event time. In the context of survival data, left censoring is most likely to occur when you begin observing a sample at a time when some of the individuals may have already experienced the event. If you are studying menarche (the onset of menstruation), for example and you begin following girls at age 12, you may find that some of them have already begun menstruating. Unless you can obtain information on the starting date for those girls, the age of menarche is left censored at age 12. (In the social sciences, *left censoring* often means something quite different. Observations are said to be left censored if the *origin time*, not the event time, is known only to be less than some value. According to the definitions used here, such observations are actually right censored).

In both the natural and social sciences, right censoring is far more common than left censoring, and most computer programs for survival analysis do not allow for left censored data. Note, however, that the LIFEREG procedure *will* handle left censoring as well as *interval censoring*. Interval censoring combines both right and left censoring. An observation on a variable T is interval censored if all you know about T is that $a < T < b$, for some values of a and b. For survival data, this sort of censoring is likely to occur when observations are made at infrequent intervals and there is no way to get retrospective information on the exact timing of events. Suppose, for example, that a sample of people is tested annually for HIV infection. If a person who was not infected at the end of year 2 is then found to be infected at the end of year 3, the time of infection is interval censored between 2 and 3. When all observations are interval censored and the intervals are equally spaced, it is often convenient to treat such data as discrete-time data, which is the subject of Chapter 7, "Analysis of Tied or Discrete Data Using the LOGISTIC, PROBIT, and GENMOD Procedures."

I won't say anything more about left censoring and interval censoring until Chapter 4, "Estimating Parametric Regression Models with PROC LIFEREG." The rest of this section is about the various patterns of right-censored data and the possible mechanisms generating such data. The distinctions are important because some kinds of censoring are unproblematic, while other kinds require some potentially dubious assumptions.

The simplest and most common situation is depicted in Figure 2.1. For concreteness, suppose that this figure depicts some of the data from a study in which all persons receive heart surgery at time 0 and are followed for 3 years thereafter. The horizontal axis represents time. Each of the horizontal lines labeled A through E represents a single person. An X indicates that a death occurred at that point in time. The vertical line at 3 is the point at which we stop following the patients. Any deaths occurring at time 3 or earlier are observed and, hence, those death times are uncensored. Any deaths occurring after 3 are not observed, and those death times are censored at time 3. Therefore, persons A, C, and D have uncensored death times, while persons B and E have right-censored death times. Observations that are censored in this way are referred to as *singly Type I censored*.

Figure 2.1   *Singly Right-Censored Data*

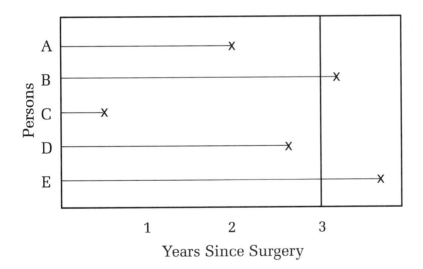

Years Since Surgery

Type I means that the censoring time is fixed (that is, under the control of the investigator), and *singly* refers to the fact that all the observations had the same censoring time. Even observations that are not censored are said to have a censoring time, in this case three years. It's just that their death times did not exceed their censoring time. Of course, censoring times can also vary across individuals. For example, you might want to combine data from two experiments, one with observation terminating after three years and another with observation terminating after five years. This is still Type I censoring, provided the censoring time is fixed by the design of the experiment.

Type II censoring occurs when observation is terminated after a prespecified number of events have occurred. Thus, a researcher running an experiment with 100 laboratory rats may decide that the experiment will stop when 50 of them have died. This sort of censoring is uncommon in the social sciences.

Random censoring occurs when observations are terminated for reasons that are *not* under the control of the investigator. There are many possible reasons why this might happen. Suppose you are interested in divorces, so you follow a sample of couples for 10 years beginning with the marriage, and you record the timing of all divorces. Clearly, couples that are still married after 10 years are censored by a Type I mechanism. But for some couples, either the husband or the wife may die before the 10 years are up. Some couples may move out of state or to another country, and it may be impossible to contact them. Still other couples may refuse to participate in the study after, say, five years. These kinds of censoring are depicted in Figure 2.2 where the O for couples B and C indicates that observation is censored at that point in time. Regardless of the subject matter, nearly all prospective studies end up with some cases that didn't make it to the maximum observation time for one reason or another.

Figure 2.2   *Randomly Censored Data*

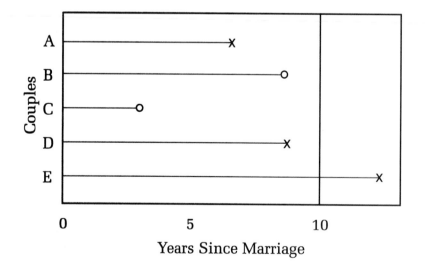

Random censoring can also be produced when there is a single termination time, but entry times vary *randomly* across individuals. Consider again the example in which people are followed from heart surgery until death. A more likely scenario is one in which people receive heart surgery at various points in time, but the study has to be terminated on a single date, say, December 31, 1993. All persons still alive on that date are considered censored, but their survival times from surgery will vary. This censoring is considered random because the entry times are typically not under the control of the investigator.

Standard methods of survival analysis do not distinguish among Type I, Type II, and random censoring. They are all treated as generic right-censored observations. Why make the distinctions, then? Well, if you have only Type I or Type II censoring, you're in good shape. The maximum likelihood and partial likelihood methods discussed in this book handle these types of censoring with no appreciable bias. Things are not so simple with random censoring, however. Standard methods require that random censoring be *noninformative*. Here's how Cox and Oakes (1984) describe this condition:

> A crucial condition is that, conditionally on the values
> of any explanatory variables, the prognosis for any
> individual who has survived to c_i should not be affected
> if the individual is censored at c_i. That is, an individual
> who is censored at c should be representative of all
> those subjects with the same values of the explanatory
> variables who survive to c (p. 5).

The best way to understand this condition is to think about possible violations. Suppose you follow a cohort of new graduate students to see what factors affect how long it takes them to get a Ph.D. Many students drop out before completing the degree, and these observations are randomly censored. Unfortunately, there is good reason to suspect that those who drop out are among those who would take a long time to finish if they stayed until completion. This is called *informative* censoring. In the divorce example mentioned earlier, it is plausible that those couples who refuse to continue participating in the study are more likely to be experiencing marital difficulties and, hence, are at greater risk of divorce. Again, the censoring is informative (assuming that measured covariates do not fully account for the association between drop-out and marital difficulty).

Informative censoring can, at least in principle, lead to severe biases, but it is difficult in most situations to gauge the magnitude or direction of those biases. In the case of graduate student drop out, where the censored

cases are likely to be those who would have had long times to the event, one consequence of censoring is to underestimate the median survival time. Furthermore, if men are more likely to drop out than women, there can be an artifactual tendency for women to have longer survival times than men.

An easy solution to censoring that is random because of random entry times is to include entry time as a covariate in a regression model. This solution should work well in most situations, but it can lead to computational difficulties if a large proportion of the observations is censored.

Unfortunately, there is no statistical test for informative censoring versus noninformative censoring. The best you can do is a kind of sensitivity analysis that is described in Chapter 8, "Heterogeneity, Repeated Events, and Other Topics." Aside from that, there are three important lessons here. First, in designing and conducting studies, you should do everything possible to reduce the amount of random censoring. You can't rely on statistical methods to adjust automatically for such censoring. Second, you should make an effort to measure and include in the model any covariates that are likely to affect the rate of censoring. Third, in studies with high levels of random censoring, you should place less confidence in your results than calculated confidence intervals indicate.

DESCRIBING SURVIVAL DISTRIBUTIONS

All of the standard approaches to survival analysis are *probabilistic* or *stochastic*. That is, the times at which events occur are assumed to be realizations of some random process. It follows that T, the event time for some particular individual, is a random variable having a probability distribution. There are many different models for survival data, and what often distinguishes one model from another is the probability distribution for T. Before looking at these different models, you need to understand the three different ways of describing probability distributions.

Cumulative Distribution Function

One way that works for all random variables is the *cumulative distribution function*, or *c.d.f.* The c.d.f. of a variable T, denoted by $F(t)$, is a function that tells us the probability that the variable will be less than or equal to any value t that we choose. Thus, $F(t) = \Pr\{T \le t\}$. If we know the value of F for every value of t, then we know all there is to know about the distribution of T. In survival analysis, it is more common to work with a closely related function called the *survivor function*, defined as $S(t) = \Pr\{T > t\} = 1 - F(t)$. If the

event of interest is a death, the survivor function gives the probability of surviving beyond t. Because S is a probability, we know that it is bounded by 0 and 1. And because T cannot be negative, we know that $S(0) = 1$. Finally, as t gets larger, S never increases (and usually decreases). Within these restrictions, S can have a wide variety of shapes.

Chapter 3, "Estimating and Comparing Survival Curves with PROC LIFETEST," explains how to estimate survivor functions using life-table and Kaplan-Meier methods. Often, the objective is to compare survivor functions for different subgroups in a sample. If the survivor function for one group is always higher than the survivor function for another group, then the first group clearly lives longer than the second group. If survivor functions cross, however, the situation is more ambiguous.

Probability Density Function

When variables are continuous, another common way of describing their probability distributions is the *probability density function,* or *p.d.f.* This function is defined as

$$f(t) = \frac{dF(t)}{dt} = -\frac{dS(t)}{dt}.$$

(2.1)

That is, the p.d.f. is just the derivative or slope of the c.d.f. Although this definition is considerably less intuitive than that for the c.d.f., it is the p.d.f. that most directly corresponds to our intuitive notions of distributional shape. For example, the familiar bell-shaped curve that is associated with the normal distribution is given by its p.d.f., not its c.d.f.

Hazard Function

For continuous survival data, the *hazard function* is actually more popular than the p.d.f. as a way of describing distributions. The hazard function is defined as

$$h(t) = \lim_{\Delta t \to 0} \frac{\Pr\{t \le T < t+\Delta t \mid T \ge t\}}{\Delta t}.$$

(2.2)

Instead of $h(t)$, some authors denote the hazard by $\lambda(t)$ or $r(t)$. Because the hazard function is so central to survival analysis, it is worth taking some time to explain this definition. The aim of the definition is to quantify the instantaneous risk that an event will occur at time t. Since time is continuous, the probability that an event will occur at exactly time t is necessarily 0. But we *can* talk about the probability that an event occurs in the small interval between t and $t + \Delta t$. We also want to make this probability *conditional* on the individual surviving to time t. Why? Because if individuals have already *died* (that is, experienced the event), they are clearly no longer at

risk of the event. Thus, we only want to consider those individuals who have made it to the beginning of the interval $[t, t + \Delta t)$. These considerations point to the numerator in equation (2.2): $\Pr\{t \le T < t+\Delta t \mid T \ge t\}$.

The numerator is still not quite what we want, however. First, the probability is a nondecreasing function of Δt—the longer the interval, the more likely it is that an event will occur in that interval. To adjust for this, we divide by Δt, as in equation (2.2). Second, we want the risk for event occurrence at *exactly* time t, not in some interval beginning with t. So we shrink the interval down by letting Δt get smaller and smaller, until it reaches a limiting value.

The definition of the hazard function in equation (2.2) is similar to an alternative definition of the p.d.f:

$$f(t) = \lim_{\Delta t \to 0} \frac{\Pr\{t \le T < t+\Delta t\}}{\Delta t}. \tag{2.3}$$

The only difference is that the probability in the numerator of equation (2.3) is an unconditional probability, whereas the probability in equation (2.2) is conditional on $T \ge t$. For this reason, the hazard function is sometimes described as a *conditional density*. When events are repeatable, the hazard function is often referred to as the *intensity function*.

The survivor function, the probability density function, and the hazard function are equivalent ways of describing a continuous probability distribution. Given any one of them, we can recover the other two. The relationship between the p.d.f. and the survivor function is given directly by the definition in equation (2.1). Another simple formula expresses the hazard in terms of the p.d.f. and the survivor function:

$$h(t) = \frac{f(t)}{S(t)}. \tag{2.4}$$

Together, equations (2.4) and (2.1) imply that

$$h(t) = -\frac{d}{dt}\log S(t). \tag{2.5}$$

Integrating both sides of equation (2.5) gives an expression for the survivor function in terms of the hazard function:

$$S(t) = \exp\left\{-\int_0^t h(u)du\right\}. \tag{2.6}$$

Together with equation (2.4), this formula leads to

$$f(t) = h(t)\exp\left\{-\int_0^t h(u)du\right\}. \tag{2.7}$$

These formulas are extremely useful in any mathematical treatment of models for survival analysis because it is often necessary to move from one representation to another.

INTERPRETATIONS OF THE HAZARD FUNCTION

Before proceeding further, three clarifications need to be made:

- Although it may be helpful to think of the hazard as the instantaneous probability of an event at time t, it's not really a probability because the hazard can be greater than 1.0. This can happen because of the division by Δt in equation (2.1). Although the hazard has no upper bound, it cannot be less than 0.

- Because the hazard is defined in terms of a probability (which is never directly observed), it is itself an unobserved quantity. We may estimate the hazard with data, but that's only an estimate.

- It's most useful to think of the hazard as a characteristic of individuals, not of populations or samples (unless everyone in the population is exactly the same). Each individual may have a hazard function that is completely different from anyone else's.

The hazard function is much more than just a convenient way of describing a probability distribution. In fact, the hazard at any point t corresponds directly to intuitive notions of the risk of event occurrence at time t. With regard to numerical magnitude, the hazard is a dimensional quantity that has the form *number of events per interval of time*, which is why the hazard is sometimes called a *rate*. To interpret the value of the hazard, then, you must know the units in which time is measured. Suppose, for example, that I somehow know that my hazard for contracting influenza at some particular point in time is .015, with time measured in months. This means that if my hazard stays at that value over a period of one month, I would expect to contract influenza .015 times. Remember, this is not a probability. If my hazard was 1.3 with time measured in years, then I would expect to contract influenza 1.3 times over the course of a year (assuming that my hazard stays constant during that year).

To make this more concrete, consider a simple but effective way of estimating the hazard. Suppose that we observe a sample of 10,000 people over a period of one month, and we find 75 cases of influenza. If every person is observed for the full month, the total exposure time is 10,000 months. Assuming that the hazard is constant over the month and across individuals, an optimal estimate of the hazard is 75/10000=.0075. If some people died or withdrew from the study during the one-month interval, we have to subtract their *unobserved* time from the denominator.

The assumption that the hazard is constant may bother some readers since one thing known about hazards is that they can vary continuously with time. That's why I introduced the hazard *function* in the first place. Yet, this sort of hypothetical interpretation is one that is familiar to everyone. If we examine the statement "This car is traveling at 30 miles per hour," we are actually saying that "*If* the car continued at this constant speed for a period of one hour, it would travel 30 miles." But cars never maintain exactly the same speed for a full hour.

The interpretation of the hazard as the expected number of events in a one-unit interval of time is sensible when events are repeatable. But what about a nonrepeatable event like death? Taking the reciprocal of the hazard, $1/h(t)$, gives the expected length of time until the event occurs, again assuming that $h(t)$ remains constant. If my hazard for death is .018 per year at this moment, then I can expect to live another $1/.018 = 55.5$ years. Of course, this calculation assumes that everything about me and my environment stays exactly the same. Actually, my hazard of death will certainly increase (at an increasing rate) as I age. The reciprocal of the hazard is useful for repeatable events as well. If I have a constant hazard of .015 per month of contracting influenza, the expected length of time between influenza episodes is 66.7 months.

In thinking about the hazard, I find it helpful to imagine that each of us carries around hazards for different kinds of events. I have a hazard for accidental death, a hazard for coronary infarction, a hazard for quitting my job, a hazard for being sued, and so on. Furthermore, each of these hazards changes as conditions change. Right now, as I sit in front of my computer, my hazard for serious injury (one requiring hospitalization) is very low, but not zero. The ceiling could collapse, my chair could tip over, etc. It surely goes up substantially as I leave my office and walk down the stairs. And it goes up even more when I get in my car and drive onto the expressway. Then it goes down again when I get out of my car and walk into my home.

This example illustrates the fact that the true hazard function for a specific individual and a specific event varies greatly with the ambient conditions. In fact, it is often a step function with dramatic increases or decreases as an individual moves from one situation to another. When we estimate a hazard function for a group of individuals, these micro-level changes typically cancel out so that we end up capturing only the gross trends with age or calendar time. On the other hand, by including changing conditions as time-dependent covariates in a regression model (Chapter 5, "Estimating Cox Regression Models with PROC PHREG"), we *can* estimate their effects on the hazard.

SOME SIMPLE HAZARD MODELS

We have seen that the hazard function is a useful way of describing the probability distribution for the time of event occurrence. Every hazard function has a corresponding probability distribution. But hazard functions can be extremely complicated, and the associated probability distributions may be rather esoteric. This section examines some rather simple hazard functions and discusses their associated probability distributions. These hazard functions are the basis for some widely-employed regression models that are introduced briefly here.

The simplest function says that the hazard is constant over time, that is, $h(t) = \lambda$ or, equivalently, $\log h(t) = \mu$. Substituting this hazard into equation (2.5) and carrying out the integration implies that the survival function is $S(t) = e^{-\lambda t}$. Then from equation (2.1) we get the p.d.f. $f(t) = \lambda e^{-\lambda t}$. This is the p.d.f. for the well-known exponential distribution with parameter λ. Thus, a constant hazard implies an exponential distribution for the time until an event occurs (or the time between events).

The next step up in complexity is to let the natural logarithm of the hazard be a linear function of time:

$$\log h(t) = \mu + \alpha t .$$
(2.8)

Taking the logarithm is a convenient and popular way to ensure that $h(t)$ is nonnegative, regardless of the values of μ, α, and t. Of course, we can rewrite the equation as

$$h(t) = \lambda \gamma^t$$
(2. 9)

where $\lambda = e^\mu$ and $\gamma = e^\alpha$. This hazard function implies that the time of event occurrence has a *Gompertz* distribution. Alternatively we can assume that

$$\log h(t) = \mu + \alpha \log t$$
(2.10)

which can be rewritten as

$$h(t) = \lambda t^\alpha$$
(2.11)

with $\lambda = e^{\mu}$. This equation implies that the time of event occurrence follows a *Weibull* distribution.

Figures 2.3 and 2.4 show some typical hazard functions for the Weibull and Gompertz distributions. Both distributions give the exponential distribution as a special case when α is 0. When α is not 0, the hazard is either always increasing or always decreasing with time for both distributions. One difference between them is that, for the Weibull model, when $t = 0$, the hazard is either 0 or infinite. With the Gompertz model, on the other hand, the initial value of the hazard is just λ, which can be any nonnegative number.

Figure 2.3 *Typical Hazard Functions for the Weibull Distribution*

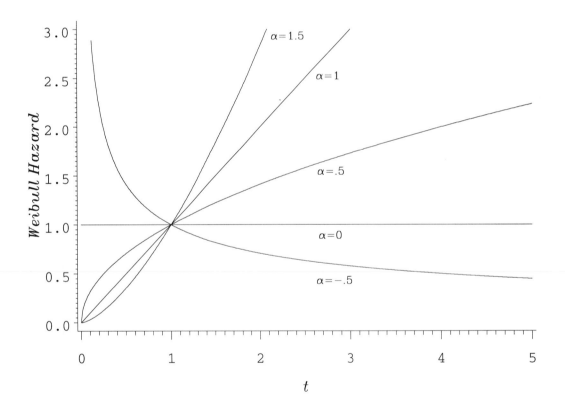

Figure 2.4   *Typical Hazard Functions for the Gompertz Distribution*

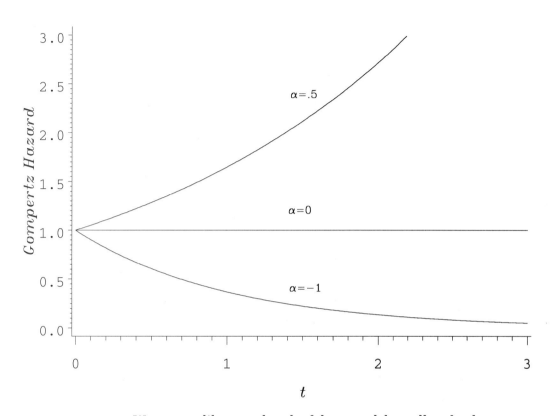

We can readily extend each of these models to allow for the influence of covariates (explanatory variables). Thus, if we have covariates $x_1, x_2,\ldots, x_k$, we can write

Exponential: $\log h(t) = \mu + \beta_1 x_1 + \beta_2 x_2 + \ldots + \beta_k x_k$

Gompertz: $\log h(t) = \mu + \alpha t + \beta_1 x_1 + \beta_2 x_2 + \ldots + \beta_k x_k$

Weibull: $\log h(t) = \mu + \alpha \log t + \beta_1 x_1 + \beta_2 x_2 + \ldots + \beta_k x_k.$

(2.12)

We can estimate the Weibull and exponential models (along with a number of other models) with PROC LIFEREG, as described in Chapter 4. The Gompertz model is not standardly available in SAS. All three models are members of a general class known as *proportional hazards models*. Chapter 5 explains how to use Cox's partial likelihood method to estimate the coefficients of the covariates for any proportional hazards model without having to specify exactly which model it is.

THE ORIGIN OF TIME

All models for survival data are fundamentally concerned with the timing of events. In assigning a number to an event time, we implicitly choose both a scale and an origin. The scale is just the units in which time is measured: years, days, minutes, hours, or seconds. We have already seen that the numerical value of the hazard depends on the units of measurement for time. In practice, however, the choice of units makes little difference for the regression models discussed in later chapters. Because those models are linear in the *logarithm* of the hazard or event time, a change in the units of measurement affects only the intercept, leaving the coefficients unchanged.

The choice of origin (0 point) is more problematic, however, for three reasons. First, it *does* make a difference—often substantial—in coefficient estimates and fit of the models. Second, the preferred origin is sometimes unavailable, and you must use some proxy. Third, many situations occur in which two or more possible time origins are available, but there is no unambiguous criterion for deciding among them.

Consider the problem of unavailability of the preferred origin. Many medical studies measure time of death as the length of time between the *point of diagnosis* and death. Most medical researchers prefer, if possible, to measure time from the point of infection or the onset of the disease. Since there is often wide variation in how long it takes before a disease is diagnosed, the use of diagnosis time as a proxy may introduce a substantial amount of random noise into the measurement of death times. A likely consequence is attenuation of coefficients toward 0. Worse yet, since variation in time of diagnosis may depend on such factors as age, sex, race and social class, there is also the possibility of systematic bias. Thus, if African Americans tend to be diagnosed later than Caucasians, they will appear to have shorter times to death. Unfortunately, if the point of disease onset is unavailable (as it usually is), you cannot do much about this problem except to be aware of the potential biases that might result.

On the other hand, the point of disease onset may *not* be the ideal choice for the origin. If the risk of death is heavily dependent on treatment—which cannot begin until the disease is diagnosed—then the point of diagnosis may actually be a better choice for the origin. This fact brings up the third issue. What criteria can be used to choose among two or more possible origins? Before attempting to answer that question, consider some of the possibilities:

■ *Age*. Demographers typically study the *age* at death, implicitly using the individual's birth as the point of origin.

- *Calendar time.* Suppose we begin monitoring a population of deer on October 1, 1993, and follow them for one year, recording any deaths that occur in that interval. If we know nothing about the animals prior to the starting date, then we have no choice but to use that as the origin for measuring death time.

- *Time since some other event.* In studying the determinants of divorce, it is typical to use the date of marriage as the origin time. Similarly, in studying criminal recidivism, the natural starting date is the date at which the convict is released from prison.

- *Time since the last occurrence of the same type of event.* When events are repeatable, it is common to measure the time of an event as the time since the most recent occurrence. Thus, if the event is a hospitalization, we may measure the length of time since the most recent hospitalization.

In principle, the hazard for the occurrence of a particular kind of event can be a function of *all* of these times or any subset of them. Nevertheless, the continuous-time methods considered in this book require a choice of a single time origin. (The discrete time methods discussed in Chapter 7 are more flexible in that regard). Although you can sometimes include time measurements based on other origins as covariates, that strategy usually restricts the choice of models and may require more demanding computation.

So how do you choose the principal time origin? Here are some criteria that researchers commonly use, although not always with full awareness of the rationale or the implications.

1. *Choose a time origin that marks the onset of continuous exposure to risk of the event.* If the event of interest is a divorce, the natural time origin is the date of the marriage. Prior to marriage, the risk (or hazard) of divorce is 0. After marriage, the risk is some positive number. In the case of recidivism, a convict is not at risk of recidivating until he or she is actually released from prison, so the point of release is an obvious time origin.

   This criterion is so intuitively appealing that most researchers instinctively apply it. But the justification is important because there are sometimes attractive alternatives. The most compelling argument for this criterion is that it automatically excludes earlier periods of time when the hazard is necessarily 0. If these periods are not excluded, and if they vary in length across individuals, then bias may result. (Chapter 5 shows how to exclude periods of zero hazard using PHREG).

Often this criterion is qualified to refer only to some subset of a larger class of events. For example, people are continuously at risk of death from the moment they are born. Yet, in studies of deaths due to radiation exposure, the usual origin is the time of first exposure. That is the point at which the individual is first exposed to risk of that particular kind of death—a death due to radiation exposure. Similarly, in a study of why some patients die sooner than others after cardiac surgery, the natural origin is the time of the surgery. The event of interest is then *death following cardiac surgery.* On the other hand, if the aim is to estimate the effect of surgery itself on the death rate among cardiac patients, the appropriate origin is time of diagnosis, with the occurrence of surgery as a time dependent covariate.

2. *In experimental studies, choose the time of randomization to treatment as the time origin.* In such studies, the main aim is usually to estimate the differential risk associated with different treatments. It is only at the point of assignment to treatment that such risk differentials become operative. Equally important, randomization should ensure that the distribution of other time origins (for example, onset of disease) is approximately the same across the treatment groups.

This second criterion ordinarily overrides the first. In an experimental study of the effects of different kinds of marital counseling on the likelihood of divorce, the appropriate time origin would be the point at which couples were randomly assigned to treatment modality, *not* the date of the marriage. On the other hand, length of marriage at the time of treatment assignment can be included in the analysis as a covariate. This inclusion is *essential* if assignment to treatment was not randomized.

3. *Choose the time origin that has the strongest effect on the hazard.* The main danger in choosing the *wrong* time origin is that the effect of time on the hazard may be inadequately controlled, leading to biased estimates of the effects of other

covariates, especially time-dependent covariates. In general, the most important variables to control are those that have the biggest effects. For example, while it is certainly the case that the hazard for death is a function of age, the percent annual change in the hazard is rather small. On the other hand, the hazard for death due to ovarian cancer is likely to increase markedly from time since diagnosis. Hence, it is more important to control for time since diagnosis (by choosing it as the time origin). Again, it may be possible to control for other time origins by including them as covariates.

DATA STRUCTURE

The LIFETEST, LIFEREG, and PHREG procedures all expect data with the same basic structure. Indeed, this structure is fairly standard across many different computer packages for survival analysis. For each case in the sample, there must be one variable (which I'll call DUR) that contains either the time that an event occurred or, for censored cases, the last time at which that case was observed, both measured from the chosen origin. A second variable (which I'll call STATUS) is necessary if some of the cases are censored or if you want to distinguish different kinds of events. The variable STATUS is assigned arbitrary values that indicate the status of the individual at the time recorded in the DUR variable. If there is only one kind of event, it is common to have STATUS=1 for uncensored cases and STATUS=0 for censored cases, but any two values will do as long as you remember which is which. For PROC LIFEREG and PROC PHREG, which estimate regression models, the record should also contain values of the covariates. This is straightforward if the covariates are constant over time. The more complex data structure needed for time-dependent covariates is discussed in Chapter 5.

The basic data structure is illustrated by Output 2.1 which gives survival times for 25 patients diagnosed with myelomatosis (Peto et al. 1977). These patients were randomly assigned to two drug treatments, as indicated by the TREAT variable. The DUR variable gives the time in days from the point of randomization to either death or censoring (which could occur either by loss to follow up or termination of the observation). The variable STATUS has a value of 1 for those who died and 0 for those who were censored. An additional covariate RENAL is an indicator variable for normal (1) versus impaired (0) renal functioning at the time of randomization. This data set is one of several that is analyzed in the remaining chapters.

Output 2.1   *Myelomatosis Data*

OBS	DUR	STATUS	TREAT	RENAL
1	8	1	1	1
2	180	1	2	0
3	632	1	2	0
4	852	0	1	0
5	52	1	1	1
6	2240	0	2	0
7	220	1	1	0
8	63	1	1	1
9	195	1	2	0
10	76	1	2	0
11	70	1	2	0
12	8	1	1	0
13	13	1	2	1
14	1990	0	2	0
15	1976	0	1	0
16	18	1	2	1
17	700	1	2	0
18	1296	0	1	0
19	1460	0	1	0
20	210	1	2	0
21	63	1	1	1
22	1328	0	1	0
23	1296	1	2	0
24	365	0	1	0
25	23	1	2	1

Although the basic data structure for survival analysis is quite simple, it can often be an arduous task to get the data into this form, especially in complex life history studies that contain information on many different kinds of repeatable events. With its extremely flexible and powerful DATA step, SAS is well suited to perform the kinds of programming necessary to process such complex data sets. Of particular utility is the rich set of date and time functions available in the DATA step. For example, suppose the origin time for some event is contained in three numeric variables: ORMONTH, ORDAY, and ORYEAR. Similarly, the event time is contained in the variables EVMONTH, EVDAY and EVYEAR. To compute the number of days between origin and event time, you need only the statement

```
dur = mdy(evmonth,evday,evyear)—mdy(ormonth,orday,oryear);
```

The MDY function converts the month, day and year into a SAS date: the number of days since January 1, 1960. Once that conversion takes place, simple subtraction suffices to get the duration in days. Many other functions are also available to convert time data in various formats into SAS date values.

CHAPTER **3**
Estimating and Comparing Survival Curves with PROC LIFETEST

p. 29 *Introduction*

p. 30 *The Kaplan-Meier Method*

p. 36 *Testing for Differences in Survivor Functions*

p. 41 *The Life-Table Method*

p. 49 *Life Tables from Grouped Data*

p. 52 *Testing for the Effects of Covariates*

p. 56 *Log Survival and Smoothed Hazard Plots*

p. 59 *Conclusion*

INTRODUCTION

Prior to 1970, the estimation of survivor functions was the predominant method of survival analysis, and whole books were devoted to its exposition (e. g., Gross and Clark 1975). Nowadays, the workhorse of survival analysis is the Cox regression method discussed in Chapter 5, "Estimating Cox Regression Models with PROC PHREG." Nevertheless, survival curves are still useful for preliminary examination of the data, for computing derived quantities from regression models (like the median survival time or the five-year probability of survival), and for evaluating the fit of regression models. For very simple experimental designs, standard tests for comparing survivor functions across treatment groups may suffice for analyzing the data. And in demography, the life-table method for estimating survivor functions still holds a preeminent place as a means of describing human mortality.

PROC LIFETEST produces estimates of survivor functions using either of two methods. The *Kaplan-Meier method* is most suitable for smaller data sets with precisely measured event times. The *life-table* or *actuarial method* may be better for large data sets or when the measurement of event times is crude. In addition to computing and graphing the estimated survivor function, PROC LIFETEST provides three methods for testing the null hypothesis that the survivor functions are identical for two or more groups (strata). Finally, PROC LIFETEST can test for associations between survival time and sets of quantitative covariates.

THE KAPLAN-MEIER METHOD

In biomedicine, the Kaplan-Meier (KM) estimator is the most widely used method for estimating survivor functions. Also known as the *product-limit estimator*, this method had been in use for many years prior to 1958 when Kaplan and Meier showed that it was, in fact, the nonparametric maximum likelihood estimator. This gave the method a solid theoretical justification.

When there are no censored data, the KM estimator is simple and intuitive. Recall from Chapter 2, "Basic Concepts of Survival Analysis," in the section **Describing Survival Distributions**, that the survivor function $S(t)$ is the probability that an event time is greater than t, where t can be any nonnegative number. When there is no censoring, the KM estimator $\hat{S}(t)$ is just the sample proportion of observations with event times greater than t. Thus, if 75 percent of the observations have event times greater than 5, we have $\hat{S}(5) = .75$.

The situation is also quite simple in the case of single right censoring, that is, when all the censored cases are censored at the same time c and all the observed event times are less than c. In that case, for all $t \le c$, $\hat{S}(t)$ is still the sample proportion of observations with event times greater than t. For $t > c$, $\hat{S}(t)$ is undefined.

Things get more complicated when some censoring times are smaller than some event times. In that instance, the observed proportion of cases with event times greater than t can be biased downward because cases that are censored before t may, in fact, have "*died*" before t without our knowledge. The solution is as follows. Suppose there are k distinct event times, $t_1 < t_2 < \ldots < t_k$. At each time t_j, there are n_j individuals who are said to be at risk of an event. *At risk* means they have not experienced an event nor have they been censored prior to time t_j. If any cases are censored at exactly t_j, they are also considered to be at risk at t_j. Let d_j be the number of individuals who die at time t_j. The KM estimator is then defined as

$$\hat{S}(t) = \prod_{j:\,t_j \le t} \left[1 - \frac{d_j}{n_j} \right] \tag{3.1}$$

for $t_1 \le t \le t_k$. In words, this formula says that for a given time t, take all the event times that are less than or equal to t. For each of those event times, compute the quantity in brackets, which can be interpreted as the conditional probability of surviving to time t_{j+1}, given that one has survived to time t_j. Then multiply all of these conditional probabilities together. For t less than t_1, (the smallest event time), $\hat{S}(t)$ is defined to be 1.0. For t greater than t_k, the largest observed event time, the definition of $\hat{S}(t)$ depends on the configuration of the censored observations. When there are no censored times greater than t_k, $\hat{S}(t)$ is set to 0 for $t > t_k$. When there *are* censored times greater than t_k, $\hat{S}(t)$ is

undefined for *t* greater than the largest censoring time. For an explanation of
the rationale for equation (3.1), see **The Life-Table Method** later in this chapter.

Here's an example of how to get the KM estimator using PROC
LIFETEST with the myelomatosis data shown in Output 2.1:

```
data myel;
   input dur status treat renal;
   cards;
      8        1        1        1
    180        1        2        0
    632        1        2        0
    852        0        1        0
     52        1        1        1
   2240        0        2        0
    220        1        1        0
     63        1        1        1
    195        1        2        0
     76        1        2        0
     70        1        2        0
      8        1        1        0
     13        1        2        1
   1990        0        2        0
   1976        0        1        0
     18        1        2        1
    700        1        2        0
   1296        0        1        0
   1460        0        1        0
    210        1        2        0
     63        1        1        1
   1328        0        1        0
   1296        1        2        0
    365        0        1        0
     23        1        2        1
run;

proc lifetest data=myel;
   time dur*status(0);
run;
```

The KM estimator is the default, so you do not need to request it.
To be explicit, you can put METHOD=KM in the PROC LIFETEST statement.
The syntax DUR*STATUS(0) is common to PROC LIFETEST, PROC LIFEREG,
and PROC PHREG. The first variable is the time of the event or censoring; the
second variable contains information on whether or not the observation was
censored; and the number (or numbers) in parentheses are values of the second
variable that correspond to censored observations. These statements produce
the results shown in Output 3.1.

Output 3.1 *Kaplan-Meier Estimates for Myelomatosis Data*

```
                        Product-Limit Survival Estimates

                                     Survival
                                     Standard       Number   Number
      DUR      Survival    Failure     Error        Failed   Left

      0.00      1.0000        0          0            0       25
      8.00         .          .          .            1       24
      8.00      0.9200     0.0800     0.0543          2       23
     13.00      0.8800     0.1200     0.0650          3       22
     18.00      0.8400     0.1600     0.0733          4       21
     23.00      0.8000     0.2000     0.0800          5       20
     52.00      0.7600     0.2400     0.0854          6       19
     63.00         .          .          .            7       18
     63.00      0.6800     0.3200     0.0933          8       17
     70.00      0.6400     0.3600     0.0960          9       16
     76.00      0.6000     0.4000     0.0980         10       15
    180.00      0.5600     0.4400     0.0993         11       14
    195.00      0.5200     0.4800     0.0999         12       13
    210.00      0.4800     0.5200     0.0999         13       12
    220.00      0.4400     0.5600     0.0993         14       11
    365.00*        .          .          .           14       10
    632.00      0.3960     0.6040     0.0986         15        9
    700.00      0.3520     0.6480     0.0970         16        8
    852.00*        .          .          .           16        7
   1296.00      0.3017     0.6983     0.0953         17        6
   1296.00*        .          .          .           17        5
   1328.00*        .          .          .           17        4
   1460.00*        .          .          .           17        3
   1976.00*        .          .          .           17        2
   1990.00*        .          .          .           17        1
   2240.00*        .          .          .           17        0
                      * Censored Observation
```

Summary Statistics for Time Variable DUR

	Point	95% Confidence Interval	
Quantile	Estimate	[Lower,	Upper)
75%	.	220.00	.
50%	210.00	63.00	1296.00
25%	63.00	18.00	195.00

Mean   562.76   Standard Error   117.32

NOTE: The last observation was censored so the estimate of the mean
      is biased.

Summary of the Number of Censored and Uncensored Values

Total	Failed	Censored	%Censored
25	17	8	32.0000

Each line of numbers in Output 3.1 corresponds to one of the 25 cases, arranged in ascending order (except for the first line, which is for time 0). Censored observations are starred. The crucial column is the second—labeled Survival—which gives the KM estimates. At 180 days, for example, the KM estimate is .56. We say, then, that the estimated probability that a patient will survive for 180 days or more is .56. When there are tied values (two or more cases with the same event time), as we have at 8 days and 63 days, the KM estimate is reported only for the last of the tied cases. No KM estimates are reported for the censored times.

In fact, however, the KM estimator is defined for any time between 0 and the largest event or censoring time. It's just that it only changes at an observed event time. Thus, the estimated survival probability for any time from 70 days up to (but not including) 76 days is .64. The one-year (365 days) survival probability is .44, the same as it was at 220 days. After 2240 days (the largest censoring time), the KM estimate is undefined.

The third column, labeled Failure, is just 1 minus the KM estimate, which is the estimated probability of a death prior to the specified time. The fourth column, labeled Survival Standard Error, is an estimate of the standard error of the KM estimate, obtained by the well-known Greenwood's formula (Collett 1994, p. 23). You can use this estimated standard error to construct confidence intervals around the KM estimates.

The fifth column, labeled Number Failed, is just the cumulative number of cases that experienced events prior to and including each point in time. The column labeled Number Left is the number of cases that have neither experienced events nor been censored prior to each point in time. This is the size of the *risk set* for each time point. Below the main table, you find the estimated 75th, 50th, and 25th percentiles (labeled Quantiles). If these were not given, you could easily determine them from the Failure column. Thus, the 25th percentile (63 in this case) is the smallest event time such that the probability of dying earlier is greater than .25. No value is reported for the 75th percentile because the KM estimator for these data never reaches a failure probability greater than .70.

Of greatest interest is the 50th percentile, which is, of course, the median death time. Here, the median is 210 days, with a 95-percent confidence interval of 63 to 1296. An estimated mean time of death is also reported. As noted on the output, the mean is biased downward when there are censoring times greater than the largest event time. Even when this is not the case, the upper tail of the distribution will be poorly estimated when a substantial number of the cases are censored, and this can greatly affect estimates of the mean. Consequently, the median is usually a much preferred measure of central tendency for censored survival data.

You can get a plot of the estimated survivor function by requesting it in the PROC LIFETEST statement:

```
proc lifetest data=myel plots=(s) graphics;
   time dur*status(0);
   symbol1 v=none;
run;
```

The GRAPHICS option requests high-resolution graphics rather than character-based graphics. The SYMBOL1 statement suppresses the symbols ordinarily placed at the data points on the graph. (The data points are apparent from the steps on the graph, and the default symbol (+) just adds clutter). Output 3.2 shows the resulting graph. At each death time, the curve steps down to a lower value. It stops at the highest censoring time (2240).

Output 3.2 *Plot of the Survivor Function for Myelomatosis Data*

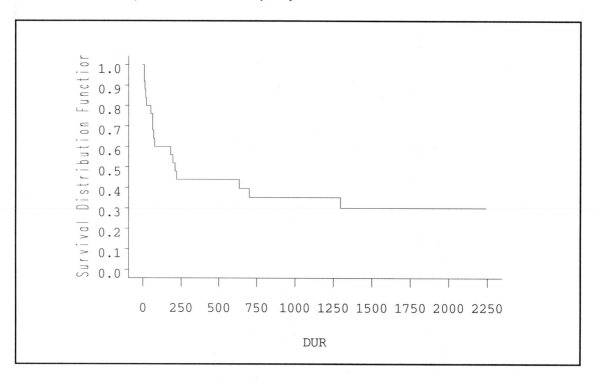

To get confidence intervals around the survival probabilities, you can calculate them by hand using the standard errors reported in the table. However, it's much easier to write the intervals to an output data set. You can do this using the OUTSURV= option in the PROC LIFETEST statement:

```
proc lifetest data=myel outsurv=a;
   time dur*status(0);
run;
```

```
proc print data=a;
run;
```

Output 3.3 shows the printed data set. The two right-hand columns give the upper and lower limits for a 95-percent confidence interval around each survival probability. (To get 90-percent intervals, use ALPHA=.10 as an option in the PROC LIFETEST statement.)

Output 3.3 *Data Set Produced by the OUTSURV= Option*

OBS	DUR	_CENSOR_	SURVIVAL	SDF_LCL	SDF_UCL
1	0	0	1.00000	1.00000	1.00000
2	8	0	0.92000	0.81366	1.00000
3	13	0	0.88000	0.75262	1.00000
4	18	0	0.84000	0.69629	0.98371
5	23	0	0.80000	0.64320	0.95680
6	52	0	0.76000	0.59259	0.92741
7	63	0	0.68000	0.49715	0.86285
8	70	0	0.64000	0.45184	0.82816
9	76	0	0.60000	0.40796	0.79204
10	180	0	0.56000	0.36542	0.75458
11	195	0	0.52000	0.32416	0.71584
12	210	0	0.48000	0.28416	0.67584
13	220	0	0.44000	0.24542	0.63458
14	365	1	0.44000	.	.
15	632	0	0.39600	0.20271	0.58929
16	700	0	0.35200	0.16192	0.54208
17	852	1	0.35200	.	.
18	1296	0	0.30171	0.11498	0.48845
19	1296	1	0.30171	.	.
20	1328	1	0.30171	.	.
21	1460	1	0.30171	.	.
22	1976	1	0.30171	.	.
23	1990	1	0.30171	.	.
24	2240	1	0.30171	.	.

It is important to realize that each of these confidence intervals applies only to a particular point in time. You may be tempted to interpret the entire series of confidence intervals as a confidence *region* such that you have 95-percent confidence that the whole survivor function falls within that region. This is misleading, however, because the probability that a single interval covers the true value may be much higher than the probability that *all* such intervals contain their respective true values. Harris and Albert (1991) describe methods for constructing confidence regions for the entire survivor function, and their book includes a disk containing SAS macros for those methods.

Another problem with confidence intervals is that the calculated intervals may extend outside the bounds of 0 or 1. The usual solution is to truncate the interval at 1 or 0, as with the upper confidence limits for lines 2 and 3 in Output 3.3. A preferable approach described by Collett (1994) is to find confidence intervals for the transformation $\log(-\log \hat{S}(t))$ and then transform the limits back to the original metric.

TESTING FOR DIFFERENCES IN SURVIVOR FUNCTIONS

If an experimental treatment has been applied to one group but not another, the obvious question to ask is "Did the treatment make a difference in the survival experience of the two groups?" Since the survivor function gives a complete accounting of the survival experience of each group, a natural approach to answering this question is to test the null hypothesis that the survivor functions are the same in the two groups; that is, $S_1(t) = S_2(t)$ for all t, where the subscripts distinguish the two groups. PROC LIFETEST calculates two alternative statistics for testing this null hypothesis: the log-rank test (also known as the Mantel-Haenszel test) and the Wilcoxon test. A third test, the likelihood-ratio statistic, is calculated under the additional assumption that the event times have an exponential distribution.

For the myelomatosis data, it is clearly desirable to test whether the treatment variable (TREAT) has any effect on the survival experience of the two groups. To do that with PROC LIFETEST, simply add a STRATA statement after the TIME statement:

```
proc lifetest data=myel plots=(s) graphics;
   time dur*status(0);
   strata treat;
   symbol1 v=none color=black line=1;
   symbol2 v=none color=black line=2;
run;
```

Using this statement has three consequences. First, instead of a single table with KM estimates, separate tables (not shown here) are produced for each of the two treatment groups. Second, corresponding to the two tables are two graphs of the survivor function, superimposed on the same axes for easy comparison. (The SYMBOL statements are optional, but if you omit them, the two survival curves will be distinguished only by color—not too useful for a monochrome printer—and will contain the annoying plus signs at each data point). Third, PROC LIFETEST reports several statistics related to testing for differences between the two groups.

Look at the graphs in Output 3.4. Before 220 days, the two survival curves are virtually indistinguishable, with little visual evidence of a treatment effect. The gap that develops after 220 days reflects the fact that no additional deaths occur in treatment group 1 after that time.

Output 3.4 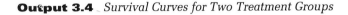 *Survival Curves for Two Treatment Groups*

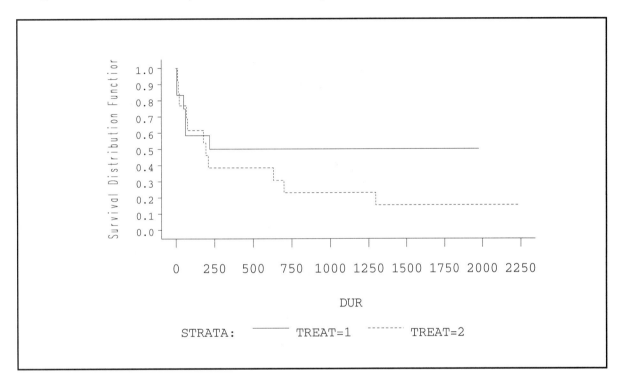

Next, PROC LIFETEST prints log-rank and Wilcoxon statistics for each treatment group, followed by an estimate of their sampling variances and covariances. These are used to compute the chi-square statistics shown near the bottom of Output 3.5. In most cases, you can ignore the preliminaries and look only at the *p*-values. Here they are far from significant, which is hardly surprising given the graphical results and the small sample size. The *p*-value for a likelihood-ratio test is also reported; this test is usually inferior to the other two tests because it requires the typically implausible assumption that the hazard function is constant in each group, implying an exponential distribution for event times.

Output 3.5 *Statistics for Testing for Differences between Two Groups*

```
                Testing Homogeneity of Survival Curves over Strata

                              Rank Statistics

              TREAT            Log-Rank         Wilcoxon

               1                -2.3376            -18
               2                2.337597            18

          Covariance Matrix for the Log-Rank Statistics
              TREAT                    1                 2

               1                    4.16301          -4.16301
               2                   -4.16301           4.16301

          Covariance Matrix for the Wilcoxon Statistics

              TREAT                    1                 2

               1                    1301.00          -1301.00
               2                   -1301.00           1301.00

                  Test of Equality over Strata

                                                 Pr >
              Test        Chi-Square     DF    Chi-Square

              Log-Rank       1.3126       1      0.2519
              Wilcoxon       0.2490       1      0.6178
              -2Log(LR)      1.5240       1      0.2170
```

What about the Wilcoxon test versus the log-rank test? Are there any reasons for choosing one over the other? Each statistic can be written as a function of deviations of observed numbers of events from expected numbers. For group 1, the log-rank statistic can be written as

$$\sum_{j=1}^{r} \left(d_{1j} - e_{1j} \right)$$

where the summation is over all unique event times (in both groups), and there are a total of r such times. d_{1j} is the number of deaths that occur in group 1 at time j, and e_{1j} is the expected number of events in group 1 at time j. The expected number is given by $n_{1j} d_j / n_j$, where n_j is the total number of cases that are at risk just prior to time j; n_{1j} is the number at risk just prior to time j in group 1, and d_j is the total number of deaths at time j in both groups. (This is just the usual formula for computing expected cell counts in a 2×2 table, under the hypothesis of independence.) As shown in Output 3.5, the log-rank statistic in group 1 is −2.3376. The chi-square statistic is calculated by squaring this number and dividing by the estimated variance, which is 4.16301 in this case.

The Wilcoxon statistic, given by

$$\sum_{j=1}^{r} n_j (d_{1j} - e_{1j}),$$

differs from the log-rank statistic only by the presence of n_j, the total number at risk at each time point. Thus, it is a *weighted* sum of the deviations of observed numbers of events from expected numbers of events. (A whole family of such statistics could be constructed by allowing for other possible weights). As with the log-rank statistic, the chi-square test is calculated by squaring the Wilcoxon statistic for either group (−18 for group 1 in this example) and dividing by the estimated variance (1301).

Since the Wilcoxon test gives more weight to early times than to late times (n_j always decreases), it is less sensitive than the log-rank test to differences between groups that occur at later points in time. To put it another way, although both statistics test the same null hypothesis, they differ in their sensitivity to various kinds of departures from that hypothesis. In particular, the log-rank test is more powerful for detecting differences of the form

$$S_1(t) = [S_2(t)]^\gamma$$

where γ is some positive number other than 1.0. This equation defines a *proportional hazards model,* which is discussed in detail in Chapter 5. (As we will see in that chapter, the log-rank test is closely related to tests for differences between two groups that are performed within the framework of Cox's proportional hazards model.) In contrast, the Wilcoxon test is more powerful than the log-rank test in situations where event times have log-normal distributions with a common variance but with different means in the two groups. Neither test is particularly good at detecting differences when survival curves cross.

Now let's see an example where the survival distributions clearly differ across two groups. Using the same data set, we can stratify on RENAL, the variable that has a value of 1 if renal functioning was impaired at the time of randomization; otherwise, the variable has a value of 0. Output 3.6 shows that the survival curve for those with impaired renal functioning drops precipitously, while the curve for those with normal functioning declines much more gradually. The three hypothesis tests are unanimous in rejecting the null hypothesis of no difference between the two groups.

Output 3.6 *Graphs and Tests for Stratifying by Renal Functioning*

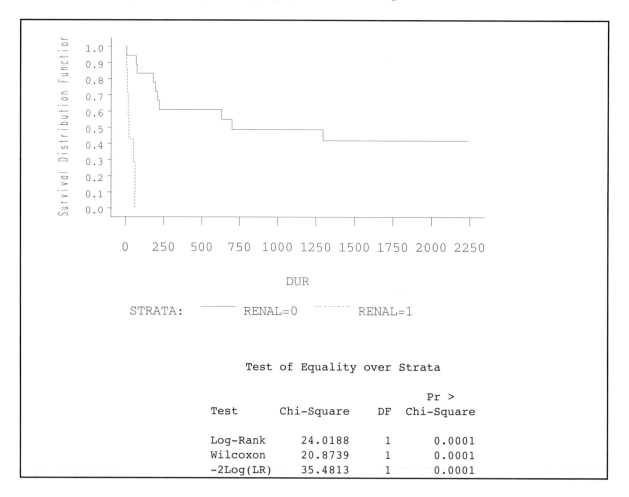

So far, we have only tested for differences between two groups. The tests readily generalize to three or more groups, with the null hypothesis that all groups have the same survivor function. If the null hypothesis is true, the test statistics all have chi-square distributions with degrees of freedom (d. f.) equal to the number of groups minus 1. The STRATA statement provides great flexibility in defining those groups. PROC LIFETEST constructs a stratum corresponding to each unique value of the variable in the STRATA statement. That variable may be either numeric or character. If the STRATA statement contains two or more variable names, PROC LIFETEST constructs one group for every unique combination of values of the variables. In the myelomatosis example, if we had specified the following STRATA statement, PROC LIFETEST would have constructed four groups corresponding to the cross classification of the two treatment groups with the two renal functioning categories.

```
strata treat renal;
```

Of course, with only 25 cases in the data set, it would be unwise to subdivide the sample to this extent. In general, you should be cautious about specifying multiple variables in the STRATA statement because the number of groups can easily grow very large.

For numeric variables, you can use the STRATA statement to define groups by intervals rather than by unique values. For example, if you have a variable AGE, you can specify

```
strata age (20 30 40 50);
```

This statement produces five groups corresponding to the intervals

```
(−∞, 20), [20, 30), [30, 40), [40, 50), [50, ∞).
```

Other options for defining intervals are described in the *SAS/STAT User's Guide*.

Later in this chapter (**Testing for Effects of Covariates**), we'll see how to test whether two groups differ while controlling (stratifying) for another variable.

THE LIFE-TABLE METHOD

If the number of observations is large and if event times are precisely measured, there will be many unique event times. The KM method then produces long tables that may be unwieldy for presentation and interpretation. You can avoid this problem with the life-table method because event times are grouped into intervals that can be as long or short as you please. In addition, the life-table method (also known as the *actuarial method*) can produce estimates and plots of the hazard function, which are not available in PROC LIFETEST with the KM method. The downside to the life-table method is that the choice of intervals is usually somewhat arbitrary, leading to arbitrariness in the results and possible uncertainty about how to choose the intervals. There is inevitably some loss of information as well. Note, however, that PROC LIFETEST computes the log-rank and Wilcoxon statistics from the *ungrouped* data (if available) so they are unaffected by the choice of intervals for the life-table method.

Let's first see what the life-table method produces in PROC LIFETEST, and then we'll discuss some details of the calculations. Output 3.7 displays the first 20 observations from a recidivism study that was briefly described in Chapter 1, "Introduction," in the section **Why Use Survival Analysis?** The sample consisted of 432 male inmates who were released from Maryland state prisons in the early 1970s (Rossi et al. 1980). These men were followed for one year after their release, and the dates of any arrests were recorded. We'll only look at the first arrest here. (In fact, there weren't enough men with two or more arrests to use the techniques for repeated events discussed in Chapter 8, "Heterogeneity, Repeated Events, and Other Topics.") The WEEK variable contains the week of the first arrest after release. The variable ARREST has a value of 1 for those arrested during the one-year follow-up, and it has a value of 0 for those who were not. Only 26 percent of the men were arrested. The data are singly right censored so that all the censored cases have a value of 52 for WEEK.

Output 3.7 *Recidivism Data (First 20 Cases Out of 432)*

OBS	WEEK	FIN	AGE	RACE	WEXP	MAR	PARO	PRIO	ARREST
1	52	1	24	1	1	0	1	1	0
2	52	0	29	1	1	0	1	3	0
3	52	1	20	1	1	1	1	1	0
4	52	0	20	1	0	0	1	1	0
5	52	1	31	0	1	0	1	3	0
6	12	1	22	1	1	1	1	2	1
7	52	0	24	1	1	0	1	2	0
8	19	0	18	1	0	0	0	2	1
9	52	0	18	1	0	0	1	3	0
10	15	1	22	1	0	0	1	3	1
11	8	1	21	1	1	0	1	4	1
12	52	1	21	1	0	0	1	1	0
13	52	1	21	0	1	0	1	1	0
14	36	1	19	1	0	0	1	2	1
15	52	0	33	1	1	0	1	2	1
16	4	0	18	1	1	0	0	1	1
17	45	1	18	1	0	0	0	5	1
18	52	0	21	1	0	0	0	0	1
19	52	1	20	1	0	1	0	1	0
20	52	0	22	1	1	0	0	1	0

The covariates shown in Output 3.7 have the following interpretation:

FIN has a value of 1 if the inmate received financial aid after release; otherwise, FIN has a value of 0. This variable was randomly assigned with equal numbers in each category.

AGE specifies age in years at the time of release.

RACE   has a value of 1 if the person was black; otherwise, RACE has a value of 0.

WEXP   has a value of 1 if the inmate had full-time work experience before incarceration; otherwise, WEXP has a value of 0.

MAR   has a value of 1 if the inmate was married at the time of release; otherwise, MAR has a value of 0.

PARO   has a value of 1 if the inmate was released on parole; otherwise, PARO has a value of 0.

PRIO   specifies the number of convictions an inmate had prior to incarceration.

We now request a life table, using the default specification for interval lengths:

```
proc lifetest data=recid method=life;
   time week*arrest(0);
run;
```

Output 3.8 shows the results. PROC LIFETEST constructs six intervals, starting at 0 and incrementing by periods of 10 weeks. The algorithm for the default choice of intervals is fairly complex (see the *SAS/STAT User's Guide* for details). You can override the default by specifying WIDTH=w in the PROC LIFETEST statement. The intervals will then begin with [0, w) and will increment by w. Alternatively, you can get more control over the intervals by specifying INTERVALS=a b c ... in the PROC LIFETEST statement, where a, b, and c are cut points. For example, INTERVALS= 15 20 30 50 produces the intervals [0, 15), [15, 20), [20, 30), [30, 50), [50, ∞). See the *SAS/STAT User's Guide* for other options. Note that intervals do not have to be the same length. It's often desirable to make later intervals longer so that they include enough events to give reliable estimates of the hazard and other statistics.

Output 3.8 *Applying the Life-Table Method to the Recidivism Data*

```
                    Life Table Survival Estimates

                                           Effective   Conditional
            Interval       Number   Number    Sample   Probability
         [Lower,  Upper)   Failed  Censored     Size    of Failure

              0      10       14        0      432.0       0.0324
             10      20       21        0      418.0       0.0502
             20      30       23        0      397.0       0.0579
             30      40       23        0      374.0       0.0615
             40      50       26        0      351.0       0.0741
             50      60        7      318      166.0       0.0422
```

continued on next page

Output 3.8 continued

Interval [Lower,	Upper)	Conditional Probability Standard Error	Survival	Failure	Survival Standard Error	Median Residual Lifetime
0	10	0.00852	1.0000	0	0	.
10	20	0.0107	0.9676	0.0324	0.00852	.
20	30	0.0117	0.9190	0.0810	0.0131	.
30	40	0.0124	0.8657	0.1343	0.0164	.
40	50	0.0140	0.8125	0.1875	0.0188	.
50	60	0.0156	0.7523	0.2477	0.0208	.

Evaluated at the Midpoint of the Interval

Interval [Lower,	Upper)	Median Standard Error	PDF	PDF Standard Error	Hazard	Hazard Standard Error
0	10	.	0.00324	0.000852	0.003294	0.00088
10	20	.	0.00486	0.00103	0.005153	0.001124
20	30	.	0.00532	0.00108	0.005966	0.001244
30	40	.	0.00532	0.00108	0.006345	0.001322
40	50	.	0.00602	0.00114	0.007692	0.001507
50	60	.	0.00317	0.00118	0.004308	0.001628

For each interval, 14 different statistics are reported. The four statistics displayed in the first panel, while not of major interest in themselves, are necessary for calculating the later statistics. Number Failed and Number Censored should be self-explanatory. Effective Sample Size is straightforward for the first five intervals because they contain no censored cases. The effective sample size for these intervals is just the number of persons who had not yet been arrested at the start of the interval. For the last interval, however, the effective sample size is only 166, even though 351 persons made it to the 50th week without an arrest. Why? The answer is a fundamental property of the life-table method. The method treats any cases censored within an interval as if they were censored *at the midpoint of the interval.* This treatment is equivalent to assuming that the distribution of censoring times is uniform within the interval. Since censored cases are only at risk for half of the interval, they only count for half in figuring the effective sample size. Thus, the effective sample size for the last interval is thus 7+318/2=166. The 7 corresponds to the seven men who *were* arrested in the interval; they are treated as though they were at risk for the whole interval.

The Conditional Probability of Failure is an estimate of the probability that a person will be arrested in the interval, given that he made it to the start of the interval. This estimate is calculated as (number failed)/(effective sample size). An estimate of its standard error is given in the next panel. The Survival column is the life-table estimate of the survivor function, that is, the probability that the event occurs at a time greater than or equal to the start time of each interval. For example, the estimated probability that an inmate will not be arrested until week 30 or later is .8657.

The survival estimate is calculated from the conditional probabilities of failure in the following way. For interval i, let t_i be the start time and q_i be the conditional probability of failure. The probability of surviving to t_i or beyond is then

$$\hat{S}(t_i) = \prod_{j=1}^{i-1} (1 - q_j).$$

(3.2)

For $i = 1$ and, hence, $t_i = 0$, the survival probability is set to 1.0.

The rationale for equation (3.2) is a fairly simple application of conditional probability theory. Suppose we want an expression for the probability of surviving to t_4 or beyond. To obtain this, let's define the following events:

A = survival to t_2 or beyond.

B = survival to t_3 or beyond.

C = survival to t_4 or beyond.

We want the probability of C. But since you can't get past t_4 without getting past t_2 and t_3, we can write $\Pr(C) = \Pr(A, B, C)$. By the definition of conditional probability, we can rewrite this as

$\Pr(A, B, C)=\Pr(C \mid A, B)\Pr(B \mid A)\Pr(A)=(1 - q_3)(1 - q_2)(1 - q_1).$

Extending this argument to other intervals yields the formula in equation (3.2). Note the similarity between this formula and equation (3.1) for the KM estimator. In equation (3.1), d_j / n_j is equivalent to q_j in equation (3.2); both are estimates of the probability of failure in an interval given survival to the start of the interval. The major differences between the two formulas are as follows:

- The number of censored observations in an interval is not halved in the KM estimator.
- The interval boundaries for the KM estimator are determined by the event times themselves.

Thus, each interval for KM estimation extends from one unique event time up to, but not including, the next unique event time.

Continuing with the second panel of Output 3.8, the Failure column is just 1 minus the Survival column. We are also given the standard errors of the Survival probabilities. As with the KM method, these standard errors are calculated by Greenwood's formula, and we can use them to construct confidence intervals around the survival probabilities. The Median Residual Lifetime column is, in principle, an estimate of the remaining time until an event for an individual who survived to the start of the interval. For this example, however, the estimates are all missing. To calculate this statistic for a given interval, it is necessary that there be a later interval whose survival probability is less than half the survival probability associated with the interval of interest. It is apparent from Output 3.8 that no interval satisfies this criterion. For any set of data, there will nearly always be some later intervals for which this statistic cannot be calculated.

The PDF column is an estimate of the probability density function at the midpoint of the interval. Of greater interest is the Hazard column, which gives estimates of the hazard function at the midpoint of each interval. This is calculated as

$$h(t_{im}) = \frac{d_i}{b_i\left(n_i - \frac{w_i}{2} - \frac{d_i}{2}\right)} \qquad (3.3)$$

where for the ith interval, t_{im} is the midpoint, d_i is the number of events, b_i is the width of the interval, n_i is the number still at risk at the beginning of the interval, and w_i is the number of cases withdrawn (censored) within the interval. A better estimate of the hazard could be obtained by d_i/T_i, where T_i is the total exposure time within interval i. For each individual, exposure time is the amount of time actually observed within the interval. For an individual who is known to have survived the whole interval, exposure time is just the interval width b_i. For individuals who had events or who withdrew in the interval, exposure time is the time from the beginning of the interval until the event or withdrawal. *Total exposure time* is the sum of all the individual exposure times. The denominator in equation (3.3) is an approximation to total exposure time, such that all events and all withdrawals are presumed to occur at the midpoint of the interval (thus, the division by 2). Why use an inferior estimator? Well, exact exposure times are not always available (see the next section), so the estimator in equation (3.3) has become the standard for life tables.

Output 3.9 *Hazard Estimates for Recidivism Data*

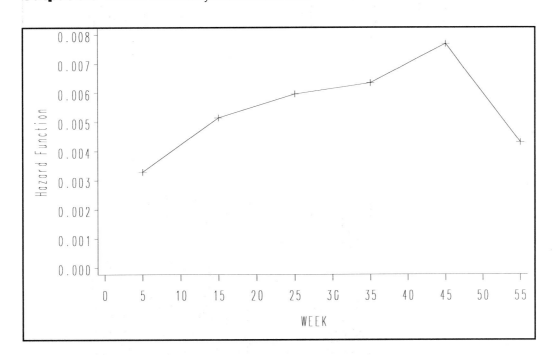

You can get plots of the survival and hazard estimates by putting PLOTS=(S,H) in the PROC LIFETEST statement. Output 3.9 displays the graph of the hazard function. Apparently the hazard of arrest increases steadily until the 50-60 week interval, when it drops precipitously from .077 to .043. This drop is an artifact of the way the last interval is constructed, however. Although the interval runs from 50 to 60, in fact, no one was at risk of an arrest after week 52 when observation was terminated. As a result, the denominator in equation (3.3) is a gross overestimate of the exposure time in the interval.

We can fix this by explicitly setting the last interval to end at 53. (If we set it at 52, the interval will not include arrests that occurred in week 52 because the interval is open on the right). At the same time, it is better to recode the censored times from 52 to 53 because they are not censored *within* the interval but rather at the end. The recode has the effect of crediting the full interval (rather than only half) as exposure time for the censored cases.

Here's the revised SAS code:

```
data;
   set recid;
   if arrest=0 then week=53;
run;
```

```
proc lifetest method=life plots=(s,h) graphics
             intervals=10 20 30 40 50 53;
   time week*arrest(0);
run;
```

The resulting hazard estimates and plot in Output 3.10 show only a slight tendency for the hazard to decline at the end of the one-year observation period.

Output 3.10   *Corrected Hazard Estimates and Plot for Recidivism Data*

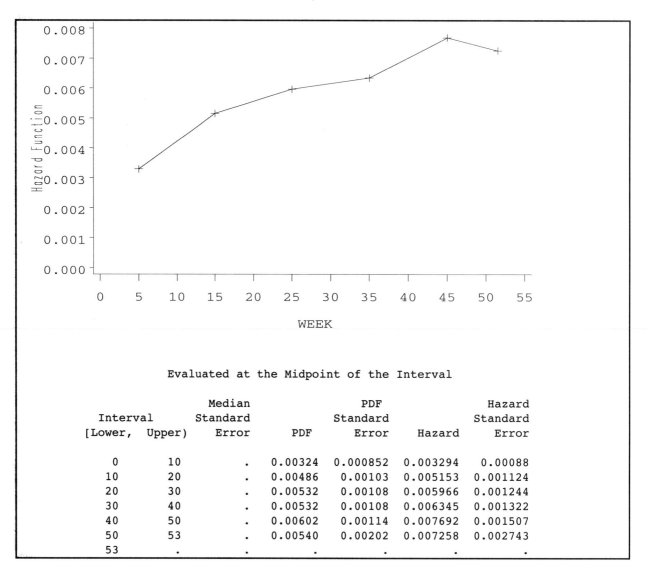

Evaluated at the Midpoint of the Interval

Interval [Lower, Upper)	Median Standard Error	PDF	PDF Standard Error	Hazard	Hazard Standard Error
0 10	.	0.00324	0.000852	0.003294	0.00088
10 20	.	0.00486	0.00103	0.005153	0.001124
20 30	.	0.00532	0.00108	0.005966	0.001244
30 40	.	0.00532	0.00108	0.006345	0.001322
40 50	.	0.00602	0.00114	0.007692	0.001507
50 53	.	0.00540	0.00202	0.007258	0.002743
53	.	.	.	.	.

LIFE TABLES FROM GROUPED DATA

Although PROC LIFETEST estimates survival probabilities from individual-level data with exact event times, you can also easily construct life tables from published data that provide only

- the boundaries of the intervals
- the number of events in each interval
- the number of censored cases in each interval.

Consider the following survival data for 68 patients from the Stanford Heart Transplantation Program, as reported by Elandt-Johnson and Johnson (1980):

Number of Days	Number of Deaths	Number Censored
0-50	16	3
50-100	11	0
100-200	4	2
200-400	5	4
400-700	2	6
700-1000	4	3
1000-1300	1	3
1300-1600	1	1
1600+	0	1

Time is measured from the date of the transplant. Although this sample is rather small for constructing a life table, it will do fine for illustration. The trick is to create a separate observation for each of the frequency counts in the table. For each observation, the value of the time variable (TIME) can be anywhere within the interval—we'll use the midpoint. A second variable (STATUS) is created with a value of 1 for death counts and a value of 0 for the censored counts. The frequency count (NUMBER) is used as a weight variable with the FREQ statement in PROC LIFETEST. Here's the SAS code:

```
data;
   input time status number;
   cards;
25 1 16
25 0 3
75 1 11
75 0 0
150 1 4
150 0 2
300 1 5
300 0 4
550 1 2
550 0 6
850 1 4
850 0 3
1150 1 1
1150 0 2
```

```
       1450 1 1
       1450 0 3
       1700 1 0
       1700 0 1
       ;

       proc lifetest method=life intervals=50 100 200 400 700
                   1000 1300 1600 plots=(s,h) graphics;
          time time*status(0);
          freq number;
       run;
```

Two of the data lines (75 0 0, 1700 1 0) are unnecessary because the frequency is 0, but they are included here for completeness. Output 3.11 shows the tabular results. The hazard plot is in Output 3.12.

The most striking fact about this example is the rapid decline in the hazard of death from the origin to about 200 days after surgery. After that, the hazard is fairly stable. This decline is reflected in the Median Residual Lifetime column. At time 0, the median residual lifetime of 257.7 days is an estimate of the median survival time for the entire sample. However, of those patients still alive at 50 days, the median residual lifetime rises to 686.6 days. The median remaining life continues to rise until it reaches a peak of 982.9 days for those who were still alive 400 days after surgery.

Output 3.11   *Life-Table Estimates from Grouped Data*

```
Life Table Survival Estimates
```

Interval [Lower, Upper)		Number Failed	Number Censored	Effective Sample Size	Conditional Probability of Failure
0	50	16	3	66.5	0.2406
50	100	11	0	49.0	0.2245
100	200	4	2	37.0	0.1081
200	400	5	4	30.0	0.1667
400	700	2	6	20.0	0.1000
700	1000	4	3	13.5	0.2963
1000	1300	1	2	7.0	0.1429
1300	1600	1	3	3.5	0.2857
1600	.	0	1	0.5	0

continued on next page

Output 3.11 continued

Interval [Lower,	Upper)	Conditional Probability Standard Error	Survival	Failure	Survival Standard Error	Median Residual Lifetime
0	50	0.0524	1.0000	0	0	257.7
50	100	0.0596	0.7594	0.2406	0.0524	686.6
100	200	0.0510	0.5889	0.4111	0.0608	855.7
200	400	0.0680	0.5253	0.4747	0.0620	910.5
400	700	0.0671	0.4377	0.5623	0.0628	982.9
700	1000	0.1243	0.3939	0.6061	0.0637	779.6
1000	1300	0.1323	0.2772	0.7228	0.0664	.
1300	1600	0.2415	0.2376	0.7624	0.0677	.
1600	.	0	0.1697	0.8303	0.0750	.

Evaluated at the Midpoint of the Interval

Interval [Lower,	Upper)	Median Standard Error	PDF	PDF Standard Error	Hazard	Hazard Standard Error
0	50	140.1	0.00481	0.00105	0.00547	0.001355
50	100	139.4	0.00341	0.000935	0.005057	0.001513
100	200	124.4	0.000637	0.000308	0.001143	0.00057
200	400	363.2	0.000438	0.000186	0.000909	0.000405
400	700	216.3	0.000146	0.0001	0.000351	0.000248
700	1000	236.9	0.000389	0.000175	0.001159	0.000571
1000	1300	.	0.000132	0.000126	0.000513	0.000511
1300	1600	.	0.000226	0.000202	0.001111	0.001096
1600	.	.	.	.	.	.

Output 3.12 *Hazard Plot for Grouped Data*

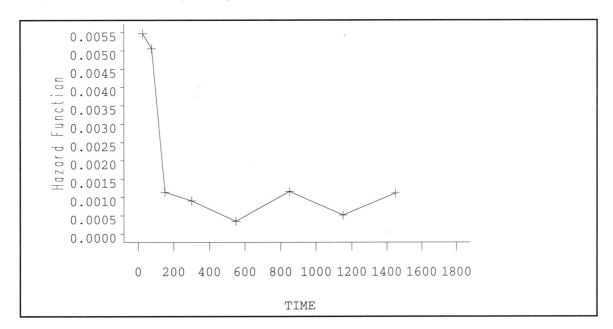

TESTING FOR EFFECTS OF COVARIATES

Besides tests of differences between groups, PROC LIFETEST can test whether quantitative covariates are associated with survival time. Given a list of covariates, PROC LIFETEST produces a test statistic for each one, ignoring the others. It also treats them as a set, testing the null hypothesis that they are jointly unrelated to survival time and testing for certain incremental effects of adding variables to the set. The statistics are generalizations of the log-rank and Wilcoxon tests discussed earlier in this chapter. They can also be interpreted as nonparametric tests of the coefficients of the accelerated failure time model discussed in Chapter 4, "Estimating Parametric Regression Models with PROC LIFEREG."

You can test the same sorts of hypotheses with PROC LIFEREG or PROC PHREG. In fact, the log-rank chi-square reported by PROC LIFETEST is identical to the score statistic given by PROC PHREG for the null hypothesis that all coefficients are 0 (using Breslow's approximation for tied data). In most cases, however, you are better off switching to the regression procedures, for two reasons. First, PROC LIFETEST doesn't give coefficient estimates, so there is no way to quantify the effect of a covariate on survival time. Second, the incremental tests do not really test the effect of each variable controlling for all the others. Instead, you get a test of the effect of each variable controlling for those variables that have already been included; since you have no control over the order of inclusion, these tests can be misleading. Nevertheless, PROC LIFETEST can be useful for screening a large number of covariates before proceeding to estimate regression models. Since the log-rank and Wilcoxon tests do not require iterative calculations, they require relatively little computer time. (This is also true for the SELECTION=SCORE option in PROC PHREG).

Let's look at the recidivism data as an example. The covariate tests are invoked by listing the variable names in a TEST statement:

```
proc lifetest data=recid;
   time week*arrest(0);
   test fin age race wexp mar paro prio;
run;
```

Output 3.13 shows selections from the output. I have omitted the Wilcoxon statistics since they are nearly identical to the log-rank statistics for this example. I also omitted the variance-covariance matrix for the statistics because it is primarily useful as input to other analyses.

Output 3.13 *Covariate Tests for the Recidivism Data*

```
                 Univariate Chi-Squares for the LOG RANK Test

                      Test                                      Pr >
    Variable        Statistic      Variance     Chi-Square    Chi-Square

     FIN             10.4256       28.4744        3.8172        0.0507
     AGE             233.2          4305.3       12.6318        0.0004
     RACE            -2.7093       12.8100        0.5730        0.4491
     WEXP            16.4141       27.3305        9.8580        0.0017
     MAR              7.1773       13.1535        3.9164        0.0478
     PARO             2.9471       26.7927        0.3242        0.5691
     PRIO          -108.8           812.3        14.5602        0.0001


           Forward Stepwise Sequence of Chi-Squares for the LOG RANK Test

                                          Pr >        Chi-Square       Pr >
    Variable       DF    Chi-Square    Chi-Square     Increment      Increment

     PRIO           1     14.5602        0.0001        14.5602         0.0001
     AGE            2     25.4905        0.0001        10.9303         0.0009
     FIN            3     28.8871        0.0001         3.3966         0.0653
     MAR            4     31.0920        0.0001         2.2050         0.1376
     RACE           5     32.4214        0.0001         1.3294         0.2489
     WEXP           6     33.2800        0.0001         0.8585         0.3541
     PARO           7     33.3828        0.0001         0.1029         0.7484
```

The top panel shows that age at release (AGE), work experience (WEXP), and number of prior convictions (PRIO) have highly significant associations with time to arrest. The effects of marital status (MAR) and financial aid (FIN) are more marginal, while race and parole status (PARO) are apparently unrelated to survival time. The signs of the log-rank test statistics tell you the direction of the relationship. The negative sign for PRIO indicates that inmates with more prior convictions tend to have shorter times to arrest. On the other hand, the positive coefficient for AGE indicates that older inmates have longer times to arrest. As already noted, none of these tests controls or adjusts for any of the other covariates.

The lower panel displays results from a forward inclusion procedure. PROC LIFETEST first finds the variable with the highest chi-square statistic in the top panel—in this case PRIO—and puts it in the set to be tested. Since PRIO is the only variable in the set, the results for PRIO are the same in both panels. Then PROC LIFETEST finds the variable that produces the largest increment in the joint chi-square for the set of two variables—in this case AGE. The joint chi-square of 25.49 in line 2 tests the null hypothesis that the coefficients of AGE and PRIO in an accelerated-failure time model are both 0.

The chi-square increment of 10.93 is merely the difference between the joint chi-square in lines 1 and 2. It is a test of the null hypothesis that the coefficient for AGE is 0 when PRIO is controlled. On the other hand, there is no test for the effect of PRIO controlling for AGE.

This process is repeated until all the variables are added. For each variable, we get a test of the hypothesis that the variable has no effect on survival time controlling for all the variables above it (but none of the variables below it). For variables near the end of the sequence, the incremental chi-square values are likely to be similar to what you might find with PROC LIFEREG or PROC PHREG. For variables near the beginning of the sequence, however, the results can be quite different.

For this example, the forward inclusion procedure leads to some substantially different conclusions from the univariate procedure. While WEXP has a highly significant effect on survival time when considered by itself, there is no evidence of such an effect when other variables are controlled. The reason is that work experience is moderately correlated with age and the number of prior convictions, both of which have substantial effects on survival time. Marital status also loses its statistical significance in the forward inclusion test.

What is the relationship between the STRATA statement and the TEST statement? For a dichotomous variable like FIN, the statement TEST FIN is a possible alternative to STRATA FIN. Both produce a test of the null hypothesis that the survivor functions are the same for the two categories of FIN. In fact, if there are no ties in the data (no cases with exactly same event time), the two statements will produce identical chi-square statistics and p-values. In the presence of ties, however, STRATA and TEST use somewhat different formulas, which may result in slight differences in the p-values. (If you're interested in the details, see Collett 1994, p. 284). In the recidivism data, for example, the 114 arrests occurred at only 49 unique arrest times, so the number of ties was substantial. The STRATA statement produces a log-rank chi-square of 3.8376 for a p-value of .0501, and a Wilcoxon chi-square of 3.7495 for a p-value of .0528. The TEST statement produces a log-rank chi-square of 3.8172 for a p-value of .0507 and a Wilcoxon chi-square of 3.7485 for a p-value of .0529. Obviously the differences are minuscule in this case.

Other considerations should govern the choice between STRATA and TEST. While STRATA produces separate tables and graphs of the survivor function for the two groups, TEST produces only the single table and graph for the entire sample. With TEST, you can test for the effects of many dichotomous variables with a single statement, but STRATA requires a new PROC LIFETEST step for each variable tested. Of course, if a variable has more than two values, STRATA treats each value as a separate group while TEST treats the variable as a quantitative measure.

What happens when you include both a STRATA statement and a TEST statement? Adding a TEST statement has no effect whatever on the results from the STRATA statement. This fact implies that the hypothesis test produced by the STRATA statement in no way controls for the variables listed in the TEST statement. On the other hand, the TEST statement can produce quite different results, depending on whether you also have a STRATA statement. When you have a STRATA statement, the log-rank and Wilcoxon statistics produced by the TEST statement are first calculated within strata and then averaged across strata. In other words, they are stratified statistics that control for whatever variable or variables are listed in the STRATA statement. Suppose, for example, that for the myelomatosis data we want to test the effect of the treatment while controlling for renal functioning. We can submit these statements:

```
proc lifetest data=renal;
   time dur*censor(0);
   strata renal;
   test treat;
run;
```

The resulting log-rank chi-square for TREAT was 5.791 with a *p*-value of .016. This result is in sharp contrast with the unstratified chi-square of only 1.3126 that we saw earlier in this chapter (Output 3.5). As we'll see in Chapter 5, "Estimating Cox Regression Models with PROC PHREG" (Output 5.17), you can obtain identical results using PROC PHREG with stratification and the score test.

Clearly, there is no point in listing a variable in both a STRATA and a TEST statement. If you do it anyway, the TEST statement will not give meaningful results for that variable.

LOG SURVIVAL AND SMOOTHED HAZARD PLOTS

PROC LIFETEST produces two other plots that give useful information about the shape of the hazard function, the log-survival (LS) plot and the log-log survival (LLS) plot. In this section, we'll see how these plots help determine whether the hazard function can be accurately described by certain parametric models discussed in Chapter 2. We'll also see how to get smoothed estimates of the hazard function with ungrouped data.

Suppose we specify PLOTS=(S, LS, LLS) in the PROC LIFETEST statement. The S gives us the now-familiar survival curve. LS produces a plot of $-\log \hat{S}(t)$ versus t. To explain what this plot is good for, we need a little background. From equation (2.5), you can readily see that

$$-\log S(t) = \int_0^t h(u)du.$$

Because of this relationship, the log survivor function is commonly referred to as the *cumulative hazard function*, frequently denoted by $\Lambda(t)$. Now, if $h(t)$ is a constant with a value of λ (which corresponds to an exponential distribution), then the cumulative hazard function is just $\Lambda(t) = \lambda t$. This result implies that a plot of $-\log \hat{S}(t)$ versus t should yield a straight line with an origin at 0. Moreover, an examination of the log-survival plot can tell us whether the hazard is constant, increasing, or decreasing with time.

Output 3.14 displays the LS plot for the myelomatosis data. Instead of a straight line, the graph appears to increase at a *decreasing* rate. This fact suggests that the hazard is *not* constant, but rather declines with time. If the plot had curved upward rather than downward, it would suggest that the hazard was *increasing* with time. Of course, since the sample size is quite small, caution is advisable in drawing any conclusions. A formal test, such as the one described in the next chapter, might not show a significant decrease in the hazard.

Output 3.14 *Log-Survival Plot for Myelomatosis Data*

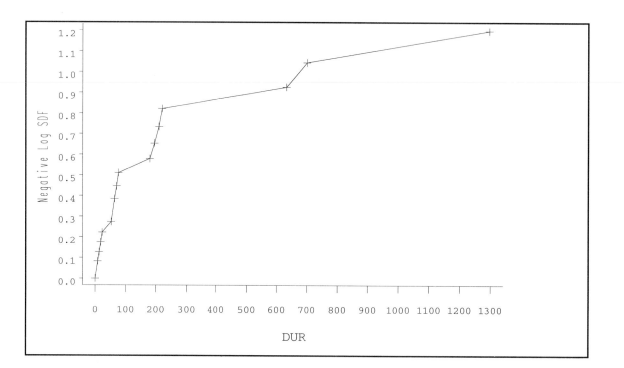

The LLS keyword produces a plot of $\log[-\log \hat{S}(t)]$ versus $\log t$. If survival times follow a Weibull distribution with a hazard given by $\log h(t) = \alpha + \beta \log t$, then the log-log survival plot (log cumulative hazard plot) should be a straight line with a slope of β. Examining Output 3.15, we see a rather rough plot with a slight tendency to turn downward at later times. Again, however, the data are so sparse that this is probably not sufficient evidence for rejecting the Weibull distribution.

In Chapter 4, we'll see how to construct similar plots for other distributions such as the log-normal and log-logistic. We'll also see how to apply the log-survival plot to *residuals* from a regression analysis, thereby testing the fit of the model.

Output 3.15 *Log-Log Survival Plot for Myelomatosis Data*

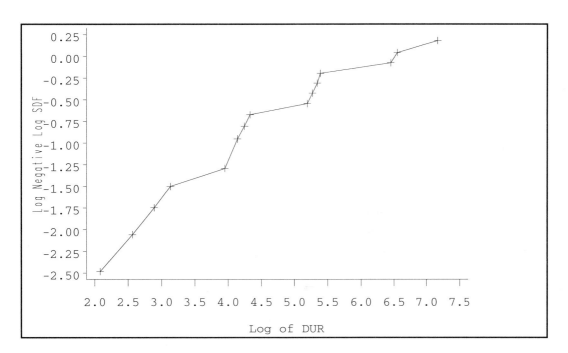

Although graphs based on the survivor function are certainly useful, they are ultimately rather frustrating. What we really want to see is a graph of the hazard function. We got that from the life-table method, but at the cost of grouping the event times into arbitrarily chosen intervals. While it's possible to estimate hazards from ungrouped data, the estimates usually vary so wildly from one time to the next as to be almost useless. There are several ways to smooth these estimates by calculating some sort of moving average. One method, known as *kernel smoothing*, has been shown to have good properties for hazard functions (Ramlau-Hansen 1983). I've written a SAS macro called SMOOTH that calculates and graphs kernel estimates of the hazard function using output from PROC LIFETEST. See Appendix 1, "Macro Programs," for detailed information.

For the recidivism data, you use the macro as follows:

```
proc lifetest outsurv=a data=recid;
   time week*arrest(0);
run;

%smooth(data=a,time=week,width=8)
```

In this example, PROC LIFETEST calculates Kaplan-Meier estimates of the survivor function and outputs them to data set A. Three parameters are passed to the SMOOTH macro: DATA=A gives the name of the input data set; TIME=WEEK provides the name of the variable containing event times; and WIDTH=8 sets the bandwidth for the smoothing function. This means that data points more than eight weeks away from the point being estimated are not used in the smoothing function. This is, of course, an arbitrary choice. In practice, you can try out various widths until you find a value that eliminates extreme choppiness but still leaves distinctive features of the curve. If you do not specify a value for WIDTH, SMOOTH uses one-fifth the range of the event times, which is often a pretty good start.

Output 3.16 shows the smoothed hazard function. The graph bears some resemblance to the grouped hazard estimates in Output 3.10, although here we see a rather pronounced trough at about 27 weeks. Note that the graph is truncated at about 8 weeks and 44 weeks. To avoid artifactual peaks or dips at the end of the curve, the SMOOTH macro does not produce estimates for times less than one bandwidth above the minimum event time or more than one bandwidth below the maximum event time.

Output 3.16 *Smoothed Hazard Function Estimate for Recidivism Data*

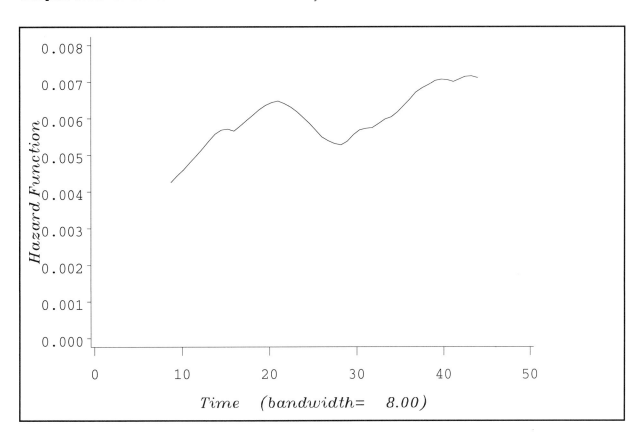

CONCLUSION

PROC LIFETEST is a useful procedure for preliminary analysis of survival data and for testing simple hypotheses about differences in survival across groups. For experimental studies, PROC LIFETEST gives results that are analogous to a one-way analysis of variance. But the procedure is not adequate for two-factor designs because there is no way to test for interactions. Similarly, while the TEST statement in PROC LIFETEST may be useful for screening large numbers of quantitative covariates, it is not adequate for examining the effects of variables controlling for other covariates. In most cases, therefore, you will need to move to the estimation of regression models with PROC LIFEREG or PROC PHREG.

It is also important to recognize that survival curves and their associated hazard functions can be misleading when the sample is heterogeneous. As explained in Chapter 8, uncontrolled heterogeneity tends to make hazard functions look as though they are declining, even when there is no real decline for any individual in the sample. One way to reduce the effect of heterogeneity is to estimate survivor functions on *residuals* from regression models, as shown in Chapter 4. Alternatively, you can estimate and plot baseline survivor functions after fitting Cox regression models, as shown in Chapter 5. Also in Chapter 4, we'll see how to use PROC LIFETEST to decide among the several parametric models that can be estimated with PROC LIFEREG.

CHAPTER **4**
Estimating Parametric Regression Models with PROC LIFEREG

p. 61   *Introduction*

p. 62   *The Accelerated Failure Time Model*

p. 66   *Alternative Distributions*

p. 78   *Categorical Variables and the CLASS Statement*

p. 79   *Maximum Likelihood Estimation*

p. 85   *Hypothesis Tests*

p. 88   *Goodness-of-Fit Tests with the Likelihood-Ratio Statistic*

p. 91   *Graphical Methods for Evaluating Model Fit*

p. 97   *Left Censoring and Interval Censoring*

p.101   *Generating Predictions and Hazard Functions*

p.104   *The Piecewise Exponential Model*

p.109   *Conclusion*

INTRODUCTION

The LIFEREG procedure produces estimates of parametric regression models with censored survival data using the method of maximum likelihood. In recent years, PROC LIFEREG has been eclipsed by the PHREG procedure, which does *semiparametric* regression analysis using a method known as *partial* likelihood. The reasons for PROC PHREG's popularity will become apparent in the next chapter. PROC LIFEREG is by no means obsolete, however. It can do some things better than PROC PHREG, and it can do other things that PROC PHREG can't do at all:

- PROC LIFEREG accommodates left censoring and interval censoring. PROC PHREG only allows right censoring.
- With PROC LIFEREG, you can test certain hypotheses about the shape of the hazard function. PROC PHREG only gives you nonparametric estimates of the *survivor* function, which can be difficult to interpret.

■ If the shape of the survival distribution is known, PROC LIFEREG produces more efficient estimates (with smaller standard errors) than PROC PHREG.

■ PROC LIFEREG automatically creates sets of dummy (indicator) variables to represent categorical variables with multiple values. PROC PHREG requires that you create such variables in the DATA step.

PROC LIFEREG's greatest limitation is that it does not handle time-dependent covariates, something at which PROC PHREG excels. Compared with parametric procedures in other statistical packages, the most attractive features of PROC LIFEREG are its ability to handle left and interval censoring, and its rich array of survival distributions. In particular, the availability of the generalized gamma distribution makes it possible to perform likelihood-ratio goodness-of-fit tests for many of the other probability distributions.

THE ACCELERATED FAILURE TIME MODEL

The class of regression models estimated by PROC LIFEREG is known as the *accelerated failure time* (AFT) model. In its most general form, the AFT model describes a relationship between the survivor functions of any two individuals. If $S_i(t)$ is the survivor function for individual i, then for any other individual j, the AFT model holds that

$$S_i(t) = S_j(\phi_{ij}t) \quad \text{for all } t \tag{4.1}$$

where ϕ_{ij} is a constant that is specific to the pair (i, j). This model says, in effect, that what makes one individual different from another is the rate at which they age. A good example is the conventional wisdom that a year for a dog is equivalent to seven years for a human. This example can be represented by equation (4.1), with S_i being the survival probability for a dog, S_j the survival probability for a human, and $\phi_{ij} = 7$.

What PROC LIFEREG actually estimates is a special case of this model that is quite similar in form to an ordinary linear regression model. Let T_i be a random variable denoting the event time for the ith individual in the sample, and let $x_{i1}, \ldots, x_{ik}$ be the values of k covariates for that same individual. The model is then

$$\log T_i = \beta_0 + \beta_1 x_{i1} + \ldots + \beta_k x_{ik} + \sigma \varepsilon_i \qquad (4.2)$$

where ε_i is a random disturbance term, and $\beta_0, \ldots, \beta_k$, and σ are parameters to be estimated. Exponentiating both sides of equation (4.2) gives an alternative way of expressing the model:

$$T_i = \exp\{\beta_0 + \beta_1 x_{i1} + \ldots + \beta_k x_{ik} + \sigma \varepsilon_i\}.$$

So far, the only differences between the model in equation (4.2) and the usual linear regression model are that (a) there is a σ before the ε and (b) the dependent variable is logged. The σ can be omitted, which requires that the variance of ε be allowed to vary from one data set to another. But it is simpler to fix the variance of ε at some standard value (e.g., 1.0) and let σ change in value to accommodate changes in the disturbance variance. (This notational strategy could also be used for linear models). As for the log transformation of T, its main purpose is to ensure that predicted values of T are positive, regardless of the values of the x's and the β's.

In a linear regression model, it is typical to assume that ε_i has a normal distribution with a mean and variance that is constant over i, and that the εs are independent across observations. One member of the AFT class, the *log-normal model*, has exactly these assumptions. It is called the log-normal model because if $\log T$ has a normal distribution, then T has a log-normal distribution. Other AFT models allow distributions for ε besides the normal distribution but retain the assumptions of constant mean and variance, as well as independence across observations. We will consider these alternative models in some detail, but for the moment let's stick with the log-normal.

If there are no censored data, we can readily estimate this model by ordinary least squares (OLS). Simply create a new variable in the DATA step that is equal to the log of the event time, and use the REG procedure with the transformed variable as the dependent variable. This process yields the best linear unbiased estimates of the β coefficients, regardless of the shape of the distribution of ε. If ε is normal, the OLS estimates will also be maximum likelihood estimates and will have minimum variance among all estimators, both linear and nonlinear. In fact, the coefficients and standard errors produced by PROC REG will be identical to those produced by PROC LIFEREG with a log-normal specification.

But survival data typically have at least some censored observations, and these are difficult to handle with OLS. Alternatively, we can use maximum likelihood estimation. Later, this chapter examines the theory of maximum likelihood (ML) for censored regression models in some detail. First, let's look at an example of how a regression application is set up with PROC LIFEREG and what results it produces. In the section **The Life Table Method** in Chapter 3, "Estimating and Comparing Survival Curves with PROC LIFETEST", I describe the recidivism data set in which 432 inmates were followed for one year after release. That data set is used throughout this chapter, so you may want to reread the earlier description (or see Appendix 2, "Data Sets").

In this recidivism example, the variable WEEK contains the week of the first arrest or censoring. The variable ARREST is equal to 1 if WEEK is uncensored or 0 if censored. There are seven covariates. To estimate the log-normal model, we specify

```
proc lifereg data=recid;
   model week*arrest(0)=fin age race wexp mar paro prio
         / dist=lnormal;
run;
```

Note that WEEK*ARREST(0) in the MODEL statement follows the same syntax as the TIME statement in PROC LIFETEST. However, it is now followed by an equal sign and a list of covariates. The slash (/) separates the variable list from the specification of options, of which there are several possibilities. Here, we have merely indicated our choice of the log-normal distribution.

Output 4.1 displays the results. The output first provides some preliminary information: the names of the time and censoring variables, the values that correspond to censoring, and the numbers of cases with each type of censoring. Then the output shows that the log-likelihood for the model is −322.6946. This is an important statistic that we will use later to test various hypotheses. Next, we get a table of estimated coefficients, their standard errors, chi-square statistics for the null hypothesis that each coefficient is 0, and a *p*-value associated with that statistic. The chi-squares are calculated by dividing each coefficient by its estimated standard error and squaring the result.

Output 4.1 *Results from Fitting a Log-Normal Model to the Recidivism Data*

```
LIFEREG  PROCEDURE

Data Set           =WORK.DATA10
Dependent Variable=Log(WEEK)
Censoring Variable=ARREST
Censoring Value(s)=      0
Noncensored Values=  114  Right Censored Values=    318
Left Censored Values=   0  Interval Censored Values=   0


Log Likelihood for LNORMAL -322.6945851


Variable  DF   Estimate  Std Err ChiSquare  Pr>Chi Label/Value

INTERCPT  1   4.2676657  0.46169  85.44385  0.0001 Intercept
FIN       1  0.34284768  0.164086  4.365737  0.0367
AGE       1  0.02720184  0.015756  2.980621  0.0843
RACE      1    -0.36316  0.264692  1.882413  0.1701
WEXP      1  0.26813206  0.178889  2.246619  0.1339
MAR       1  0.46035337  0.295148  2.432778  0.1188
PARO      1  0.05587938  0.169111  0.109184  0.7411
PRIO      1  -0.0655175  0.027091  5.848919  0.0156
SCALE     1  1.29456993  0.098952            Normal scale parameter
```

Two variables meet the .05 criterion for statistical significance: FIN
(whether the inmate received financial aid) and PRIO (number of prior
convictions). The signs of the coefficients tell us the direction of the
relationship. The positive coefficient for FIN indicates that those who received
financial aid had longer times to arrest than those who did not. The negative
coefficient for PRIO indicates that additional convictions were associated with
shorter times to arrest. As in any regression procedure, these coefficients adjust
or control for the other covariates in the model.

The numerical magnitudes of the coefficients are not very
informative in the reported metrics, but a simple transformation leads to a very
intuitive interpretation. For a 1-0 variable like FIN, if we simply take e^β, we get
the estimated ratio of the expected (mean) survival times for the two groups.
Thus, $e^{.3428} = 1.41$. Therefore, controlling for the other covariates, the
expected time to arrest for those who received financial aid is 41 percent
greater than for those who did not receive financial aid. (This statement
also applies to the median time to arrest, or any other percentile for that
matter). For a quantitative variable like PRIO, we can use the transformation
$100(e^\beta - 1)$, which gives the percent increase in the expected survival time for
each one-unit increase in the variable. Thus, $100(e^{-.0655} - 1) = -6.34$.
According to the model, then, each additional prior conviction is associated
with a 6.34 percent decrease in expected time to arrest, holding other

covariates constant. We can also interpret the coefficients for any of the other AFT models discussed in this chapter in this way.

The output line labeled SCALE is an estimate of the σ parameter in equation (4.2), along with its estimated standard error. For some distributions, changes in the value of this parameter can produce qualitative differences in the shape of the hazard function. For the log-normal model, however, changes in σ merely compress or stretch the hazard function.

ALTERNATIVE DISTRIBUTIONS

In ordinary linear regression, the assumption of a normal distribution for the disturbance term is routinely invoked for a wide range of applications. Yet PROC LIFEREG allows for four additional distributions for ε: extreme value (2 parameter), extreme value (1 parameter), log-gamma, and logistic. For each of these distributions, there is a corresponding distribution for T:

Distribution of ε	Distribution of T
extreme value (2 par.)	Weibull
extreme value (1 par.)	exponential
log-gamma	gamma
logistic	log-logistic
normal	log-normal

Incidentally, all AFT models are named for the distribution of T rather than the distribution of ε or log T. You might expect that since the logistic and normal lead to the log-logistic and log-normal, the gamma will lead to the log-gamma. But it is just the reverse. This is one of those unfortunate terminological inconsistencies that we just have to live with.

What is it about survival analysis that makes these alternatives worth considering? The main reason for allowing other distributions is that they have different implications for *hazard functions* that may, in turn, lead to different substantive interpretations. The remainder of this section explores each of these alternatives in some detail.

The Exponential Model

The simplest model that PROC LIFEREG estimates is the exponential model, invoked by DIST=EXPONENTIAL in the MODEL statement. This model specifies that ε has a standard extreme-value distribution, and constrains $\sigma = 1$. If ε has an extreme-value distribution, then log T also has an extreme-value distribution, conditional on the covariates. This implies that T itself has an exponential distribution, which is why we call it the *exponential model*. The standard extreme value distribution is also known as a *Gumbel distribution* or a *double exponential distribution*. It has a p.d.f. of $f(\varepsilon) = \exp[\varepsilon - \exp(\varepsilon)]$. Like the normal distribution, this is a unimodal distribution defined on the entire real line. Unlike the normal, however, it is not symmetrical, being slightly skewed to the left.

As we saw in Chapter 2, "Basic Concepts of Survival Analysis," an exponential distribution for T corresponds to a *constant hazard function*, which is the most characteristic feature of this model. However, equation (2.12) expresses the exponential regression model as

$$\log h(t) = \beta_0^\bullet + \beta_1^\bullet x_1 + \ldots + \beta_k^\bullet x_k \tag{4.3}$$

where the $\bullet$s have been added to distinguish these coefficients from those in equation (4.2). Although the dependent variable in equation (4.2) is the log of time, in equation (4.3) it is the log of the hazard. It turns out that the two models are completely equivalent. Furthermore, there is a simple relationship between the coefficients in equation (4.2) and equation (4.3), namely that $\beta_j = -\beta_j^\bullet$ for all j.

The change in signs makes intuitive sense. If the hazard is high, then events occur quickly and survival times are short. On the other hand, when the hazard is low, events are unlikely to occur and survival times are long. It is important to be able to shift back and forth between these two ways of expressing the model so that you can compare results across different computer programs. In particular, since PROC PHREG reports coefficients in log-hazard form, we need to make the conversion in order to compare PROC LIFEREG output with PROC PHREG output.

You may wonder why there is no disturbance term in equation (4.3) (a characteristic it shares with the more familiar logistic regression model). No disturbance term is needed because there is implicit random variation in the relationship between $h(t)$, the unobserved hazard, and the observed event time T. Even if two individuals have exactly the same covariate values (and therefore the same hazard), they will not have the same event time. Nevertheless, in Chapter 8, "Heterogeneity, Repeated Events, and Other Topics," we will see that there have been some attempts to add a disturbance term to models like this to represent *unobserved heterogeneity*.

Output 4.2 shows the results of fitting the exponential model to the recidivism data. Comparing this with the log-normal results in Output 4.1, we see some noteworthy differences. The coefficient for AGE is about twice as large in the exponential model, and its *p*-value declines from .08 to .01. Similarly, the coefficient for PRIO increases somewhat in magnitude, and its *p*-value also goes down substantially. On the other hand, the *p*-value for FIN increases to slightly above the .05 level.

Output 4.2 *Exponential Model Applied to Recidivism Data*

```
LIFEREG  PROCEDURE

Log Likelihood for EXPONENT -325.8259007

Variable  DF    Estimate   Std Err  ChiSquare  Pr>Chi Label/Value

INTERCPT  1  4.05069154   0.58604   47.77542   0.0001 Intercept
FIN       1  0.36626434  0.191116    3.672793   0.0553
AGE       1  0.05559804  0.021841    6.479813   0.0109
RACE      1  -0.3049391   0.30794    0.980603   0.3220
WEXP      1  0.14674614    0.2117    0.480499   0.4882
MAR       1  0.42698669  0.381382    1.253453   0.2629
PARO      1  0.08264792  0.195604    0.178529   0.6726
PRIO      1  -0.0856592  0.028313    9.153053   0.0025
SCALE     0           1         0               Extreme value scale parameter
  Lagrange Multiplier ChiSquare for Scale 24.93017 Pr>Chi is 0.0001.
```

Clearly, the choice of model can make a substantive difference. Later, this chapter considers some criteria for choosing among these and other models. Notice that the SCALE parameter σ is forced equal to 1.0; the last line says that the "Lagrange Multiplier ChiSquare for Scale" is 24.93017 with a *p*-value of .0001. This is a 1 degree-of-freedom test for the null hypothesis that $\sigma = 1$. Here the null hypothesis is soundly rejected, indicating that the hazard function is *not* constant over time. While this might suggest that the log-normal model is superior, things are not quite that simple. There are other models to consider as well.

The Weibull Model

The Weibull model is a slight modification of the exponential model, with big consequences. By specifying DIST=WEIBULL in the MODEL statement, we retain the assumption that ε has a standard extreme-value distribution, but we relax the assumption that $\sigma = 1$. When $\sigma > 1$, the hazard decreases with time. When $.5 < \sigma < 1$, the hazard is increasing at a decreasing rate. When $0 < \sigma < .5$, the hazard is increasing at an increasing rate. And when $\sigma = .5$, the hazard function is an increasing straight line with an origin at 0. Graphs of these hazard functions appear in Figure 2.3 (with the α in the figure equal to $1/\sigma - 1$).

We call this the Weibull model because T has a Weibull distribution, conditional on the covariates. The Weibull distribution has long been the most popular parametric model in the biostatistical literature, for two reasons. First, it has a relatively simple survivor function that is easy to manipulate mathematically:

$$S_i(t) = \exp\left\{-[t_i e^{-\beta x_i}]^{\frac{1}{\sigma}}\right\}.$$

Second, in addition to being an AFT model, the Weibull model is also a proportional hazards model. This means that its coefficients (when suitably transformed) can be interpreted as relative hazard ratios. In fact, the Weibull model (and its special case, the exponential model) is the only model that is simultaneously a member of both these classes.

As with the exponential model, there is an exact equivalence between the log-hazard form of the model

$$\log h(t) = \alpha \log t + \beta_0^{\bullet} + \beta_1^{\bullet} x_1 + \ldots + \beta_k^{\bullet} x_k$$

and the log-survival time model

$$\log T = \beta_0 + \beta_1 x_1 + \ldots + \beta_k x_k + \sigma\varepsilon.$$

The relationship between the parameters is slightly more complicated, however. Specifically, for the Weibull model

$$\beta_j^{\bullet} = \frac{-\beta_j}{\sigma} \quad \text{for } j = 0, \ldots, k$$

and $\alpha = 1/\sigma - 1$. Since $\beta_j = 0$ if and only if $\beta_j^{\bullet} = 0$, a test of the null hypothesis that a coefficient is 0 will be the same regardless of which form you use. On the other hand, standard errors and confidence intervals for coefficients in the log-survival time format are not so easily converted to the log-hazard format. Collett (1994, p. 282) gives formulas for accomplishing this.

Output 4.3 shows the results from fitting the Weibull model to the recidivism data. Compared with the exponential model in Output 4.2, the coefficients are all somewhat attenuated. But the standard errors are also smaller, so the chi-square statistics and p-values are hardly affected at all. Furthermore, if we convert the coefficients to the log-hazard format by changing sign and dividing by $\hat{\sigma}$ (the SCALE estimate of .7124 in the output), we get

FIN	-0.382
AGE	-0.057
RACE	0.316
WEXP	-0.150
MAR	-0.437
PARO	-0.083
PRIO	0.092.

These coefficients are much closer to the log-hazard coefficients for the exponential model (which differ only in sign from the log-survival time coefficients).

Output 4.3 *Weibull Model Applied to Recidivism Data*

```
L I F E R E G   P R O C E D U R E

Log Likelihood for WEIBULL -319.3765238

Variable  DF    Estimate  Std Err ChiSquare  Pr>Chi Label/Value

INTERCPT   1   3.9901348 0.419095  90.64624  0.0001 Intercept
FIN        1  0.27216336 0.137962   3.891714  0.0485
AGE        1   0.0407138 0.016004   6.472179  0.0110
RACE       1  -0.2248024 0.220159   1.042629  0.3072
WEXP       1  0.10655659 0.151541   0.494425  0.4820
MAR        1  0.31127326 0.273302   1.297171  0.2547
PARO       1  0.05882725 0.139638    0.17748  0.6735
PRIO       1  -0.0658169 0.020941   9.878652  0.0017
SCALE      1  0.71240533 0.063423            Extreme value scale parameter
```

Since $\hat{\sigma}$ (labeled SCALE in Output 4.3) is between .5 and 1, we conclude that the hazard is increasing at a decreasing rate. We can also calculate $\hat{\alpha} = (1/.7124) - 1 = 0.4037$, which is the coefficient for log t in the log-hazard model. Because both the dependent and independent variables are logged, this coefficient can be interpreted as follows: a 1-percent increase in time since release produces a 0.40-percent increase in the hazard for arrest.

The Log-Normal Model

Although we have already discussed the log-normal model and applied it to the recidivism data, we have not yet considered the shape of its hazard function. Unlike the Weibull model, the log-normal model has a nonmonotonic hazard function. The hazard is 0 when $t=0$. It rises to a peak and then declines toward 0 as t goes to infinity. The log-normal is *not* a proportional hazards model, and its hazard cannot be expressed in closed form (it involves the c.d.f. of a standard normal variable). It can, however, be expressed as a regression model in which the dependent variable is the logarithm of the hazard. Specifically,

$$\log h(t) = \log h_0(te^{-\beta x}) - \beta x$$

where $h_0(.)$ is the hazard function for an individual with $\mathbf{x} = \mathbf{0}$. This equation also applies to the log-logistic and gamma models to be discussed shortly, except that $h_0(.)$ will be different in each case.

Some typical log-normal hazard functions are shown in Figure 4.1. All three functions correspond to distributions with a median of 1.0. When σ is large, the hazard peaks so rapidly that the function is almost indistinguishable from those like the Weibull and log-logistic that may have an infinite hazard when $t = 0$.

The inverted U-shape of the log-normal hazard is often appropriate for repeatable events. Suppose, for example, that the event of interest is a residential move. Immediately after a move, the hazard of another move is likely to be extremely low. People need to rest and recoup the substantial costs involved in moving. The hazard will certainly rise with time, but much empirical evidence indicates that it eventually begins to decline. One explanation is that, as time goes by, people become increasingly invested in a particular location or community. However, Chapter 8 shows how the declining portion of the hazard function may also be a consequence of unobserved heterogeneity.

Figure 4.1   *Typical Hazard Functions for a Log-Normal Model*

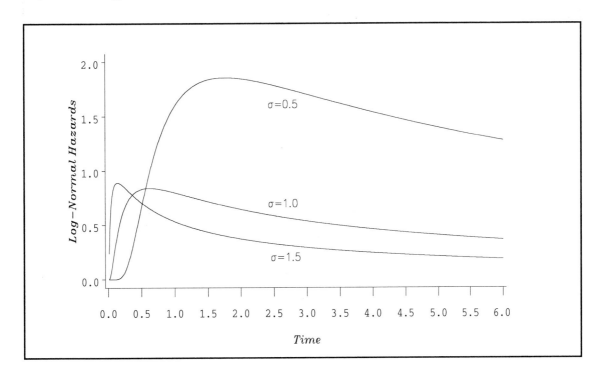

The Log-Logistic Model

Another model that allows for an inverted U-shaped hazard is the log-logistic model, which assumes that ε has a logistic distribution with p.d.f.

$$f(\varepsilon) = \frac{e^{\varepsilon}}{(1 + e^{\varepsilon})^2} \; .$$

A symmetric distribution with a mean of 0, the logistic distribution is quite similar in shape to the normal distribution. The logistic distribution is well known to students of the logistic (logit) regression model, which can be derived by assuming (a) a linear model with a logistically distributed error term and (b) a dichotomization of the dependent variable.

If ε has a logistic distribution, then so does log T (although with a nonzero mean). It follows that T has a log-logistic distribution. The log-logistic hazard function is

$$h(t) = \frac{\lambda \gamma (\lambda t)^{\gamma - 1}}{1 + (\lambda t)^{\gamma}}$$

where $\gamma = 1/\sigma$ and $\lambda = \exp\{-[\beta_0 + \beta_1 x_1 + \dots + \beta_k x_k]\}$. This produces the characteristic shapes shown in Figure 4.2, all of which correspond to distributions with a median of 1.0.

Figure 4.2. *Typical Hazard Functions for the Log-Logistic Model*

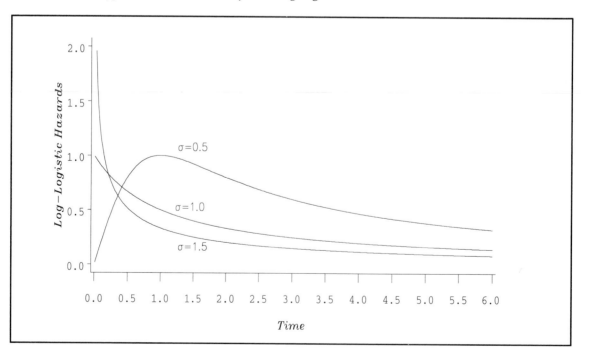

When $\sigma < 1$, the log-logistic hazard is similar to the log-normal hazard: it starts at 0, rises to a peak, and then declines toward 0. When $\sigma > 1$, the hazard behaves like the decreasing Weibull hazard: it starts at infinity and declines toward 0. When $\sigma =1$, the hazard has a value of λ at $t=0$, and then declines toward 0 as t goes to infinity.

The log-logistic model has a rather simple survivor function,

$$S(t) \; = \; \frac{1}{1 + (\lambda t)^{\gamma}} \; .$$

As before, $\gamma = 1/\sigma$ and $\lambda = \exp\{-[\beta_0 + \beta_1 x_1 + \dots + \beta_k x_k]\}$. A little algebra shows that this can be written as

$$\log\left[\frac{S(t)}{1-S(t)}\right] \; = \beta_0^\bullet + \beta_1^\bullet x_1 + \dots + \; \beta_k^\bullet x_k - \gamma \log t$$

where $\beta_i^\bullet = \beta_j/\sigma$ for $i = 1,\dots,k$. This is nothing more than a logistic (logit) regression model, which means that we can estimate the log-logistic model for the recidivism data by fitting a logit model to the dichotomy arrested versus not arrested in the first year after release. (Because t is a constant 52 weeks, the term $\gamma \log t$ gets absorbed into the intercept.) Of course, this estimation method is not fully efficient because we are not using the information on the exact timing of the arrests, and we certainly will not get the same estimates. The point is that the two apparently different methods are actually estimating the same underlying model.

Because $S(t)$ is the probability of surviving to time t, $S(t)/[1-S(t)]$ is the *odds* of surviving to time t. Thus, we have a model that is linear in the log-odds. Equivalently, we can say that the log-logistic model is a member of a general class of models called *proportional odds models*. This class can be defined in the following way. Let $S_i(t)$ and $S_j(t)$ be the survivor functions for any two individuals i and j. The proportional odds model says that

$$\frac{S_i(t)}{1-S_i(t)} \; = \; \phi_{ij}\left(\frac{S_j(t)}{1-S_j(t)}\right) \qquad \text{for all } t$$

where ϕ_{ij} is some constant that is specific to the pair (i, j). In fact, the log-logistic model is the *only* model that is both a proportional odds model and an AFT model.

To fit the log-logistic model with PROC LIFEREG, you specify DIST=LLOGISTIC as an option in the MODEL statement. Output 4.4 shows the results for the recidivism data. The first thing to notice is that the estimate of σ (labeled SCALE) is less than 1.0, implying that the estimated hazard function follows the inverted U-shaped form shown in Figure 4.2. Given what I just said about the similarity of the log-normal and log-logistic hazards, you might expect the other results to be most similar to the log-normal output in Output 4.1. But the coefficients and test statistics actually appear to be closer to those for the Weibull model in Output 4.3.

Output 4.4 *Log-Logistic Model Applied to Recidivism Data*

```
L I F E R E G   P R O C E D U R E

Log Likelihood for LLOGISTC -319.3983709

Variable   DF   Estimate   Std Err   ChiSquare   Pr>Chi  Label/Value

INTERCPT    1   3.91830423  0.427434  84.03459   0.0001  Intercept
FIN         1   0.28887608  0.145585   3.937211  0.0472
AGE         1   0.03636558  0.015572   5.453767  0.0195
RACE        1  -0.2791492   0.229654   1.477496  0.2242
WEXP        1   0.17842379  0.157185   1.288494  0.2563
MAR         1   0.34730388  0.269669   1.658665  0.1978
PARO        1   0.05079816  0.149574   0.115341  0.7341
PRIO        1  -0.0691822   0.022742   9.254181  0.0023
SCALE       1   0.64713465  0.055923   .                Logistic scale parameter
```

The Gamma Model

Survival analysis literature discusses two different gamma models: the standard (2-parameter) model and the generalized (3-parameter) model. PROC LIFEREG fits the generalized model. Because the generalized gamma model has one more parameter than any of the other models we have considered, its hazard function can take on a wide variety of shapes. In particular, the exponential, Weibull, standard gamma, and log-normal models (but not the log-logistic) are all special cases of the generalized gamma model. This fact is exploited later in this chapter when we consider likelihood ratio tests for comparing the different models. But the generalized gamma model can also take on shapes that are unlike any of these special cases. Most important, it can have hazard functions with U or *bathtub* shapes in which the hazard declines, reaches a minimum, and then increases. It is well known that the hazard for human mortality, considered over the whole life span, has such a shape. On the other hand, the generalized gamma model cannot represent hazard functions that have more than one peak.

Given the richness of the generalized gamma model, why not always use it instead of the other models? There are two reasons. First, the formula for the hazard function for the generalized gamma model is rather complicated, involving the gamma function and the incomplete gamma function. Consequently, you may often find it difficult to judge the shape of the hazard function from the estimated parameters. By contrast, hazard functions for the specific submodels can be rather simply described, as we have already seen. Second, computation for the generalized gamma model is considerably more difficult. For example, it took more than five times as much computer time to estimate the generalized gamma model for the recidivism data as compared with the exponential model. This fact can be an important consideration when you are working with large data sets. The generalized gamma model also has a reputation for convergence problems, although the parameterization and numerical algorithms used by PROC LIFEREG seem to have reduced these to a minimum.

To fit the generalized gamma model with PROC LIFEREG, you specify DIST=GAMMA as an option in the MODEL statement. Output 4.5 shows the results from fitting this model to the recidivism data. As usual, the SCALE parameter is the estimate of σ in equation (4.2). The estimate labeled SHAPE is the additional shape parameter that is denoted by δ in the PROC LIFEREG documentation. (In the output for earlier releases of PROC LIFEREG, this parameter is labeled GAMMA). When the shape parameter is 0, we get the log-normal distribution. When it is 1.0, we have the Weibull distribution. And when the shape parameter and the scale parameter are equal, we have the standard gamma distribution. In Output 4.5, the shape estimate is almost exactly 1.0, so we are very close to the Weibull distribution. The shape and scale parameters are also similar, so the standard gamma model is also quite plausible for these data. Later, we'll make these comparisons more rigorous.

Output 4.5 *Generalized Gamma Model Applied to the Recidivism Data*

```
     L I F E R E G   P R O C E D U R E

Log Likelihood for GAMMA  -319.3764549

Variable  DF    Estimate  Std Err  ChiSquare  Pr>Chi  Label/Value

INTERCPT  1  3.99149155  0.434907  84.23224   0.0001  Intercept
FIN       1  0.27244327  0.140118   3.780636  0.0518
AGE       1  0.04066435  0.016546   6.039829  0.0140
RACE      1 -0.2254894   0.227983   0.978241  0.3226
WEXP      1  0.10734828  0.16595    0.418444  0.5177
MAR       1  0.31179029  0.276896   1.267921  0.2602
PARO      1  0.05878877  0.139813   0.176805  0.6741
PRIO      1 -0.0658616   0.021303   9.558375  0.0020
SCALE     1  0.71511922  0.239598                     Gamma scale parameter
SHAPE     1  0.99429204  0.484882                     Gamma shape parameter
```

As for the standard gamma model, there is no direct way of fitting this in PROC LIFEREG. Ideally, you fit the generalized model while imposing the constraint SCALE=SHAPE, but PROC LIFEREG doesn't handle equality constraints. PROC LIFEREG does allow you to fix both the scale and shape parameters at specific values. So if you're desperate to fit the standard gamma model, you can try out a bunch of different values (for example, with a line search) until you find the common value for the shape and scale parameters that maximizes the log-likelihood. When I did this for the recidivism data, I ended up with scale and shape parameters equal to .811. Without going into the details of the search, the code to fit the final model is as follows:

```
proc lifereg data=recid;
  model week*arrest(0)=fin age race wexp
        mar paro prio /dist=gamma noshape1 shape1=.811
        noscale scale=.811;
run;
```

Output 4.6 shows the results. The coefficients show little change from Output 4.5, which is not surprising since the log-likelihood hardly changes at all. The standard errors are probably slight underestimates because they do not take account of the sampling variation in the SCALE-SHAPE estimate.

Output 4.6 *Standard Gamma Model Applied to the Recidivism Data*

```
                    L I F E R E G   P R O C E D U R E
Log Likelihood for GAMMA -319.4636775

 Variable  DF    Estimate  Std Err  ChiSquare  Pr>Chi Label/Value

 INTERCPT   1  4.03969532 0.426895  89.54781   0.0001 Intercept
 FIN        1  0.28319316 0.141064   4.030268  0.0447
 AGE        1  0.03902397 0.015661   6.209049  0.0127
 RACE       1 -0.2498191  0.227472   1.206139  0.2721
 WEXP       1  0.13482081  0.15585   0.748343  0.3870
 MAR        1  0.33229455 0.275574   1.454021  0.2279
 PARO       1   0.0579843 0.145018   0.159874  0.6893
 PRIO       1 -0.0673115  0.021468   9.830681  0.0017
 SCALE      0       0.811         0                    Gamma scale parameter
 SHAPE      0       0.811         0                    Gamma shape parameter
    Lagrange Multiplier ChiSquare for Scale 0.002124 Pr>Chi is 0.9632.
```

What is the interpretation of the standard gamma model? Under this model, the survival time T has the gamma p.d.f.

$$f(t) = \frac{\lambda(\lambda t)^{K-1} e^{-\lambda t}}{\Gamma(K)}$$

where $K = 1/\delta^2$ (δ is the shape parameter reported by LIFEREG). The λ parameter is a function of the covariates: $\lambda = \exp\{-[\beta_0 + \beta_1 x_1 + \dots + \beta_k x_k]\}$. $\Gamma(.)$ is the gamma function, a well-known function in mathematics that is defined by an integral. When K is an integer, $\Gamma(K) = (K-1)!$ and, in particular, $\Gamma(1) = 0! = 1$.

Both the survivor and hazard functions of the standard gamma distribution are awkward because they involve incomplete gamma functions, which are expressed as integrals. When $K > 1$, the hazard is 0 at time 0, and increases thereafter. When $0 < K < 1$, the hazard is infinite at time 0 and decreases thereafter. When $K = 1$, the hazard is constant, and we are back to the exponential model. So far, this is similar to the Weibull hazard. The big difference is that the increasing Weibull hazard increases without limit, while the standard gamma hazard approaches λ as an upper limit. (Clearly, if there is an upper limit, the hazard cannot increase at an increasing rate). Similarly, while the decreasing Weibull hazard approaches 0 as a lower limit, the decreasing gamma hazard has a lower limit of λ. Figure 4.3 shows examples of such hazards with $\lambda = 1$. Since λ is a log-linear function of the covariates, we can think of the covariates as raising or lowering the boundary of the hazard. The K parameter determines how quickly the limit is approached and whether it approaches from above or below. For the model in Output 4.6, we can get the ML estimate of K by taking $1/(.811)^2 = 1.52$. Since this is greater than 1, we have evidence for an increasing hazard.

Figure 4.3 *Typical Hazard Functions for the Standard Gamma Model*

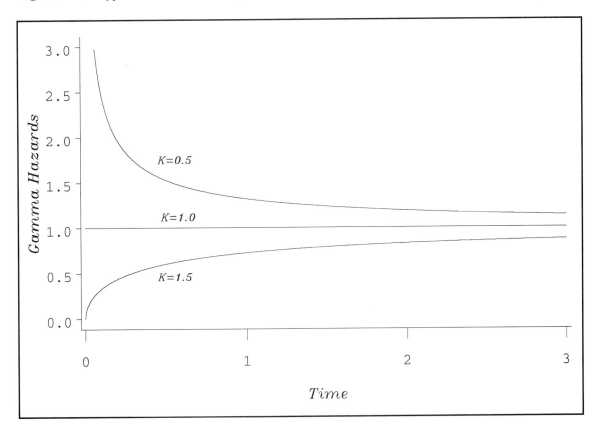

CATEGORICAL VARIABLES AND THE CLASS STATEMENT

In the recidivism example, several of the covariates—race, marital status, work experience, and parole status—are dichotomous variables that are coded as indicator (dummy) variables. For categorical covariates with more than two categories, the standard approach is to create a *set* of indicator variables, one for each category (except for one). You can do this in the DATA step, but PROC LIFEREG does it automatically if the variable (or variables) is listed in a CLASS statement. Here's an example. Another covariate in the recidivism data set is education, which was originally coded like this:

2 = 6th grade or less	24 cases
3 = 7th to 9th grade	239 cases
4 = 10th to 11th grade	119 cases
5 = 12th grade	39 cases
6 = some college	11 cases

Due to the small numbers of cases in the two extreme categories, I combined them (in a DATA step) with the adjacent categories to produce a variable EDUC with values of 3 (9th or less), 4 (10th to 11th) and 5 (12th or more). I then specified a Weibull model in PROC LIFEREG with the following statements:

```
proc lifereg data=recid;
   class educ;
   model week*arrest(0)=fin age race wexp mar paro
        prio educ/dist=weibull covb;
   run;
```

The COVB option requests the covariance matrix for the parameter estimates, which we'll discuss later in the chapter. Output 4.7 shows other results (some output lines have been omitted). For any variables listed in the CLASS statement, PROC LIFEREG first reports the number of levels found, and values for those levels.

In the table of estimates, there are four lines for the EDUC variable. The first line is a chi-square test of the null hypothesis that all the coefficients associated with EDUC are 0. In this case, the chi-square statistic is 3.20 with 2 d.f., yielding a *p*-value of .20—clearly not significant. The next two lines contain coefficients, standard errors, and hypothesis tests for levels 3 and 4 of EDUC, while the last line merely informs us that level 5 is the omitted category. Hence, each of the estimated coefficients is a contrast with level 5. (The default in PROC LIFEREG is to take the highest formatted value as the omitted category, but you can get some control over this with the ORDER option in the PROC LIFEREG statement.)

Output 4.7 *Recidivism Model with Education as a CLASS Variable*

```
L I F E R E G   P R O C E D U R E
                 Class Level Information

              Class     Levels     Values

              EDUC         3        3 4 5

Log Likelihood for WEIBULL -317.4956184

Variable  DF   Estimate   Std Err  ChiSquare   Pr>Chi  Label/Value

INTERCPT   1   4.46799186 0.517139  74.64661   0.0001  Intercept
FIN        1   0.26898413 0.137861   3.806899   0.0510
AGE        1   0.03920003 0.015947   6.042594   0.0140
RACE       1  -0.252407   0.22293    1.281928   0.2575
WEXP       1   0.07729428 0.152151   0.258073   0.6114
MAR        1   0.30129792 0.273231   1.215999   0.2701
PARO       1   0.06579323 0.139592   0.222148   0.6374
PRIO       1  -0.0585497  0.021336   7.530823   0.0061

EDUC       2                         3.202349   0.2017
           1  -0.5115662 0.309022    2.740463   0.0978            3
           1  -0.3536199 0.324266    1.18924    0.2755            4
           0   0          0          .          .                5

SCALE      1   0.7118726 0.063398              Extreme value scale parameter
```

Unlike the GLM procedure, PROC LIFEREG does not have facilities for specifying interactions between two CLASS variables or between a CLASS variable and a quantitative covariate. To do this, you must create appropriate variables representing the interaction, either in the DATA step or with the GLMMOD procedure.

MAXIMUM LIKELIHOOD ESTIMATION

All models in PROC LIFEREG are estimated by the method of maximum likelihood. This section explores some of the basics of ML estimation, with an emphasis on how it handles censored observations. The discussion is not intended to be rigorous. If you want a more complete and careful treatment of ML, you should consult one of the many texts available on the subject. (Kalbfleisch and Prentice, 1980, Chapter 3, gives a more detailed introduction in the context of survival analysis).

ML is a quite general approach to estimation that has become popular in many different areas of application. There are two reasons for this popularity. First, ML produces estimators that have good large-sample properties. Provided that certain regularity conditions are met, ML estimators are consistent, asymptotically efficient, and asymptotically normal. *Consistency* means that the estimates converge *in probability* to the true values as the sample gets larger, implying that the estimates will be approximately unbiased in large samples. *Asymptotically efficient* means that, in large samples, the estimates will have standard errors that are (approximately) at least as small as those for any other estimation method. And, finally, *asymptotically normal* means that the sampling distribution of the estimates will be approximately normal in large samples, which means that you can use the normal and chi-square distributions to compute confidence intervals and *p*-values.

All these approximations get better as the sample size gets larger. The fact that these desirable properties have only been proven for large samples does *not* mean that ML has bad properties for small samples. It simply means that we usually don't *know* what the small-sample properties are. And in the absence of attractive alternatives, researchers routinely use ML estimation for both large and small samples. Although I won't argue against that practice, I do urge caution in interpreting *p*-values and confidence intervals when samples are small. Despite the temptation to accept *larger* *p*-values as evidence against the null hypothesis in small samples, it is actually more reasonable to demand *smaller* values to compensate for the fact that the approximation to the normal or chi-square distributions may be poor.

The other reason for ML's popularity is that it is often straightforward to derive ML estimators when there are no other obvious possibilities. As we will see, one case that ML handles nicely is data with censored observations. While you can use least squares with certain adjustments for censoring (Lawless 1982, p. 328), such estimates often have much larger standard errors, and there is little available theory to justify the construction of hypothesis tests or confidence intervals.

The basic principle of ML is to choose as estimates those values that will maximize the probability of observing what we have, in fact, observed. There are two steps to this: (1) write down an expression for the probability of the data as a function of the unknown parameters, and (2) find the values of the unknown parameters that make the value of this expression as large as possible.

The first step is known as *constructing the likelihood function*. To accomplish this, you must specify a model, which amounts to choosing a probability distribution for the dependent variable and choosing a functional form that relates the parameters of this distribution to the values of the covariates. We have already considered those two choices.

The second step—*maximization*—typically requires an iterative numerical method, that is, one involving successive approximations. Such methods are often computationally demanding, which explains why ML estimation has become popular only in the last two decades.

In the next section, I work through the basic mathematics of constructing and maximizing the likelihood function. You can skip this part without loss of continuity if you're not interested in the details or if you simply want to postpone the effort. Immediately after this section, I discuss some of the practical details of ML estimation with PROC LIFEREG.

Maximum Likelihood Estimation: Mathematics

Assume that we have n independent individuals ($i = 1,....,n$). For each individual i, the data consist of three parts: t_i, δ_i, and x_i, where t_i is the time of the event or the time of censoring, δ_i, is an indicator variable with a value of 1 if t_i is uncensored or 0 if censored, and $x_i = [1 \; x_{i1} \; ... \; x_{ik}]'$ is a vector of covariate values (the 1 is for the intercept). For simplicity, we will treat δ_i and x_i as fixed rather than random. We could get equivalent results if δ_i were random but noninformative, and if the distributions of δ_i and t_i were expressed conditional on the values of x_i. But that would just complicate the notation.

For the moment, suppose that all the observations are uncensored. Since we are assuming independence, it follows that the probability of the entire data is found by taking the product of the probabilities of the data for every individual. Because t_i is assumed to be measured on a continuum, the probability that it will take on any specific value is 0. Instead, we represent the probability of each observation by the p.d.f. $f(t_i)$. Thus, the probability (or likelihood) of the data is given by the following, where Π indicates repeated multiplication:

$$L = \prod_{i=1}^{n} f_i(t_i) \; .$$

Notice that f_i is subscripted to indicate that each individual has a different p.d.f. that depends on the covariates.

To proceed further, we need to substitute an expression for $f_i(t_i)$ that involves the covariates and the unknown parameters. Before we do that, however, let's see how this likelihood is altered if we have censored cases. If an individual is censored at time t_i, all we know is that this individual's event time is greater than t_i. But the probability of an event time greater than t_i is given by the survivor function $S(t)$ evaluated at time t_i. Now suppose that we have r uncensored observations and $n - r$ censored observations. If we arrange the data so that all the uncensored cases come first, we can write the likelihood as

$$L = \prod_{i=1}^{r} f_i(t_i) \prod_{i=r+1}^{n} S_i(t_i)$$

where, again, we subscript the survivor function to indicate that it depends on the covariates. Using the censoring indicator δ, we can equivalently write this as

$$L = \prod_{i=1}^{n} [f_i(t_i)]^{\delta_i}[S_i(t_i)]^{1-\delta_i}.$$

Here δ_i acts as a switch, turning the appropriate function on or off, depending on whether the observation is censored. As a result, we do not need to order the observations by censoring status. This last expression, which applies to all the models that PROC LIFEREG estimates with right-censored data, shows how censored and uncensored cases are combined in ML estimation.

Once we choose a particular model, we can substitute appropriate expressions for the p.d.f. and the survivor function. Take the simplest case—the exponential model. We have

$$f_i(t_i) = \lambda_i e^{-\lambda_i t_i} \text{ and } S_i(t_i) = e^{-\lambda_i t_i}$$

where $\lambda_i = \exp\{-\boldsymbol{\beta}\mathbf{x}_i\}$ and $\boldsymbol{\beta}$ is a vector of coefficients. Substituting, we get

$$L = \prod_{i=1}^{n}[\lambda_i e^{-\lambda_i t_i}]^{\delta_i}[e^{-\lambda_i t_i}]^{1-\delta_i} = \prod_{i=1}^{n}\lambda_i^{\delta_i}e^{-\lambda_i t_i}.$$

Although this expression can be maximized directly, it is generally easier to work with the natural logarithm of the likelihood function because products get converted into sums and exponents become coefficients. Because the logarithm is an increasing function, whatever maximizes the logarithm also maximizes the original function.

Taking the logarithm of both sides, we get

$$\log L = \sum_{i=1}^{n} \delta_i \log \lambda_i - \sum_{i=1}^{n} \lambda_i t_i$$

$$= -\boldsymbol{\beta}\sum_{i=1}^{n} \delta_i \mathbf{x}_i - \sum_{i=1}^{n} t_i e^{-\boldsymbol{\beta}\mathbf{x}_i}.$$

This brings us to step 2, choosing values of $\boldsymbol{\beta}$ that make this expression as large as possible. There are many different methods for maximizing functions like this. One well-known approach is to find the derivative of the function with respect to $\boldsymbol{\beta}$, set the derivative equal to 0, and then solve for $\boldsymbol{\beta}$. Taking the derivative and setting it equal to 0 gives us

$$\sum_{i=1}^{n} \delta_i \mathbf{x}_i = \sum_{i=1}^{n} \mathbf{x}_i t_i e^{-\boldsymbol{\beta}\mathbf{x}_i}.$$

Because $\mathbf{x}_i$ is a vector, this is actually a system of $k + 1$ equations, one for each element of $\boldsymbol{\beta}$.

While these equations are not terribly complicated, the problem is that they involve nonlinear functions of $\boldsymbol{\beta}$. Consequently, except in special cases (like a single dichotomous x variable), there is no explicit solution. Instead, we have to rely on iterative methods, which amount to successive approximations to the solution until the approximations converge to the correct value. Again, there are many different methods for doing this. All give the same solution, but they differ in such factors as speed of convergence, sensitivity to starting values, and computational difficulty at each iteration.

PROC LIFEREG uses the Newton-Raphson algorithm (actually a *ridge stabilized* version of the algorithm), which is by far the most popular numerical method for solving for $\boldsymbol{\beta}$. The method is named after Isaac Newton, who devised it for a single equation and a single unknown. But who was Raphson? Some say he was Newton's programmer. Actually Joseph Raphson was a younger contemporary of Newton who generalized the algorithm to multiple equations with multiple unknowns.

The Newton-Raphson algorithm can be described as follows. Let $\mathbf{U}(\boldsymbol{\beta})$ be the vector of first derivatives of $\log L$ with respect to $\boldsymbol{\beta}$, and let $\mathbf{I}(\boldsymbol{\beta})$ be the matrix of second derivatives of $\log L$ with respect to $\boldsymbol{\beta}$. That is,

$$\mathbf{U}(\boldsymbol{\beta}) = \frac{\partial \log L}{\partial \boldsymbol{\beta}}$$

$$\mathbf{I}(\boldsymbol{\beta}) = \frac{\partial^2 \log L}{\partial \boldsymbol{\beta} \partial \boldsymbol{\beta}'} .$$

The vector of first derivatives $\mathbf{U}(\boldsymbol{\beta})$ is sometimes called the *gradient* or *score*, while the matrix of second derivatives $\mathbf{I}(\boldsymbol{\beta})$ is called the *Hessian*. The Newton-Raphson algorithm is then

$$\boldsymbol{\beta}_{j+1} = \boldsymbol{\beta}_j - \mathbf{I}^{-1}(\boldsymbol{\beta}_j)\mathbf{U}(\boldsymbol{\beta}_j) \tag{4.4}$$

where $\mathbf{I}^{-1}$ is the inverse of $\mathbf{I}$. In practice, we need a set of starting values $\boldsymbol{\beta}_0$, which PROC LIFEREG calculates by using ordinary least squares, treating the censored observations as though they were uncensored. These starting values are substituted into the right side of equation (4.4), which yields the result for the first iteration, $\boldsymbol{\beta}_1$. These values are then substituted back into the right side, the first and second derivatives are recomputed, and the result is $\boldsymbol{\beta}_2$. This process is repeated until the maximum change in the parameter estimates from one step to the next is less than .001. (This is an absolute change if the current parameter value is less than .01; otherwise it is a relative change.)

Once the solution is found, a byproduct of the Newton-Raphson algorithm is an estimate of the covariance matrix of the coefficients, which is just $-\mathbf{I}^{-1}(\hat{\boldsymbol{\beta}})$. This matrix, which can be printed by listing COVB as an option in the MODEL statement, is often useful for constructing hypothesis tests about linear combinations of coefficients. PROC LIFEREG computes standard errors of the parameters by taking the square roots of the main diagonal elements of this matrix.

Maximum Likelihood Estimation: Practical Details

PROC LIFEREG chooses parameter estimates that maximize the logarithm of the likelihood of the data. For the most part, the iterative methods used to accomplish this task work quite well with no attention from the data analyst. If you're curious to see how the iterative process works, you can request ITPRINT as an option in the MODEL statement. Then, for each iteration, PROC LIFEREG will print out the log-likelihood and the parameter estimates. When the iterations are complete, the final gradient vector and the negative of the Hessian matrix will also be printed (see the preceding section for definitions of these quantities). When the exponential model was fitted to the recidivism data, the ITPRINT output revealed that it took six iterations to reach a solution. The log-likelihood for the starting values was –531.1, which increased to –327.5 at convergence. Examination of the coefficient estimates showed only slight changes after the fourth iteration. By comparison, the generalized gamma model took 13 iterations to converge.

Occasionally the algorithm fails to converge, although this seems to occur much less frequently than it does with logistic regression. In general, nonconvergence is more likely to occur when samples are small, when censoring is heavy, or when many parameters are being estimated. There is one situation, in particular, that guarantees nonconvergence (at least in principle). If all the cases at one value of a dichotomous covariate are censored, the coefficient for that variable becomes larger in magnitude at each iteration. Here's why: the coefficient of a dichotomous covariate is a function of the logarithm of the ratio of the hazards for the two groups. But if all the cases in a group are censored, the ML estimate for the hazard in that group is 0. If the 0 is in the denominator of the ratio, then the coefficient tends toward plus infinity. If it's in the numerator, taking the logarithm yields a result that tends toward minus infinity. By extension, if a covariate has multiple values that are treated as a set of dichotomous variables (e.g., with a CLASS statement) and all cases are censored for one or more of the values, nonconvergence should result. When this happens, there is no ideal solution. You can remove the offending variable from the model, but that variable may actually be one of the strongest predictors. When the variable has more than two values, you can combine adjacent values or treat the variable as quantitative.

PROC LIFEREG has two ways of alerting you to convergence problems. If the number of iterations exceeds the maximum allowed (the default is 50), SAS issues the message: `WARNING: Convergence not attained in 50 iterations.  WARNING: The procedure is continuing but the validity of the model fit is questionable.` If it detects a problem before the iteration limit is reached, the software says `WARNING:  The negative of the Hessian is not positive definite.  The convergence is questionable.` Unfortunately, PROC LIFEREG sometimes reports estimates and gives no warning message in situations that are fundamentally nonconvergent. The only indication of a problem is a coefficient that is large in magnitude together with a huge standard error.

It's tempting to try to get convergence by raising the default maximum number of iterations or by relaxing the convergence criterion. This rarely works, however, so don't get your hopes up. You can raise the maximum with the MAXITER= option in the MODEL statement. You can alter the convergence criterion with the CONVERGE= option, but I don't recommend this unless you know what you're doing. Too large a value could make it seem that convergence had occurred when there is actually no ML solution.

HYPOTHESIS TESTS

PROC LIFEREG is somewhat skimpy in its facilities for hypothesis tests. It routinely reports chi-square tests for the hypothesis that each of the coefficients is 0. These are Wald tests that are calculated simply by dividing each coefficient by its estimated standard error and squaring the result. For models like the exponential that restrict the scale parameter to be 1.0, PROC LIFEREG reports a Lagrange multiplier chi-square statistic (also known as a score statistic) for the hypothesis that the parameter is, indeed, equal to 1.0. Finally, as we've seen, for categorical variables named in a CLASS statement, PROC LIFEREG gives a Wald chi-square statistic for the null hypothesis that all the coefficients associated with the variable are 0.

To test other hypotheses, you have to construct the appropriate statistic yourself. Before describing how to do this, I'll first present some background. For all the regression models considered in this book, there are three general methods for constructing test statistics: Wald statistics, score statistics, and likelihood ratio statistics. Wald statistics are calculated using certain functions (quadratic forms) of parameter estimates and their estimated variances and covariances. Score statistics are based on similar functions of the first and second derivatives of the likelihood function. Finally, likelihood-ratio statistics are calculated by maximizing the likelihood twice: under the null hypothesis and with the null hypothesis relaxed. The statistic is then twice the positive difference in the two log-likelihoods.

You can use all three methods to test the same hypotheses, and all three produce chi-square statistics with the same number of degrees of freedom. Furthermore, they are asymptotically equivalent, meaning that their approximate large-sample distributions are identical. Hence, asymptotic theory gives no basis for preferring one method over another. There is some evidence that likelihood-ratio statistics may more closely approximate a chi-square distribution in small to moderate sized samples, however, and some authors (e.g., Collett 1994) express a strong preference for these statistics. On the other hand, Wald tests and score tests are often more convenient to calculate because they don't require re-estimation of the model for each hypothesis tested.

Let's first consider a likelihood-ratio test of the null hypothesis that all the covariates have coefficients of 0. This is analogous to the usual *F*-test that is routinely reported for linear regression models. (Many authorities hold that if this hypothesis is not rejected, then there is little point in examining individual coefficients for statistical significance.) To calculate this statistic, we need only to fit a null model that includes no covariates. For a Weibull model, we can accomplish that with the following statement:

```
model week*arrest(0)= / dist=weibull;
```

For the recidivism data, this produces a log-likelihood of −338.59. By contrast, the Weibull model with seven covariates displayed in Output 4.3 has a log-likelihood of −321.85. Taking twice the positive difference between these two values yields a chi-square value of 33.48. With seven degrees of freedom (the number of covariates excluded from the null model), the *p*-value is less than .001. So we reject the null hypothesis and conclude that at least one of the coefficients is nonzero.

You can also test the same hypothesis with a Wald statistic, but that involves the following steps: (1) request that the parameter estimates and their covariance matrix be written to a SAS data set; (2) read that data set into PROC IML, the SAS matrix algebra procedure; (3) use PROC IML to perform the necessary matrix calculations. (These calculations include inverting the appropriate submatrix of the covariance matrix, and premultiplying and postmultiplying that matrix by a vector containing appropriate linear combinations of the coefficients). That's clearly a much more involved procedure. Furthermore, PROC LIFEREG will not write the parameter estimates to a data set if there are any CLASS variables in the model. That's unfortunate because testing hypotheses about CLASS variables is one of the more frequently needed applications.

Wald statistics for testing equality of any two coefficients *are* simple to calculate. The method is particularly useful for doing post-hoc comparisons of the coefficients of CLASS variables. Earlier we used a CLASS statement to include a three-category education variable in the model. As shown in Output 4.7, there is one chi-square test comparing category 3 with category 5, and another chi-square test comparing category 4 with category 5. But there is no test reported for comparing category 3 with category 4. The appropriate null hypothesis is that $\beta_3 = \beta_4$, where the subscripts refer to the values of categories. A Wald chi-square for testing this hypothesis can be computed by

$$\frac{(\hat\beta_3 - \hat\beta_4)^2}{Var(\hat\beta_3) + Var(\hat\beta_4) - 2Cov(\hat\beta_3\ \hat\beta_4)}. \tag{4.5}$$

The (estimated) variances and covariances in the denominator are easily obtained from the covariance matrix that was requested in the MODEL statement. Output 4.8 shows a portion of the printed matrix. In this printout, EDUC.1 and EDUC.2 refer to categories 3 and 4, respectively.

Output 4.8 *A Portion of the Covariance Matrix for a Model with a CLASS Variable*

```
LIFEREG  PROCEDURE

              Estimated Covariance Matrix

                    EDUC.1        EDUC.2        SCALE

     INTERCPT     -0.094637     -0.090901     0.003377
          FIN     -0.000920     -0.001186     0.001338
          AGE      0.000137      0.000285     0.000202
         RACE      0.002250     -0.003371    -0.001341
         WEXP      0.002200     -0.001100     0.000398
          MAR      0.000551      0.000826     0.001593
         PARO     -0.000617      0.000704     0.000383
         PRIO     -0.000593     -0.000131    -0.000260
       EDUC.1      0.095495      0.086663    -0.002738
       EDUC.2      0.086663      0.105149    -0.001756
        SCALE     -0.002738     -0.001756     0.004019
```

$Var(\hat\beta_3)$ is found to be .095495 at the intersection of EDUC.1 with itself, and similarly $Var(\hat\beta_4)$ is .105149 at the intersection of EDUC.2 with itself. The covariance is .086663 at the intersection of EDUC.1 and EDUC.2. Combining these numbers with the coefficient estimates in Output 4.7, we get

$$\frac{[-.5116 - (-.3536)]^2}{.09549 + .1051 - 2(.08666)} = .9154.$$

With 1 degree of freedom, the chi-square value is far from the .05 critical value of 3.84. We conclude that there is no difference in the time to arrest between those with 9th grade or less and those with 10th or 11th grade education. This should not be surprising since the overall chi-square test is not significant, nor is the more extreme comparison of category 3 with category 5. Of course, when performing post-hoc comparisons like this, it is generally advisable to adjust the alpha level for multiple comparisons. (The simplest approach is the well-known Bonferroni method: For k tests and an overall Type I error rate of α, each test uses α/k as the criterion value).

We can also test the hypothesis that $\beta_3 = \beta_4$ with the likelihood ratio statistic. To do that, we must reestimate the model while imposing the constraint that $\beta_3 = \beta_4$. We can accomplish this reestimate by recoding the education variable so that levels 3 and 4 have the same value. For example, the DATA step can contain a statement like

```
if educ = 3 then educ = 4;
```

When I estimated the model with this recoding, the log-likelihood was −317.97, compared with −317.50 with the original coding. Twice the positive difference is .94, which, again, is far from statistically significant.

GOODNESS-OF-FIT TESTS WITH THE LIKELIHOOD-RATIO STATISTIC

As we have seen, the AFT model encompasses a number of submodels that differ in the assumed distribution for T, the time of the event. When we tried out those models on the recidivism data, we found that they produced generally similar coefficient estimates and p-values. A glaring exception is the log-normal model, which yields qualitatively different conclusions for some of the covariates. Clearly, we need some way of deciding between the log-normal and the other models. Even if all the models agree on the coefficient estimates, they still have markedly different implications for the shape of the hazard function. Again we may need methods for deciding which of these shapes is the best description of the true hazard function.

In the next section, we'll consider some graphical methods for comparing models. Here, we examine a simple and often decisive method based on the likelihood ratio statistic. In general, likelihood-ratio statistics can be used to compare nested models. A model is said to be nested within another model if the first model is a special case of the second. More precisely, model A is nested within model B if A can be obtained by imposing restrictions on the parameters in B. For example, the exponential model is nested within both the Weibull and the standard gamma models. You get the exponential from the

Weibull by forcing $\sigma=1$, and you get the exponential from the gamma by forcing both the shape and scale parameters equal to 1.

If model A is nested within model B, we can evaluate the fit of A by taking twice the positive difference in the log-likelihoods for the two models. Of course, to evaluate a model in this way, you need to find another model that it is nested within. As previously noted, the Weibull, standard gamma, and log-normal models (but not the log-logistic) are all nested within the generalized gamma model, making it a simple matter to evaluate them with the likelihood ratio test. (PROC LIFEREG is one of the few commercial programs that will fit the generalized gamma model).

Here are the restrictions on the generalized gamma that are implied by its submodels:

$\sigma = \delta$	standard gamma
$\delta = 1$	Weibull
$\sigma = 1, \delta = 1$	exponential
$\delta = 0$	log-normal

Remember that σ is the scale parameter and δ is the shape parameter. The likelihood ratio test for each of these models is, in essence, a test for the null hypothesis that the particular restriction is true. Hence, these tests should be viewed not as omnibus tests of the fit of a model, but rather as tests of particular features of a model and its fit to the data.

Let's calculate the likelihood-ratio tests for the recidivism data. The log-likelihoods for the models fitted earlier in this chapter are

−325.83	exponential
−319.38	Weibull
−322.69	log-normal
−319.46	standard gamma
−319.40	log-logistic
−319.38	generalized gamma

Because these log-likelihoods are all negative (which will virtually always be the case), lower magnitudes correspond to better fits. Taking the differences between nested models and multiplying by 2 yields the following likelihood-ratio chi-square statistics:

12.90	exponential vs. Weibull
12.74	exponential vs. standard gamma
12.90	exponential vs. g. gamma
.00	Weibull vs. g. gamma
6.62	log-normal vs. g. gamma
.16	standard gamma vs. g. gamma

With the exception of the exponential model versus the generalized gamma model (which has 2 d.f.), all these tests have a single degree of freedom corresponding to the single restriction being tested.

The conclusions are clear cut. The exponential model must be rejected (p=.002), implying that the hazard of arrest is not constant over the one-year interval. This is consistent with the results we saw earlier for the Lagrange multiplier test, although that test produced a chi-square value of 24.93, more than twice as large as the likelihood ratio statistic. The log-normal model must also be rejected, although somewhat less decisively (p=.01). On the other hand, both the standard gamma and the Weibull models fit the data very well. Apparently, we can safely ignore the discrepant coefficient estimates for the log-normal model because the model is not consistent with the data.

The Weibull and the standard gamma models are similar insofar as both have monotonic hazards that, in this case, are increasing. The principal difference is that the standard gamma model has an upper limit on the hazard while the Weibull model does not. For many applications, it is difficult to empirically discriminate between these two models. If forced to choose between them, most statisticians would pick the Weibull model because it is mathematically simpler and is also a proportional hazards model. Before embracing either of these models, however, remember that the log-logistic model, which has a nonmonotonic hazard function, does not fit into our nesting scheme. In fact, its log-likelihood is only trivially lower than that for the generalized gamma model, suggesting a very good fit to the data. While this fact should lead us to retain the log-logistic model as one of our possible candidates, we cannot use it in a formal test of significance.

In interpreting these likelihood ratio statistics, you should keep in mind that the validity of each test rests on the (at least approximate) truth of the more general model. If that model does not fit the data well, then the test can be quite misleading. I have seen several examples in which the test for the exponential model versus the Weibull model is not significant, but the test for the Weibull model versus the generalized gamma model is highly significant. Without seeing the second test, you might conclude that the hazard is constant when, in fact, it is not. But what about the generalized gamma model itself? How do we know that it provides a decent fit to the data? Unfortunately, we can't get a likelihood ratio test of the generalized gamma model unless we can fit an even *more* general model. And even if we could fit a more general model, how would we know *that* model was satisfactory? Obviously you have to stop somewhere. As noted earlier, the generalized gamma model is a rich family of distributions, so we expect it to provide a reasonably good fit in the majority of cases.

GRAPHICAL METHODS FOR EVALUATING MODEL FIT

Another way to discriminate between different probability distributions is to use graphical diagnostics. In Chapter 3 we saw how to use plots of the estimated survivor function to evaluate two of the distributional models considered in this chapter. Specifically, if the distribution of event times is exponential, a plot of $-\log \hat{S}(t)$ versus t should yield a straight line with an origin at 0. If event times have a Weibull distribution, a plot of $\log[-\log \hat{S}(t)]$ versus $\log t$ should also be a straight line. These plots can be requested in PROC LIFETEST with the PLOTS=(LS, LLS) option in the PROC LIFETEST statement.

Output 4.9 shows the log-survivor plot for the recidivism data. The graph is approximately linear with a slight tendency to bow upward. This tendency is consistent with earlier indications that the hazard tends to increase with time. Output 4.10 shows the log-log survivor plot for the same data. There is little evidence of nonlinearity (except for the jag in the middle), which is consistent with the Weibull model.

Output 4.9 *Log-Survivor Plot for Recidivism Data*

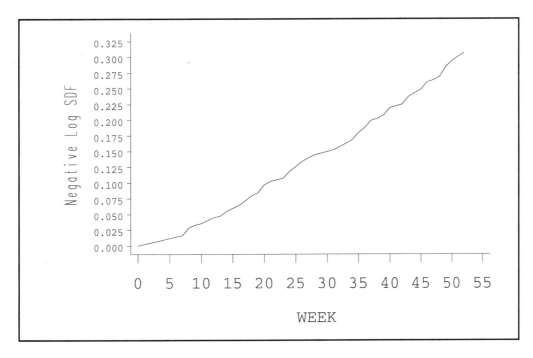

Output 4.10 *Log-Log Survivor Plot for Recidivism Data*

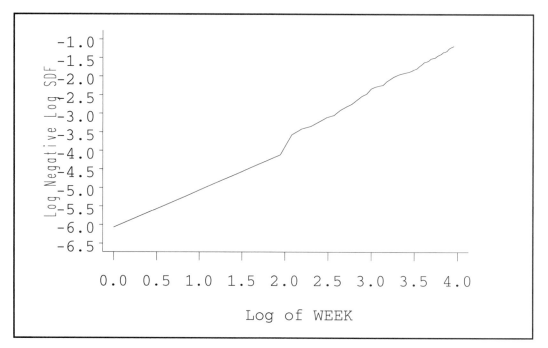

We can use a similar approach to evaluate the log-normal and log-logistic distributions, but it's a little more trouble to produce the graphs. The steps are as follows:

1. Use PROC LIFETEST to get the Kaplan-Meier estimate of the survivor function and output it to a SAS data set.
2. In a new DATA step, apply appropriate transformations to the survivor estimates.
3. Use the PLOT or GPLOT procedures to produce the desired graphs.

For the log-normal distribution, a plot of $\Phi^{-1}[1-\hat{S}(t)]$ versus log t should be linear, where $\Phi(.)$ is the c.d.f of a standard normal variable and Φ^{-1} is its inverse. Similarly, a log-logistic distribution implies that a plot of $\log[(1-\hat{S}(t))/\hat{S}(t)]$ versus log t will be linear. Here's the SAS code for producing these plots for the recidivism data:

```
proc lifetest data=recid outsurv=a;
   time week*arrest(0);
run;
```

```
data;
   set a;
   s=survival;
   logit=log((1-s)/s);
   lnorm=probit(1-s);
   lweek=log(week);
run;

proc gplot;
   symbol1 value=none i=join;
   plot logit*lweek lnorm*lweek;
run;
```

The OUTSURV option on the first line produces a data set (named A in this example) that includes the KM estimates of the survivor function in a variable called SURVIVAL. See Output 3.3 for an example of what's contained in such data sets. In the DATA step that follows, the variable SURVIVAL is renamed S to make it easier to specify the transformations. Next, the two transformations are calculated, along with the logarithm of the time variable (PROBIT is the built-in SAS function that gives the inverse of the standard normal c.d.f.) Finally, the two plots are requested. These are shown in Output 4.11 and Output 4.12. The plot for the log-logistic distribution shows some minor deviations from linearity, while the log-normal plot appears to be more seriously bowed upward.

Output 4.11 *Plot for Evaluating Log-Logistic Model*

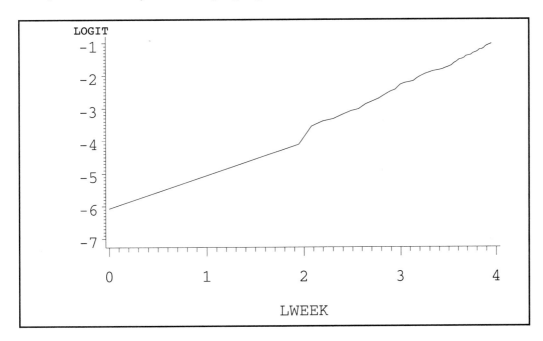

Output 4.12 *Plot for Evaluating Log-Normal Model*

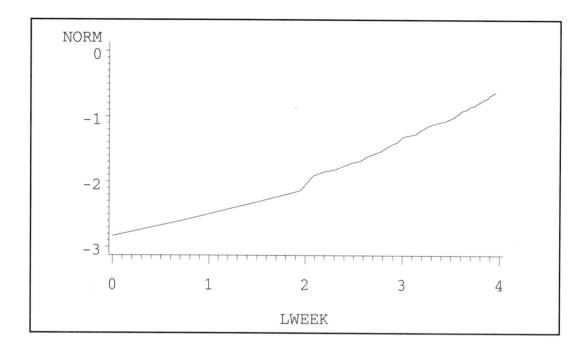

One difficulty with all these plots is that they are based on the assumption that the sample is drawn from a homogeneous population, implying that no covariates are related to survival time. In practice, that means that a model that looks fine on the plots may not fit well when covariates are taken into account. Similarly, a model that is rejected on the basis of the plots may be quite satisfactory when survival time is allowed to depend on covariates. One solution to this problem is to create plots on the *residuals* from the regression models. Not only does this take the covariates into account in judging model fit, it also leads to a single type of transformation and plot regardless of the model fitted.

Several different kinds of residuals have been proposed for survival models (Collett 1994), but the ones most suitable for this purpose are *Cox-Snell residuals*, defined as

$$e_i = -\log \hat{S}(t_i | \mathbf{x}_i)$$

where t_i is the observed event time or censoring time for individual i, $\mathbf{x}_i$ is the vector of covariate values for individual i, and $\hat{S}(t)$ is the estimated probability of surviving to time t, *based on the fitted model*. Now the e_is are rather unlike the usual residuals calculated from a linear regression model. For one thing, they're always positive. For our purposes, however, what's important about these residuals if that, if the fitted model is correct, the e_is have (approximately) an exponential distribution with parameter $\lambda=1$. (If t_i is a censoring time, then e_i is also treated as a censored observation.) But we already have a graphical method for evaluating exponential distributions with censoring: compute the KM estimator of the survivor function, take minus the log of the estimated survivor function, and plot that against t (actually e in this case). The resulting graph should be a straight line, with a slope of 1 and an origin at 0.

Here's an example of how to do this for a Weibull model fitted to the recidivism data:

```
proc lifereg data=recid;
   model week*arrest(0)=fin age race wexp mar paro prio
        / dist=weibull;
   output out=a cdf=f;
run;

data b;
   set a;
   e=-log(1-f);
run;

proc lifetest data=b plots=(ls) notable graphics;
   time e*arrest(0);
   symbol1 v=none;
run;
```

Output 4.13 *Residual Plot for Weibull Model*

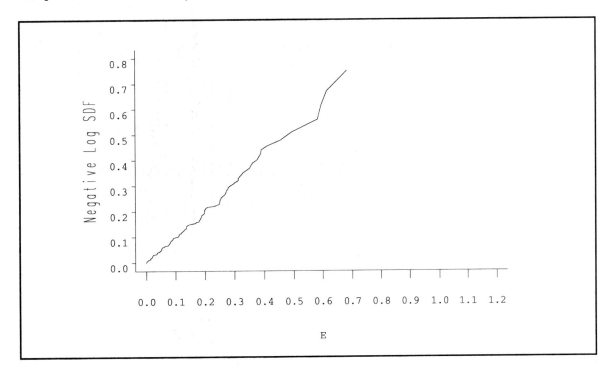

The OUTPUT statement in the LIFEREG procedure defines an output data set (here named A) containing all of the original data and selected additional variables. By specifying CDF=F, we request the estimated c.d.f. evaluated at t_i, and we give that variable the name F (or any other name we choose). Since the c.d.f. is just 1 minus the survivor function, we're halfway there in getting the residuals. In the DATA step, we take minus the log of 1− F to get the Cox-Snell residuals. Finally, in PROC LIFETEST we request the log-survivor plot for the residuals (the NOTABLE option suppresses the KM table). We can repeat this set of statements for each choice of distribution, changing only the DIST option in the MODEL statement.

Output 4.14   *Residual Plot for Log-Normal Model*

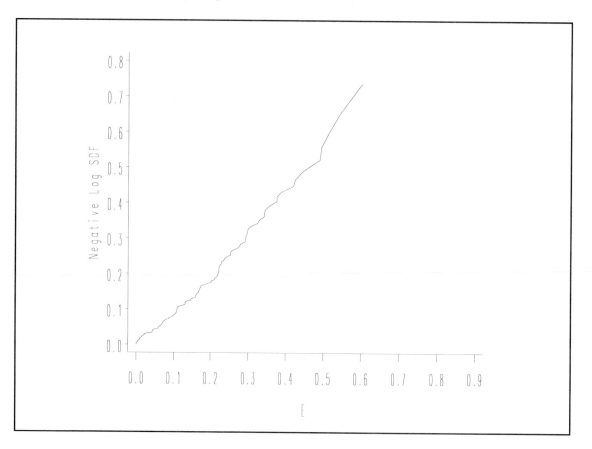

Unfortunately, while this method is attractive in theory and is easy to implement, I have not found it to be sensitive to differences in model fit. Output 4.13 shows the plot for the Weibull model, which fit the data well according to the earlier likelihood ratio test. To my eye, it looks pretty straight. Output 4.14 for the log-normal model also looks fairly straight, even though the likelihood ratio test indicated rejection. Any differences between the two plots are quite subtle. Plots for the other models are also similar.

LEFT CENSORING AND INTERVAL CENSORING

One of PROC LIFEREG's more useful features is its ability to handle left censoring and interval censoring. Recall that left censoring occurs when we know that an event occurred earlier than some time t, but we don't know exactly when. Interval censoring occurs when the time of event occurrence is known to be somewhere between times a and b, but we don't know exactly when. Left censoring can be seen as a special case of interval censoring in which $a = 0$; right censoring is a special case in which $b=\infty$.

Interval-censored data are readily incorporated into the likelihood function. The contribution to the likelihood for an observation censored between a and b is just

$$S_i(a) - S_i(b)$$

where $S_i(.)$ is the survivor function for observation i. (This difference is always positive because $S_i(t)$ is a decreasing function of t.) In words, the probability of an event occurring in the interval (a, b) is the probability of an event occurring after a minus the probability of it occurring after b. For left-censored data, $S_i(a) = 1$; for right-censored data $S_i(b)=0$.

PROC LIFEREG can handle any combination of left-censored, right-censored, and interval-censored data, but a different MODEL syntax is required if there are any left-censored or interval-censored observations. Instead of a time variable and a censoring variable, PROC LIFEREG needs two time variables, an upper time and a lower time. Let's call them UPPER and LOWER. The MODEL statement then reads as follows:

MODEL (LOWER,UPPER)=*list of covariates*;

The censoring status is determined by whether the two values are equal and whether either is coded as missing data:

Uncensored:	LOWER and UPPER are both present and equal.
Interval Censored:	LOWER and UPPER are present and different.
Right Censored:	LOWER is present, but UPPER is missing.
Left Censored:	LOWER is missing, but UPPER is present.

You might think that left censoring could also be indicated by coding LOWER as 0, but PROC LIFEREG *excludes* any observations with times that are 0 or negative. Observations are also excluded if both UPPER and LOWER are missing, or if LOWER > UPPER. Here are some examples:

Observation	Lower	Upper	Status
1	3.9	3.9	Uncensored
2	7.2	.	Right Censored
3	4.1	5.6	Interval Censored
4	.	2.0	Left Censored
5	0	5.8	Excluded
6	3.2	1.9	Excluded

Let's look at a hypothetical example of left censoring for the recidivism data. Suppose that of the 114 arrests, the week of arrest was unavailable for 30 cases. In other words, we know that an arrest occurred between 0 and 52 weeks, but we don't know when. To illustrate this, I modified the recidivism data by recoding the WEEK variable as missing for the first 30 arrests in the data set. Then, I estimated a Weibull model with the following program:

```
data;
   set recidlft;

      /* uncensored cases: */
   if arrest=1 and week ne . then do;
      upper=week;
      lower=week;
   end;

      /* left-censored cases: */
   if arrest=1 and week = . then do;
      upper=52;
      lower=.;
   end;

      /* right-censored cases: */
   if arrest=0 then do;
      upper=.;
      lower=52;
   end;
run;

proc lifereg;
   model (lower,upper)=fin age race wexp mar paro prio
         / dist=weibull;
run;
```

You should compare the results in Output 4.15 with those in Output 4.3, for which there were no left-censored cases. Although the results are quite similar, the chi-square statistics are nearly all smaller when some of the data are left censored. This is to be expected since left censoring entails some loss of information. Note that you cannot compare the log-likelihood for this model with the log-likelihood for the model with no left censoring. Whenever you alter the data, the log-likelihoods are no longer comparable.

Output 4.15 *Results for the Weibull Model with Left-Censored Data*

```
                    L I F E R E G    P R O C E D U R E

Data Set            =WORK.DATA5
Dependent Variable=Log(LOWER)
Dependent Variable=Log(UPPER)
Noncensored Values=     84  Right Censored Values=    318
Left Censored Values=  30  Interval Censored Values=   0


Log Likelihood for WEIBULL -304.7419068

Variable  DF    Estimate  Std Err ChiSquare   Pr>Chi Label/Value

INTERCPT   1   3.9656454 0.458605  74.77401   0.0001 Intercept
FIN        1  0.29116771 0.151256  3.705626   0.0542
AGE        1  0.04471953  0.01772  6.368647   0.0116
RACE       1  -0.2312236 0.240799  0.922055   0.3369
WEXP       1  0.12310271 0.166282  0.548081   0.4591
MAR        1  0.31904485 0.300374  1.128183   0.2882
PARO       1  0.07010297 0.152682  0.210814   0.6461
PRIO       1  -0.0699893 0.022929  9.317426   0.0023
SCALE      1  0.77869005 0.080329                    Extreme value scale parameter
```

Now consider an application of *interval* censoring. We can actually view the recidivism data as discrete since we only know the week of the arrest, not the exact day. Although Petersen (1991) has shown that some bias can result from treating discrete data as continuous, there's probably no danger with 52 different values for the measurement of arrest time. Nevertheless, you can use the interval-censoring option to get a slightly improved estimate. For an arrest that occurs in week 2, the actual interval in which the arrest occurred is (1, 2). Similarly, the interval is (2, 3) for an arrest occurring in week 3. This suggests the following recoding of the data:

```
data;
   set recid;

      /* interval censored cases: */
   if arrest=1 then do;
      upper=week;
      lower=week-.9999;
   end;
```

```
                        /* right censored cases: */
             if arrest=0 then do;
                upper=.;
                lower=52;
             end;
         run;

         proc lifereg;
            model (lower, upper) = fin age race wexp mar paro prio
                   / dist=weibull;
         run;
```

To get the lower value for the interval-censored cases, I subtract .9999 instead of 1 so that the result is not 0 for those persons with WEEK=1.

The results in Output 4.16 are very close to those in Output 4.3, which assumed that time was measured exactly. If the intervals had been larger, we might have found more substantial differences. The magnitude of the log-likelihood is nearly doubled for the interval-censored version but, again, log-likelihoods are not comparable when the data are altered.

Output 4.16 *Results Treating Recidivism Data as Interval Censored*

```
                   L I F E R E G   P R O C E D U R E

Data Set            =RECID
Dependent Variable=Log(LOWER)
Dependent Variable=Log(UPPER)
Noncensored Values=      0   Right Censored Values=     318
Left Censored Values=    0   Interval Censored Values= 114


Log Likelihood for WEIBULL -680.9846402


Variable  DF    Estimate  Std Err ChiSquare  Pr>Chi Label/Value

INTERCPT   1 3.99060867  0.437423  83.22915  0.0001 Intercept
FIN        1 0.28371327  0.143999  3.881861  0.0488
AGE        1   0.0425244 0.016707  6.478366  0.0109
RACE       1 -0.2342767  0.229784   1.03949  0.3079
WEXP       1 0.11058711  0.158172  0.488822  0.4845
MAR        1 0.32458763  0.285258  1.294761  0.2552
PARO       1 0.06182479   0.14573   0.17998  0.6714
PRIO       1 -0.0684968  0.021843  9.833993  0.0017
SCALE      1 0.74354156  0.066542           Extreme value scale parameter
```

GENERATING PREDICTIONS AND HAZARD FUNCTIONS

After fitting a model with PROC LIFEREG, it's sometimes desirable to generate predicted survival times for the observations in the data set. If you want a single point estimate for each individual, the predicted median survival time is probably the best. You can get this easily with the OUTPUT statement, as shown in the following example:

```
proc lifereg data=recid;
   model week*arrest(0)=fin age race wexp mar paro prio
         / dist=weibull;
   output out=a p=median std=s;
run;
proc print data=a;
   var week arrest _prob_ median s;
run;
```

The P= keyword in the OUTPUT statement requests percentiles. By default, PROC LIFEREG calculates the 50th percentile, that is, the median. (The word *median* in the OUTPUT statement is just the variable name I chose to hold the quantiles). You can request other percentiles with the QUANTILE keyword, as described in the PROC LIFEREG documentation. The STD keyword requests the standard errors of the medians.

Output 4.17 shows the first 20 cases in the new data set. In the output, _PROB_ is the quantile (i.e., percentile divided by 100) requested, and S is the standard error of the median. Note that these predicted medians are all beyond the observation limit of 52 weeks, which is not surprising given the heavy censoring of the data. Therefore, you should use extreme caution in interpreting these medians because the model is being extrapolated to times that are far beyond those that are actually observed.

Output 4.17 *Predicted Median Survival Times for Recidivism Data (First 20 Cases)*

OBS	WEEK	ARREST	_PROB_	MEDIAN	S
1	52	0	0.5	128.135	21.4610
2	52	0	0.5	104.885	17.9065
3	52	0	0.5	148.637	45.7291
4	52	0	0.5	74.553	10.6380
5	52	0	0.5	187.027	55.7407
6	12	1	0.5	150.975	44.9887
7	52	0	0.5	91.387	13.0158
8	19	1	0.5	60.670	9.9230

continued on next page

Output 4.11   continued

9	52	0	0.5	60.247	8.0057
10	15	1	0.5	93.081	14.0860
11	8	1	0.5	93.083	15.5320
12	52	0	0.5	101.941	16.8422
13	52	0	0.5	141.989	38.4758
14	36	1	0.5	87.983	13.8664
15	52	1	0.5	131.832	28.3005
16	4	1	0.5	72.083	13.8307
17	45	1	0.5	65.376	10.3499
18	52	1	0.5	78.196	13.9176
19	52	0	0.5	125.980	42.6774
20	52	0	0.5	84.832	14.4458

You may also get predicted values for sets of covariate values that are not in the original data set. Before estimating the model, simply append to the data set artificial observations with the desired covariate values and with the event time set to missing. These artificial observations are not used in estimating the model, but predicted values will be generated for them. If you only want predictions for a subset of the observations (either real or artificial), create a variable (e.g., USE) that is equal to 1 if you want a prediction and that is equal to 0 otherwise. Then, in the OUTPUT statement, include CONTROL=USE.

Instead of predicted survival times, researchers often want to predict the probability of surviving to some specified time (e.g., 5-year survival probabilities). While these are not directly computed by PROC LIFEREG, it's fairly straightforward to calculate them substituting linear predictor values produced by the OUTPUT statement into formulas for the survivor function (given in the PROC LIFEREG documentation). To make it easy, I've written a macro called PREDICT, which is described in detail in Appendix 1, "Macro Programs." This macro is used in the following way. When specifying the model, you must request that the parameter estimates be written to a data set using the OUTEST= option. Next, request that the linear predictor be added to another data set using the XBETA= option in the OUTPUT statement. Finally, call the macro, indicating the names of the two input data sets, the name assigned the linear predictor, and the time for calculating the survival probabilities. For example, to produce 30-week survival probabilities for the recidivism data, submit these statements:

```
proc lifereg data=recid outest=a;
   model week*arrest(0) = fin age race wexp mar paro prio
          / dist=weibull;
   output out=b xbeta=lp;
run;

%predict(outest=a,out=b,xbeta=lp,time=30)
```

Output 4.18 shows the first 20 cases of the new data set. The last column (PROB) contains the 30-week survival probabilities based on the fitted model.

Output 4.18 *Predicted 30-Week Survival Probabilities for Recidivism Data*

OBS	WEEK	FIN	AGE	RACE	WEXP	MAR	PARO	PRIO	EDUC	AGE1	ARREST	T	PROB
1	52	1	24	1	1	0	1	1	4	14	0	30	0.91365
2	52	0	29	1	1	0	1	3	4	17	0	30	0.88726
3	52	1	20	1	1	1	1	1	3	20	0	30	0.92930
4	52	0	20	1	0	0	1	1	4	18	0	30	0.82436
5	52	1	31	0	1	0	1	3	3	7	0	30	0.94827
6	12	1	22	1	1	1	1	2	4	14	1	30	0.93078
7	52	0	24	1	1	0	1	2	4	17	0	30	0.86491
8	19	0	18	1	0	0	0	2	3	13	1	30	0.77265
9	52	0	18	1	0	0	1	3	3	8	0	30	0.77068
10	15	1	22	1	0	0	1	3	4	14	1	30	0.86811
11	8	1	21	1	1	0	1	4	3	11	1	30	0.86811
12	52	1	21	1	0	0	1	1	4	16	0	30	0.88294
13	52	1	21	0	1	0	1	1	5	17	0	30	0.92479
14	36	1	19	1	0	0	1	2	3	13	1	30	0.85806
15	52	0	33	1	1	0	1	2	4	19	1	30	0.91688
16	4	0	18	1	1	0	0	1	4	13	1	30	0.81669
17	45	1	18	1	0	0	0	5	3	14	1	30	0.79275
18	52	0	21	1	0	0	0	0	3	17	1	30	0.83474
19	52	1	20	1	0	1	0	1	3	15	0	30	0.91166
20	52	0	22	1	1	0	0	1	2	21	0	30	0.85119

Since every model estimated in PROC LIFEREG has an implicit hazard function, it would be nice to see what that hazard function looks like. I've written another macro called LIFEHAZ (also described in Appendix 1) that produces a graph of the hazard as a function of time. As with the PREDICT macro, you first need to fit a PROC LIFEREG model that includes the OUTPUT statement and the OUTEST= option in the PROC statement. Using the same PROC LIFEREG specification that was used before the PREDICT macro, you then submit the following:

```
%lifehaz(outest=a,out=b,xbeta=lp)
```

For the recidivism data with the Weibull model, this macro produces the graph shown in Output 4.19. Keep in mind that this graph is heavily dependent on the specified model. If we specify a log-normal model before using the LIFEHAZ macro, the graph will look quite different.

Output 4.19 *Graph of Hazard Function for Recidivism Data*

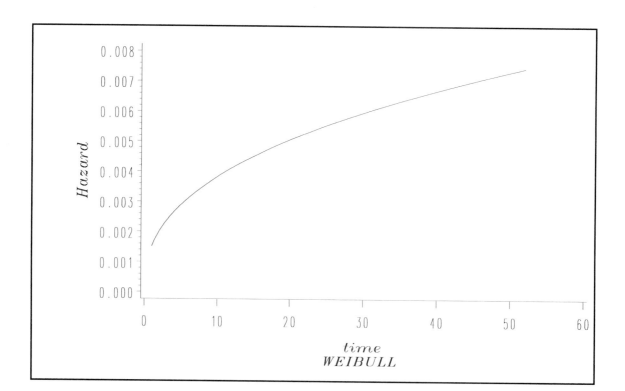

THE PIECEWISE EXPONENTIAL MODEL

All the AFT models we have considered so far assume that the hazard is a smooth, relatively simple function of time. The Cox model (estimated with the PHREG procedure) is much less restrictive in this regard, but it lacks the facility to test hypotheses about the shape of the hazard function. One way to get some of the flexibility of the Cox model without losing the hypothesis testing capability is to employ the piecewise exponential model, a method that is widely used in several fields. We can easily estimate it with PROC LIFEREG, although it requires some preliminary restructuring of the data. A bonus of this method is the ability to incorporate time dependent covariates.

The basic idea is simple. Divide the time scale into intervals. Assume that the hazard is constant within each interval but can vary across intervals. In symbols, we define a set of J intervals, with cut points $a_0, a_1, \dots, a_J$, where $a_0 = 0$, and $a_J = \infty$. Thus, interval j is given by $[a_{j-1}, a_j)$. The hazard for individual i is assumed to have the form

$$h_i(t) = \lambda_j e^{\beta x_i} \qquad \text{for } a_{j-1} \le t < a_j$$

or equivalently

$$\log h_i(t) = \alpha_j + \beta x_i$$

where $\alpha_j = \log \lambda_j$. Thus, the intercept in the log-hazard equation is allowed to vary in an unrestricted fashion from one interval to another. The choice of intervals is arbitrary, however, leading to some arbitrariness in the estimates.

The procedure for estimating this model is best explained by way of example. For the recidivism data, let's break up the 52-week observation period into four quarters of 13 weeks each and assume that the hazard is constant within each quarter. We then create a new data set with possibly multiple records for each person. One record is created for each quarter during which an individual was at risk (of the first arrest). Four records are created for persons who were arrested in the fourth quarter or who were not arrested at all. Three records are created for those arrested in the third quarter, two records are created for those arrested in the second quarter, and one record is created for those arrested in the first quarter. This yields a total of 1,573 person-quarters for the 432 ex-convicts.

Each record is treated as a distinct observation, with the time reset to 0 at the beginning of the quarter. If an arrest occurred in the quarter, a censoring indicator variable for that person-quarter is set to 1; otherwise, it is set to 0. If no arrest occurred in the quarter, a time variable is assigned the full 13 weeks. If an arrest occurred, the time variable is coded as the length of time from the start of the quarter until the arrest.

For the recidivism data, all censoring is at the end of the fourth quarter. Had there been any censoring within quarters, the time variable would be coded as the length of time from the beginning of the quarter until censoring occurred. The fixed covariates are simply replicated for each quarter. If there were any time-dependent covariates, their values at the beginning of each quarter could be assigned to the records for that quarter.

Here's a DATA step for creating such a data set:

```
data quarter;
   set recid;
   quarter=ceil(week/13);
   do j=1 to quarter;
      time=13;
      event=0;
      if j=quarter and arrest=1 then do;
            event=1;
            time=week-13*(quarter-1);
      end;
      output;
   end;
run;
```

The CEIL function, which produces the smallest integer greater than its argument, yields values of 1, 2, 3, or 4, corresponding to the quarter. The DO loop produces a record for each quarter at risk. The TIME and EVENT variables are initialized at the values appropriate for quarters in which arrests did not occur. The IF statement checks to see if an arrest occurred in the quarter. If an arrest did occur, then EVENT and TIME are appropriately recoded. Finally, a new record is output containing all the original variables plus the newly created ones.

We then call the LIFEREG procedure and specify an exponential model:

```
proc lifereg data=quarter;
   class j;
   model time*event(0)=fin age race wexp mar paro prio j
         / dist=exponential covb;
run;
```

The variable J—the index variable in the DO loop of the DATA step—has values of 1, 2, 3, or 4, corresponding to the quarter covered by each record. It is specified as a CLASS variable so that PROC LIFEREG will set up an appropriate set of indicator variables to estimate the α_j's in the piecewise exponential model (actually we estimate contrasts between the α_j's).

Results in Output 4.20 show a significant effect of J (quarter), implying that the hazard is not constant over time. The Wald chi-square value is 8.70 on 3 d.f., which is corroborated by a likelihood-ratio test with a chi-square value of 9.52. (The likelihood-ratio test is calculated by rerunning the model without J and taking twice the positive difference in the log-likelihoods.) The coefficients for the three indicator variables are all contrasts with the fourth quarter. To interpret these coefficients, it's probably best to change their signs so that they reflect hazards rather than survival times. In contrast to the Weibull model that imposed a monotonically increasing hazard, the pattern displayed here is not monotonic. The estimated hazard increases from first to second quarter, then decreases, then increases again.

Output 4.20 *Results for Piecewise Exponential Model Applied to Recidivism Data*

```
                    L I F E R E G   P R O C E D U R E

Log Likelihood for EXPONENT -476.3016845

Variable  DF   Estimate  Std Err  ChiSquare  Pr>Chi Label/Value

INTERCPT   1  3.72262227 0.608157  37.46849  0.0001 Intercept
FIN        1  0.37735383 0.191339   3.889468 0.0486
AGE        1  0.05699963 0.021964   6.734821 0.0095
RACE       1 -0.3125936  0.307985   1.030154 0.3101
WEXP       1  0.14890354  0.21219   0.492446 0.4828
MAR        1   0.4331109 0.381791   1.286904 0.2566
PARO       1  0.08362454 0.195711   0.182573 0.6692
PRIO       1 -0.0908704  0.028636  10.06989  0.0015


J          3                        8.695416  0.0336
           1  0.82018614 0.284142   8.3321    0.0039              1
           1  0.18830667 0.244603   0.592664  0.4414              2
           1  0.31340545 0.259564   1.457887  0.2273              3
           0          0        0         .        .               4

SCALE      0          1        0                 Extreme value scale parameter
```

The chi-square tests for the individual indicator variables show that the hazard of arrest in the first quarter is significantly lower than the hazard in the last quarter. Although the two middle quarters have lower estimated hazards than the last, the differences are not significant. A Wald test (constructed from the covariance matrix) comparing the first and second quarters is also significant at about the .03 level. The coefficients and *p*-values for the remaining variables are consistent with those found with the conventional exponential and Weibull models.

Of course, there is a certain arbitrariness that arises from the division of the observation period into quarters. To increase confidence in the results, you may want to try different divisions and see if the results are stable. I reestimated the model for the recidivism data with a division into 13 "months" of four weeks each, simply by changing all the 13's to 4's in the DATA step. This produces a data set with 4,991 records. Results for the fixed covariates are virtually identical. The Wald chi-square test for the overall effect of J (month) is also about the same, but, with 12 degrees of freedom, the *p*-value is well above conventional levels for statistical significance.

You can also estimate the piecewise exponential model with PROC GENMOD, which has one important advantage: the MODEL statement in GENMOD allows interactions to be freely specified in a syntax similar to that of PROC GLM. PROC LIFEREG, on the other hand, requires that you construct interactions in the DATA step. To do the analysis with PROC GENMOD, you first need to define a variable equal to the logarithm of time in the DATA step creating the multiple records. For our example, insert the following statement just before the OUTPUT statement:

```
ltime=log(time);
```

The PROC step is then

```
proc genmod data=quarter;
   class j;
   model event=fin age race wexp mar paro prio j j*fin
         / dist=poisson link=log offset=ltime type3;
run;
```

Since this chapter is not primarily about PROC GENMOD, I won't go into a detailed rationale for this specification. Note, however, that the model specified here has an interaction between FIN and J. This means that the coefficient of financial aid is allowed to vary across quarters. The TYPE3 option produces a significance test for this interaction (it was not significant).

Here are some final observations about the piecewise exponential model:

- You do not need to be concerned about the analysis of multiple records for each individual. In particular, there is no inflation of test statistics resulting from lack of independence. The fact that the results are so similar regardless of how many observations are created should reassure you on this issue. The reason it's not a problem is that the likelihood function actually factors into a distinct term for each individual-interval. This conclusion does *not* apply, however, when the data set includes multiple *events* for each individual.

- The piecewise exponential model is very similar to the discrete-time methods described in Chapter 7, "Analysis of Tied or Discrete Data Using the LOGISTIC, PROBIT, and GENMOD Procedures." The principal difference is that estimation of the piecewise exponential model uses information on the exact timing of events, while the discrete-time methods are based on interval-censored data.

- There is no requirement that the intervals have equal length, although that simplifies the DATA step somewhat. As there's some benefit in having roughly equal numbers of events occurring in each interval, this sometimes requires unequal interval lengths.

- If all the covariates are categorical, great computational economy can be obtained by estimating the model from grouped data. The basic idea is to treat the number of events occurring in a time-interval × covariate cell as having a Poisson distribution. The parameter of that distribution is then taken to be a log-linear function of the covariates, as in the PROC GENMOD program above. See Aitkin et al. (1989) for details.

- The use of time-dependent covariates in the piecewise exponential model can substantially complicate the DATA step that creates the multiple records. For examples of how to do this, see Chapter 7 on discrete-time methods. There are also a number of issues about design and interpretation of studies with time-dependent covariates that are discussed in detail in Chapters 5 and 7.

CONCLUSION

PROC LIFEREG provides effective methods for regression analysis of censored survival data, especially data with left censoring or interval censoring. These methods are somewhat less robust than the more widely used Cox regression analysis performed by PROC PHREG but, in most cases, the results produced by the two approaches are very similar. Moreover, unlike PROC PHREG, PROC LIFEREG makes it possible to test certain hypotheses about the shape of the hazard function.

The biggest limitation of the PROC LIFEREG models is the inability to incorporate time-dependent covariates, although you can accomplish this to some degree with the piecewise exponential model. We now turn to PROC PHREG, which excels at this particular task.

CHAPTER **5**
Estimating Cox Regression Models with PROC PHREG

p.111 *Introduction*

p.113 *The Proportional Hazards Model*

p.114 *Partial Likelihood*

p.127 *Tied Data*

p.138 *Time-Dependent Covariates*

p.154 *Cox Models with Nonproportional Hazards*

p.155 *Interactions with Time as Time-Dependent Covariates*

p.158 *Nonproportionality via Stratification*

p.161 *Left Truncation and Late Entry into the Risk Set*

p.165 *Estimating Survivor Functions*

p.173 *Residuals and Influence Statistics*

p.181 *Testing Linear Hypotheses with the TEST Statement*

p.183 *Conclusion*

INTRODUCTION

Although PROC PHREG is the newest SAS procedure for doing survival analysis, it is already the most widely used. PROC PHREG (pronounced P-H-REG, not FREG) implements the regression method first proposed in 1972 by the British statistician Sir David Cox in his famous paper "Regression Models and Life Tables" (*Journal of the Royal Statistical Society, Series B*). It's difficult to exaggerate the impact of this paper. In the 1992 *Science Citation Index*, it was cited over 800 times, making it the most highly cited journal article in the entire literature of statistics. In fact, Garfield (1990) reported that its cumulative citation count placed it among the top 100 papers in all of science. These citation counts undoubtedly underestimate the actual use of the method because many authors don't bother citing the original paper.

What explains this enormous popularity? Perhaps the most important reason is that, unlike the parametric methods discussed in Chapter 4, "Estimating Parametric Regression Models with PROC LIFEREG," Cox's method does not require that you choose some particular probability distribution to represent survival times. That's why it's called *semi*parametric. As a consequence, Cox's method (often referred to as *Cox regression*) is considerably more robust. A second reason for the paper's popularity is that Cox regression makes it relatively easy to incorporate time-dependent covariates, that is, covariates that may change in value over the course of the observation period.

There are other attractive features of Cox regression that are less widely known or appreciated. Cox regression permits a kind of stratified analysis that is very effective in controlling for nuisance variables. And Cox regression makes it easy to adjust for periods of time in which an individual is not at risk of an event. Finally, Cox regression can readily accommodate both discrete and continuous measurement of event times.

Despite all these desirable qualities, Cox regression should not be viewed as the universal method for regression analysis of survival data. As I indicated in Chapter 4, there are times when a parametric method is preferable. And for most applications, you can do a reasonably good job of survival analysis using only PROC LIFEREG and PROC LIFETEST. Still, if I could have only one procedure for doing survival analysis, it would be PROC PHREG.

All implementations of Cox regression are not created equal. Among the many available commercial programs, PROC PHREG stands out for its toolkit of powerful features. While some programs don't allow stratification—a fatal deficit in my view—PROC PHREG has a very flexible stratification option. Many programs don't handle time-dependent covariates at all; those that do often have severe restrictions on the number or kinds of such covariates. In contrast, PROC PHREG has by far the most extensive and powerful capabilities for incorporating time-dependent covariates. And while Cox regression can theoretically deal with discrete (*tied*) data, most programs use approximations that are inadequate in many cases. PROC PHREG is unique in its implementation of two exact algorithms for tied data.

If PROC PHREG has a weakness, it has to be the lack of built-in graphics. On the other hand, PROC PHREG will produce output data sets that allow you to program your own graphs with only a few lines of code, giving you more flexibility and extensibility than many programs with canned graphics.

THE PROPORTIONAL HAZARDS MODEL

In his 1972 paper, Cox made two significant innovations. First, he proposed a model that is standardly referred to as the *proportional hazards model*. That name is somewhat misleading, however, because the model can readily be generalized to allow for nonproportional hazards. Second, he proposed a new estimation method that was later named *partial likelihood* or, more accurately, *maximum partial likelihood*. The term *Cox regression* refers to the combination of the model and the estimation method. It didn't take any great leap of imagination to formulate the proportional hazards model—it's a relatively straightforward generalization of the Weibull and Gompertz models we considered in Chapter 2, "Basic Concepts of Survival Analysis." But the partial likelihood method is something completely different. It took years for statisticians to fully understand and appreciate this novel approach to estimation.

Before discussing partial likelihood, let's first examine the model that it was designed to estimate. We'll start with the basic model that does not include time-dependent covariates or nonproportional hazards. The model is usually written as

$$h_i(t) = \lambda_0(t)\exp\{\beta_1 x_{i1} + \ldots + \beta_k x_{ik}\}. \tag{5.1}$$

This equation says that the hazard for individual i at time t is the product of two factors:

- a baseline hazard function $\lambda_0(t)$ that is left unspecified, except that it can't be negative
- a linear function of a set of k fixed covariates, which is then exponentiated.

The function $\lambda_0(t)$ can be regarded as the hazard function for an individual whose covariates all have values of 0.

Taking the logarithm of both sides, we can rewrite the model as

$$\log h_i(t) = \alpha(t) + \beta_1 x_{i1} + \ldots + \beta_k x_{ik} \tag{5.2}$$

where $\alpha(t) = \log \lambda_0(t)$. If we further specify $\alpha(t) = \alpha$, we get the exponential model. If we specify $\alpha(t) = \alpha t$, we get the Gompertz model. Finally, if we specify $\alpha(t) = \alpha \log t$, we have the Weibull model. As we will see, however, the great attraction of Cox regression is that such choices are unnecessary. The function $\alpha(t)$ can take any form whatever, even that of a step function.

Why is this called the proportional hazards model? Because the hazard for any individual is a fixed proportion of the hazard for any other individual. To see this, take the ratio of the hazards for two individuals i and j, and apply equation (5.1):

$$\frac{h_i(t)}{h_j(t)} = \exp\{\beta_1(x_{i1} - x_{j1}) + \dots + \beta_k(x_{ik} - x_{jk})\} . \tag{5.3}$$

What's important about this equation is that $\lambda_0(t)$ cancels out of the numerator and denominator. As a result, the ratio of the hazards is constant over time. If we graph the log hazards for any two individuals, the proportional hazards property implies that the hazard functions should be strictly parallel, as in Figure 5.1.

Figure 5.1 *Parallel Hazard Functions from Proportional Hazards Model*

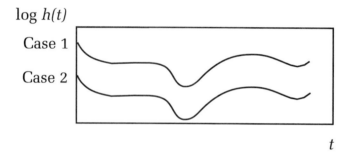

PARTIAL LIKELIHOOD

What's remarkable about partial likelihood is that you can estimate the β coefficients of the proportional hazards model without having to specify the baseline hazard function $\lambda_0(t)$. In this section, we will

- consider some general properties of partial likelihood
- look at two simple examples using PROC PHREG
- examine the mathematics of the method in some detail.

The likelihood function for the proportional hazards model of equation (5.1) can be factored into two parts:

- one part depends on both $\lambda_0(t)$ and $\boldsymbol{\beta}$ (the vector of coefficients)
- the other part depends on $\boldsymbol{\beta}$ alone.

What partial likelihood does, in effect, is discard the first part and treat the second part—the partial likelihood function—as though it were an ordinary likelihood function. You get estimates by finding values of $\boldsymbol{\beta}$ that maximize the partial likelihood. Since there is some information about β in the discarded portion of the likelihood function, the resulting estimates are not fully efficient. Their standard errors are larger than they would be if you used the entire likelihood function to obtain the estimates. In most cases, however, the loss of efficiency is quite small (Efron 1977). What you gain in return is robustness because the estimates have good properties regardless of the actual shape of the baseline hazard function. To be specific, partial likelihood estimates still have two of the three standard properties of ML estimates: they are consistent and asymptotically normal. In other words, in large samples they are approximately unbiased and their sampling distribution is approximately normal.

Another interesting property of partial likelihood estimates is that they depend only on the *ranks* of the event times, not their numerical values. This implies that any monotonic transformation of the event times will leave the coefficient estimates unchanged. For example, we could add a constant to everyone's event time, multiply the result by a constant, take the logarithm, and then take the square root—all without producing the slightest change in the coefficients.

Partial Likelihood: Examples

Let's first apply the partial likelihood method to the recidivism data that we introduced in **The Life-Table Method** in Chapter 3, "Estimating and Comparing Survival Curves with PROC LIFETEST," and that was repeatedly analyzed in Chapter 4. The syntax for PROC PHREG is almost identical to that for PROC LIFEREG, except that you do not need to specify a distribution:

```
proc phreg data=recid;
   model week*arrest(0)=fin age race wexp mar paro prio;
run;
```

Output 5.1 shows the results.

Output 5.1 *Results from Partial Likelihood Estimation with Recidivism Data*

```
The PHREG Procedure

Data Set: RECID
Dependent Variable: WEEK
Censoring Variable: ARREST
Censoring Value(s): 0
Ties Handling: BRESLOW

                     Summary of the Number of
                     Event and Censored Values

                                               Percent
               Total       Event    Censored   Censored

                432         114        318       73.61


              Testing Global Null Hypothesis: BETA=0

               Without       With
  Criterion   Covariates   Covariates   Model Chi-Square

  -2 LOG L    1351.367     1318.241      33.126 with 7 DF (p=0.0001)
  Score           .            .         33.383 with 7 DF (p=0.0001)
  Wald            .            .         31.981 with 7 DF (p=0.0001)


              Analysis of Maximum Likelihood Estimates

                  Parameter   Standard    Wald       Pr >       Risk
     Variable DF   Estimate     Error   Chi-Square Chi-Square   Ratio

       FIN     1   -0.379022   0.19136    3.92289    0.0476     0.685
       AGE     1   -0.057246   0.02198    6.78122    0.0092     0.944
       RACE    1    0.314130   0.30802    1.04008    0.3078     1.369
       WEXP    1   -0.151115   0.21212    0.50750    0.4762     0.860
       MAR     1   -0.432783   0.38179    1.28493    0.2570     0.649
       PARO    1   -0.084983   0.19575    0.18848    0.6642     0.919
       PRIO    1    0.091112   0.02863   10.12666    0.0015     1.095
```

The preliminary information is the same as in PROC LIFEREG, except for the line Ties Handling: BRESLOW. This line refers to the default method for handling *ties*—two or more observations that have exactly the same event time. Although Breslow's method is nearly universal, we'll consider three superior alternatives later in the section **Tied Data**. The middle of the output gives information on Testing Global Null Hypothesis: BETA=0. The null hypothesis is that all the coefficients are 0. Three alternative chi-square statistics are given: a likelihood-ratio test, a score test, and a Wald test. I already discussed the general properties of these tests in Chapter 4 (see **Hypothesis Tests**). Here we see that all three statistics are a bit over 30 with

7 d.f., leading to very small *p*-values. (The 7 d.f. correspond to the seven coefficients in the model.) We conclude that at least one of the coefficients is not 0. For the likelihood-ratio statistic, we are also given −2 times the (partial) log-likelihood for the model with the seven covariates as well as for a model with no covariates. The likelihood-ratio chi-square statistic is the difference between these two numbers.

In the lower part of the output, we see the coefficient estimates and associated statistics. Notice that there is no intercept estimate—a characteristic feature of partial likelihood estimation. The intercept is part of $\alpha(t)$, the arbitrary function of time, which cancels out of the estimating equations. As with PROC LIFEREG, the chi-square tests are Wald tests for the null hypothesis that each coefficient is equal to 0. These statistics are calculated simply by squaring the ratio of each coefficient to its estimated standard error. The last column, labeled Risk Ratio, is just e^{β}. For indicator (dummy) variables with values of 1 and 0, you can interpret the risk ratio as the ratio of the estimated hazard for those with a value of 1 to the estimated hazard for those with a value of 0 (controlling for other covariates). For example, the estimated risk ratio for the variable FIN (financial aid) is .685. This means that the hazard of arrest for those who received financial aid is only about 69 percent of the hazard for those who did not receive aid (controlling for other covariates). Version 7 SAS software will label this statistic as the *hazard ratio* because the term *risk ratio* is sometimes used to describe a ratio of *probabilities* rather than hazards.

For quantitative covariates, a more helpful statistic is obtained by subtracting 1.0 from the risk ratio and multiplying by 100. This gives the estimated percent change in the hazard for each one-unit increase in the covariate. For the variable AGE, the risk ratio is .944, which yields $100(.944 − 1) = − 5.6$. Therefore, for each one-year increase in the age at release, the hazard of arrest goes down by an estimated 5.6 percent.

Overall, the results are similar to those we saw in Chapter 4 with the LIFEREG procedure. There are highly significant effects of age and the number of prior offenses, and a marginally significant effect of financial aid. Comparing the coefficients with those in Output 4.2 for the exponential model, we find that all the numbers are very close, but the signs are reversed. The *p*-values are also similar. The sign reversal is not surprising since the PROC LIFEREG estimates are in log-survival time format, while the PROC PHREG estimates are in log-hazard format. The PROC PHREG estimates are all larger in magnitude than the Weibull estimates in Output 4.3, but, again, that's merely a consequence of the alternative ways of expressing the model. When we convert the Weibull estimates to log-hazard format by dividing by the scale estimate and changing the sign (as in **The Weibull Model** in Chapter 4), the results are remarkably close to the PROC PHREG estimates. Because the other PROC

LIFEREG models (gamma, log-logistic, and log-normal) are not proportional hazards models, their coefficients cannot be converted to log-hazard format. Consequently, there is no point in comparing them with the PROC PHREG coefficients.

Now let's look at a somewhat more complicated example, the famous Stanford Heart Transplant Data, as reported by Crowley and Hu (1977). The sample consists of 103 cardiac patients who were enrolled in the transplantation program between 1967 and 1974. After enrollment, patients waited varying lengths of time until a suitable donor heart was found. Thirty patients died before receiving a transplant, while another four patients had still not received transplants at the termination date of April 1, 1974. Patients were followed until death or until the termination date. Of the 69 transplant recipients, only 24 were still alive at termination. At the time of transplantation, all but four of the patients were tissue typed to determine the degree of similarity with the donor.

The following variables were input to SAS:

DOB	date of birth.
DOA	date of acceptance into the program.
DOT	date of transplant.
DLS	date last seen (dead or censored).
DEAD	coded 1 if dead at DLS; otherwise, it is coded 0.
SURG	coded 1 if patient had open-heart surgery prior to DOA; otherwise, it is coded 0.
M1	number of donor alleles with no match in recipient (1 through 4).
M2	1 if donor-recipient mismatch on HLA-A2 antigen, otherwise 0.
M3	mismatch score.

The variables DOT, M1, M2, and M3 are coded as missing for those patients who did not receive a transplant. All four date measures are coded in the form *mm/dd/yy*, where *mm* is the month, *dd* is the day, and *yy* is the year. Here is the raw data for the first 10 cases:

DOB	DOA	DOT	DLS	DEAD	SURG	M1	M2	M3
01/10/37	11/15/67	.	01/03/68	1	0	.	.	.
03/02/16	01/02/68	.	01/07/68	1	0	.	.	.
09/19/13	01/06/68	01/06/68	01/21/68	1	0	2	0	1.110
12/23/27	03/28/68	05/02/68	05/05/68	1	0	3	0	1.660
07/28/47	05/10/68	.	05/27/68	1	0	.	.	.
11/08/13	06/13/68	.	06/15/68	1	0	.	.	.
08/29/17	07/12/68	08/31/68	05/17/70	1	0	4	0	1.320
03/27/23	08/01/68	.	09/09/68	1	0	.	.	.
06/11/21	08/09/68	.	11/01/68	1	0	.	.	.
02/09/26	08/11/68	08/22/68	10/07/68	1	0	2	0	0.610

These data were read into the SAS System with the following DATA step:

```
data stan;
    infile 'c: stan.dat';
    input dob mmddyy9. doa mmddyy9. dot mmddyy9. dls mmddyy9.
        dead surg m1 m2 m3;
    surv1=dls-doa;
    surv2=dls-dot;
    ageaccpt=(doa-dob)/365.25;
    agetrans=(dot-dob)/365.25;
    wait=dot-doa;
    if dot=. then trans=0; else trans=1;
run;
```

Notice that the four date variables are read with the MMDDYY9. format, which translates the date into the number of days since January 1, 1960. (Dates earlier than that have negative values.) We then create two survival time variables, days from acceptance until death (SURV1) and days from transplant until death (SURV2). We also calculate the age (in years) at acceptance into the program (AGEACCPT), the age at transplant (AGETRANS), and the number of days from acceptance to transplant (WAIT). Finally, we create an indicator variable (TRANS) coded 1 for those who received a transplant and coded 0 for those who did not.

An obvious question is whether transplantation raised or lowered the hazard of death. A naive approach to answering this question is to do a Cox regression of SURV1 on transplant status (TRANS), controlling for AGEACCPT and SURG:

```
proc phreg data=stan;
    model surv1*dead(0)=trans surg ageaccpt;
run;
```

The results in Output 5.2 show very strong effects of both transplant status and age at acceptance. We see that each additional year of age at the time of acceptance into the program is associated with a 6 percent increase in the hazard of death. On the other hand, the hazard for those who received a transplant is only about 18 percent of the hazard for those who did not (see Risk Ratio column). Or equivalently (taking the reciprocal), those who did not receive transplants are about 5-1/2 times more likely to die at any given point in time.

Output 5.2 *Results for All Patients, No Time-Dependent Variables*

```
The PHREG Procedure

Data Set: WORK.STAN
Dependent Variable: SURV1
Censoring Variable: DEAD
Censoring Value(s): 0
Ties Handling: BRESLOW

                        Summary of the Number of
                        Event and Censored Values

                                        Percent
                Total     Event    Censored    Censored

                 103       75         28        27.18

            Testing Global Null Hypothesis: BETA=0

            Without      With
Criterion   Covariates   Covariates   Model Chi-Square

-2 LOG L     596.651      551.188      45.463 with 3 DF (p=0.0001)
Score          .            .          52.047 with 3 DF (p=0.0001)
Wald           .            .          46.670 with 3 DF (p=0.0001)

            Analysis of Maximum Likelihood Estimates

                 Parameter   Standard    Wald       Pr >       Risk
   Variable DF   Estimate    Error    Chi-Square Chi-Square   Ratio

   TRANS    1    -1.708140   0.27860   37.59048    0.0001      0.181
   SURG     1    -0.421402   0.37100    1.29018    0.2560      0.656
   AGEACCPT 1     0.058609   0.01505   15.16310    0.0001      1.060
```

While the age effect may be real, the transplant effect is almost surely an artifact. The main reason why patients did *not* get transplants is that they died before a suitable donor could be found. Thus, when we compare the death rates for those who did and did not get transplants, the rates are much higher for those who did not. In effect, the covariate is actually a *consequence* of the dependent variable: an early death prevents a patient from getting a transplant. The way around this problem is to treat transplant status as a time-dependent covariate, but that will have to wait until the section **Time-Dependent Covariates,** later in this chapter.

We can also ask a different set of questions that do not require any time-dependent covariates. Restricting the analysis to the 65 patients who *did* receive heart transplants, we can ask why some of these patients survived longer than others:

```
proc phreg data=stan;
   where trans=1;
      model surv2*dead(0)=surg m1 m2 m3 agetrans wait dot;
run;
```

Notice that we now use a different origin—the date of the transplant—in calculating survival time. (It is possible to use date of acceptance as the origin, using the methods in the section **Left Truncation and Late Entry into the Risk Set** (later in this chapter), but it is probably not worth the trouble.)

Output 5.3   *Results for Transplant Patients, No Time-Dependent Covariates*

```
                     Summary of the Number of
                    Event and Censored Values
                                              Percent
            Total       Event    Censored    Censored

             65          41          24        36.92


           Testing Global Null Hypothesis: BETA=0

              Without       With
Criterion    Covariates   Covariates    Model Chi-Square

-2 LOG L      290.896      274.311      16.586 with 7 DF (p=0.0203)
Score            .            .         15.924 with 7 DF (p=0.0258)
Wald             .            .         14.908 with 7 DF (p=0.0372)


              Analysis of Maximum Likelihood Estimates

               Parameter   Standard     Wald       Pr >      Risk
  Variable DF   Estimate    Error    Chi-Square  Chi-Square  Ratio

  SURG      1   -0.770306   0.49719    2.40042     0.1213    0.463
  M1        1   -0.248569   0.19437    1.63550     0.2009    0.780
  M2        1    0.029582   0.44268    0.00447     0.9467    1.030
  M3        1    0.644070   0.34276    3.53089     0.0602    1.904
  AGETRANS  1    0.049266   0.02282    4.66188     0.0308    1.050
  WAIT      1   -0.001969   0.00514    0.14691     0.7015    0.998
  DOT       1   -0.000165   0.0002991  0.30440     0.5811    1.000
```

Results in Output 5.3 show, again, that older patients have higher risks of dying. Specifically, each additional year of age at the time of the transplant is associated with a 5 percent increase in the hazard of death. That does not tell us whether the *surgery* is riskier for older patients, however. It merely tells us that older patients are more likely to die. There is also some evidence of higher death rates for those who have a higher level of tissue mismatch, as measured by the M3 score. None of the other variables approaches statistical significance, however.

Partial Likelihood: Mathematical and Computational Details

Now that we've seen the partial likelihood method in action, let's take a closer look at how it does what it does. Using the same notation as in Chapter 4, we have n independent individuals ($i = 1,...,n$). For each individual i, the data consist of three parts: t_i, δ_i and $\mathbf{x}_i$, where t_i is the time of the event or the time of censoring, δ_i is an indicator variable with a value of 1 if t_i is uncensored or a value of 0 if t_i is censored, and $\mathbf{x}_i = [x_{i1} \ldots x_{ik}]$ is a vector of k covariate values.

An ordinary likelihood function is typically written as a product of the likelihoods for all the individuals in the sample. On the other hand, you can write the partial likelihood as a product of the likelihoods for all the *events* that are observed. Thus, if J is the number of events, we can write

$$PL = \prod_{j=1}^{J} L_j \tag{5.4}$$

where L_j is the likelihood for the jth event. Next we need to know how the individual L_js are constructed. This is best explained by way of an example. Consider the data in Output 5.4, which is taken from Collett (1994) with a slight modification (the survival time for observation 8 is changed from 26 to 25 to eliminate ties). The variable SURV contains the survival time in months, beginning with the month of surgery, for 45 breast cancer patients. Twenty-six of the women died (DEAD=1) during the observation period, so there are 26 terms in the partial likelihood. The variable X has a value of 1 if the tumor had a positive marker for possible metastasis; otherwise, the variable has a value of 0. The cases are arranged in ascending order by survival time, which is convenient for constructing the partial likelihood.

Output 5.4 *Survival Times for Breast Cancer Patients*

OBS	EVENT	SURV	DEAD	X
1	1	5	1	1
2	2	8	1	1
3	3	10	1	1
4	4	13	1	1
5	5	18	1	1
6	6	23	1	0
7	7	24	1	1
8	8	25	1	1
9	9	26	1	1
10	10	31	1	1
11	11	35	1	1
12	12	40	1	1
13	13	41	1	1
14	14	47	1	0
15	15	48	1	1
16	16	50	1	1
17	17	59	1	1
18	18	61	1	1
19	19	68	1	1
20	20	69	1	0
21	.	70	0	0
22	21	71	1	1
23	.	71	0	0
24	.	76	0	1
25	.	100	0	0
26	.	101	0	0
27	.	105	0	1
28	.	107	0	1
29	.	109	0	1
30	22	113	1	1
31	.	116	0	1
32	23	118	1	1
33	24	143	1	1
34	25	148	1	0
35	.	154	0	1
36	.	162	0	1
37	26	181	1	0
38	.	188	0	1
39	.	198	0	0
40	.	208	0	0
41	.	212	0	0
42	.	212	0	1
43	.	217	0	1
44	.	224	0	0
45	.	225	0	1

The first death occurred to patient 1 in month 5. To construct the partial likelihood (L_1) for this event, we ask the following question: Given that a death occurred in month 5, what is the probability that it happened to patient 1 rather than to one of the other patients? The answer is the hazard for patient 1 at month 5 divided by the sum of the hazards for all the patients who were at risk of death in that same month. Now, at month 5, all 45 patients were at risk of death, so the probability is

$$L_1 = \frac{h_1(5)}{h_1(5) + h_2(5) + \ldots + h_{45}(5)}.$$

(5.5)

While this expression has considerable intuitive appeal, the derivation is actually rather involved and will not be presented here.

The second death occurred to patient 2 in month 8. Again we ask, given that a death occurred in month 8, what is the probability that it occurred to patient 2 rather than to one of the other patients at risk? Patient 1 is no longer at risk of death because she already died. So L_2 has the same form as L_1, but the hazard for patient 1 is removed from the denominator:

$$L_2 = \frac{h_2(8)}{h_2(8) + h_3(8) + \ldots + h_{45}(8)}.$$

(5.6)

The set of all individuals who are at risk at a given point in time is often referred to as the *risk set*. At time 8, the risk set consists of patients 2 through 45, inclusive.

We continue in this way for each successive death, deleting from the denominator the hazards for all those who have already died. Also deleted from the denominator are those who have been censored at an earlier point in time. That's because they are no longer at risk of an observed event. For example, the 21st death occurred to patient 22 in month 71. Patient 21 was censored at month 70, so her hazard does not appear in the denominator of L_{21}. On the other hand, if an event time is the same as a censoring time, the convention is to assume that the censored observation was still at risk at that time. Thus, patient 23 who was censored in month 71 *does* show up in the denominator of L_{21}.

The last term in the likelihood corresponds to the 26th death, which occurred to the 37th patient in month 181:

$$L_{26} = \frac{h_{37}(181)}{h_{37}(181) + h_{38}(181) + \ldots + h_{45}(181)}.$$

(5.7)

All the hazards in the denominator, except for the first, are for patients who were censored in months later than 181.

The results to this point have been completely general with no assumptions about the form of the hazard function. Now, we invoke the proportional hazards model of equation (5.1) and substitute the expression for the hazard into the expression for L_1,

$$L_1 = \frac{\lambda_0(5)e^{\beta x_1}}{\lambda_0(5)e^{\beta x_1} + \lambda_0(5)e^{\beta x_2} + \ldots + \lambda_0(5)e^{\beta x_{45}}}$$

(5.8)

where x_i is the value of x for the ith patient. This leads to a considerable simplification because the unspecified function $\lambda_0(5)$ is common to every term in the expression. Canceling, we get

$$L_1 = \frac{e^{\beta x_1}}{e^{\beta x_1} + e^{\beta x_2} + \ldots + e^{\beta x_{45}}}.$$

(5.9)

It is this cancellation of the λs that makes it possible to estimate the β coefficients without having to specify the baseline hazard function. Of course, the λs also cancel for all the other terms in the partial likelihood.

Earlier I remarked that the partial likelihood depends only on the order of the event times, not on their exact values. You can easily see this by considering each of the L_i terms. Although the first death occurred in month 5, L_1 would be exactly the same if it had occurred at any time from 0 up to (but not including) 8, the month of the second event. Similarly, L_2 would have been the same if the second death had occurred any time greater than 5 and less than 10 (the month of the third death).

A general expression for the partial likelihood for data with fixed covariates from a proportional hazards model is

$$PL = \prod_{i=1}^{n} \left[\frac{e^{\beta \mathbf{x}_i}}{\sum_{j=1}^{n} Y_{ij} e^{\beta \mathbf{x}_j}} \right]^{\delta_i}$$

(5.10)

where $Y_{ij} = 1$ if $t_j \geq t_i$; and $Y_{ij} = 0$ if $t_j < t_i$. (The Ys are just a convenient mechanism for excluding from the denominator those individuals who already experienced the event and are, thus, not part of the risk set). Although this expression has the product taken over all individuals rather than all events, the terms corresponding to censored observations are effectively excluded because $\delta_i = 0$ for those cases. This expression is not valid for tied event times, but it does allow for ties between one event time and one or more censoring times.

Once the partial likelihood is constructed, you can maximize it with respect to β just like an ordinary likelihood function. As usual, it's convenient to maximize the logarithm of the likelihood, which is

$$\log PL = \sum_{i=1}^{n} \delta_i \left[\beta \mathbf{x}_i - \log\left(\sum_{j=1}^{n} Y_{ij} e^{\beta \mathbf{x}_j} \right) \right].$$

(5.11)

Most partial likelihood programs use some version of the Newton-Raphson algorithm to maximize this function with respect to β. For details see Chapter 4 (in the section **Maximum Likelihood Estimation: Mathematics**).

As with PROC LIFEREG, there will occasionally be times when the Newton-Raphson algorithm does not converge. A message in the OUTPUT window will say WARNING: The information matrix is not positive definite and thus the convergence is questionable. Unfortunately, PROC PHREG's convergence criterion sometimes makes it look as though the algorithm has converged when, in fact, true convergence is not possible. This problem arises when one of the explanatory variables is an indicator variable (1 or 0) and all the observations are censored for one of the levels of the variable. In such cases, the log-likelihood reaches a stable value, but the coefficient of the offending variable keeps going off toward plus or minus infinity. The only indication of a problem is that the variable in question will have a large coefficient with a much larger standard error.

To complete the breast cancer example, let's take a look at the partial likelihood results in Output 5.5. With only one covariate, the Global Null Hypothesis statistics provide us with three alternative tests for the effect of that variable. The Wald and score tests have *p*-values that exceed the conventional .05 level, while the likelihood-ratio test is slightly below. This degree of discrepancy is not at all surprising with a small sample. The estimated risk ratio of 2.483 tells us that the hazard of death for those whose tumor had the positive marker was nearly 2-1/2 times the hazard for those without the positive marker.

Because the covariate is dichotomous, an alternative approach is to use PROC LIFETEST to test for differences in survival curves. When I did this, the *p*-value for the log-rank test (.0607) was identical to the *p*-value for the score test in Output 5.5. This is no accident. The log-rank test is the exact equivalent of the partial likelihood score test for a single, dichotomous covariate.

Output 5.5 *PHREG Results for Breast Cancer Data*

```
Testing Global Null Hypothesis: BETA=0

                Without        With
Criterion      Covariates    Covariates    Model Chi-Square

-2 LOG L         173.914       170.030        3.884 with 1 DF (p=0.0487)
Score               .             .           3.519 with 1 DF (p=0.0607)
Wald                .             .           3.296 with 1 DF (p=0.0695)


              Analysis of Maximum Likelihood Estimates

                  Parameter    Standard     Wald        Pr >        Risk
       Variable DF  Estimate     Error    Chi-Square  Chi-Square   Ratio

         X      1   0.909335    0.50090    3.29573      0.0695      2.483
```

TIED DATA

The formula for the partial likelihood in equation (5.10) is valid only for data in which no two events occur at the same time. It's quite common for data to contain tied event times, however, so we need an alternative formula to handle those situations. Most partial likelihood programs use a technique called *Breslow's approximation*, which works well when ties are relatively few. But when data are heavily tied, the approximation can be quite poor (Farewell and Prentice 1980; Hsieh 1995). Although PROC PHREG uses Breslow's approximation as the default, it is unique in providing a somewhat better approximation proposed by Efron (1977) as well as two *exact* methods.

This section explains the background, rationale, and implementation of these alternative methods for handling ties. Since this issue is both new and confusing, I'm going to discuss it at considerable length. Those who just want the bottom line can skip to the end of the section where I summarize the practical implications. Because the formulas can get rather complicated, I won't go into all the mathematical details. But I will try to provide some intuitive understanding of why there are different approaches and the basic logic of each one.

To illustrate the problem and the various solutions, let's turn again to the recidivism data. As output 5.6 shows, these data include a substantial number of tied survival times (weeks to first arrest). For weeks 1 through 7, there is only one arrest in each week. For these seven events, the partial likelihood terms are constructed exactly as described in the section **Partial Likelihood: Mathematical and Computational Details**. Five arrests occurred in week 8, however, so the construction of L_8 requires a different method. Two alternative approaches have been proposed for the construction of the likelihood for tied event times; these are specified in PROC PHREG by TIES=EXACT or TIES=DISCRETE as options in the MODEL statement. This terminology is somewhat misleading because both methods give exact likelihoods; the difference is that the EXACT method assumes that there is a true but unknown ordering for the tied event times (i.e., time is continuous), while the DISCRETE method assumes that the events really occurred at exactly the same time.

Output 5.6 *Week of First Arrest for Recidivism Data*

WEEK	Frequency	Percent	Cumulative Frequency	Cumulative Percent
1	1	0.2	1	0.2
2	1	0.2	2	0.5
3	1	0.2	3	0.7
4	1	0.2	4	0.9
5	1	0.2	5	1.2
6	1	0.2	6	1.4
7	1	0.2	7	1.6
8	5	1.2	12	2.8
9	2	0.5	14	3.2
10	1	0.2	15	3.5
11	2	0.5	17	3.9
12	2	0.5	19	4.4
13	1	0.2	20	4.6
14	3	0.7	23	5.3
15	2	0.5	25	5.8
16	2	0.5	27	6.2
17	3	0.7	30	6.9
18	3	0.7	33	7.6
19	2	0.5	35	8.1
20	5	1.2	40	9.3
21	2	0.5	42	9.7
22	1	0.2	43	10.0
23	1	0.2	44	10.2
24	4	0.9	48	11.1
25	3	0.7	51	11.8
26	3	0.7	54	12.5
27	2	0.5	56	13.0
28	2	0.5	58	13.4
30	2	0.5	60	13.9
31	1	0.2	61	14.1
32	2	0.5	63	14.6
33	2	0.5	65	15.0
34	2	0.5	67	15.5
35	4	0.9	71	16.4
36	3	0.7	74	17.1
37	4	0.9	78	18.1
38	1	0.2	79	18.3
39	2	0.5	81	18.8
40	4	0.9	85	19.7
42	2	0.5	87	20.1
43	4	0.9	91	21.1
44	2	0.5	93	21.5
45	2	0.5	95	22.0
46	4	0.9	99	22.9
47	1	0.2	100	23.1
48	2	0.5	102	23.6
49	5	1.2	107	24.8
50	3	0.7	110	25.5
52	322	74.5	432	100.0

The EXACT Method

Let's begin with the EXACT method since its underlying model is probably more plausible for most applications. Since arrests can occur at any point in time, it's reasonable to suppose that ties are merely the result of imprecise measurement of time and that there is a true time ordering for the five arrests that occurred in week 8. If we knew that ordering, we could construct the partial likelihood in the usual way. In the absence of any knowledge of that ordering, however, we have to consider all the possibilities. With five events, there are $5! = 120$ different possible orderings. Let's denote each of those possibilities by A_i, where $i = 1, \ldots, 120$. What we want is the probability of the *union* of those possibilities, that is, $\Pr(A_1 \text{ or } A_2 \text{ or } \ldots \text{ or } A_{120})$. Now, a fundamental law of probability theory is that the probability of the union of a set of mutually exclusive events is just the sum of the probabilities for each of the events. Therefore, we can write

$$L_8 = \sum_{i=1}^{120} \Pr(A_i). \tag{5.12}$$

Each of these 120 probabilities is just a standard partial likelihood. Suppose, for example, that we arbitrarily label the five arrests at time 8 with the numbers 8, 9, 10, 11, and 12, and suppose further that A_1 denotes the ordering {8, 9, 10, 11, 12}. Then

$$\Pr(A_1) = \left(\frac{e^{\beta x_8}}{e^{\beta x_8} + e^{\beta x_9} + \ldots + e^{\beta x_{432}}} \right) \left(\frac{e^{\beta x_9}}{e^{\beta x_9} + e^{\beta x_{10}} + \ldots + e^{\beta x_{432}}} \right) \cdots \left(\frac{e^{\beta x_{12}}}{e^{\beta x_{12}} + e^{\beta x_{13}} + \ldots + e^{\beta x_{432}}} \right).$$

On the other hand, if A_2 denotes the ordering {9, 8, 10, 11, 12}, we have

$$\Pr(A_2) = \left(\frac{e^{\beta x_9}}{e^{\beta x_8} + e^{\beta x_9} + \ldots + e^{\beta x_{432}}} \right) \left(\frac{e^{\beta x_8}}{e^{\beta x_8} + e^{\beta x_{10}} + \ldots + e^{\beta x_{432}}} \right) \cdots \left(\frac{e^{\beta x_{12}}}{e^{\beta x_{12}} + e^{\beta x_{13}} + \ldots + e^{\beta x_{432}}} \right).$$

We continue in this way for the other 118 possible orderings. Then L_8 is obtained by adding all the probabilities together.

The situation is much simpler for week 9 because only two arrests occurred, giving us two possible orderings. For L_9, then, we have

$$L_9 = \left(\frac{e^{\beta x_{13}}}{e^{\beta x_{13}} + e^{\beta x_{14}} + \ldots + e^{\beta x_{432}}} \right) \left(\frac{e^{\beta x_{14}}}{e^{\beta x_{14}} + e^{\beta x_{15}} + \ldots + e^{\beta x_{432}}} \right) +$$

$$\left(\frac{e^{\beta x_{14}}}{e^{\beta x_{13}} + e^{\beta x_{14}} + \quad + e^{\beta x_{432}}} \right) \left(\frac{e^{\beta x_{13}}}{e^{\beta x_{13}} + e^{\beta x_{15}} + \quad + e^{\beta x_{432}}} \right)$$

where the numbers 13 and 14 are arbitrarily assigned to the two events. When we get to week 10, there's only one event so we're back to the standard partial likelihood formula:

$$L_9 = \left(\frac{e^{\beta x_{15}}}{e^{\beta x_{15}} + e^{\beta x_{16}} + \ldots + e^{\beta x_{432}}} \right).$$

It's difficult to write a general formula for the exact likelihood with tied data because the notation becomes very cumbersome. For one version of a general formula, see Kalbfleisch and Prentice (1980). Be forewarned that the formula in the official PROC PHREG documentation bears no resemblance to that given by Kalbfleisch and Prentice or to the explanation given here. That's because it's based on a re-expression of the formula in terms of a definite integral, which facilitates computation (DeLong, Guirguis, and So 1994).

It should be obvious, by this point, that computation of the exact likelihood can be a daunting task. With just five tied survival times, we have seen that one portion of the partial likelihood increased from 1 term to 120 terms. If 10 events occur at the same time, there are over three million possible orderings to evaluate. Until recently, statisticians abandoned all hope that such computations might be practical (which is why no other programs calculate the exact likelihood). What makes it possible now is the development of an integral representation of the likelihood, which is much easier to evaluate numerically. Even with this innovation, however, computation of the exact likelihood when large numbers of events occur at the same time can take an enormous amount of computing time.

Early recognition of these computational difficulties led to the development of approximations. The most popular of these is widely attributed to Breslow (1974), but it was first proposed by Peto (1972). This is the default in PROC PHREG, and it is nearly universal in other programs. Efron (1977) proposed an alternative approximation that is also available in PROC PHREG. The results we saw earlier in Output 5.1 for the recidivism data were obtained with the Breslow approximation.

To use the EXACT method, we specify

```
proc phreg data=recid;
   model week*arrest(0)=fin age race wexp mar paro prio
        / ties=exact;
run;
```

This PROC step produces the results in Output 5.7. Comparing this with Output 5.1, it's apparent that the Breslow approximation works well in this case. The coefficients are generally the same to at least two (and sometimes three) decimal places. The test statistics all yield the same conclusions.

Output 5.7 *Recidivism Results Using the EXACT Method*

```
                         The PHREG Procedure
                 Testing Global Null Hypothesis: BETA=0

                 Without      With
Criterion       Covariates   Covariates    Model Chi-Square

-2 LOG L          1227.506     1194.239     33.266 with 7 DF (p=0.0001)
Score                .             .        33.529 with 7 DF (p=0.0001)
Wald                 .             .        32.112 with 7 DF (p=0.0001)


              Analysis of Maximum Likelihood Estimates

                  Parameter    Standard    Wald       Pr >      Risk
    Variable DF   Estimate      Error    Chi-Square Chi-Square  Ratio

      FIN    1    -0.379427    0.19138    3.93061    0.0474     0.684
      AGE    1    -0.057438    0.02200    6.81663    0.0090     0.944
      RACE   1     0.313906    0.30800    1.03875    0.3081     1.369
      WEXP   1    -0.149793    0.21223    0.49817    0.4803     0.861
      MAR    1    -0.433705    0.38187    1.28990    0.2561     0.648
      PARO   1    -0.084873    0.19576    0.18798    0.6646     0.919
      PRIO   1     0.091500    0.02865   10.20021    0.0014     1.096
```

Output 5.8 shows the results from using Efron's approximation (invoked by using TIES=EFRON). If Breslow's approximation is good, this one is superb. Nearly all the numbers are the same to four decimal places. In all cases where I've tried the two approximations, Efron's approximation gave results that were much closer to the exact results than Breslow's approximation. This improvement comes with only a trivial increase in computation time. For the recidivism data, Breslow's approximation took five seconds and Efron's formula took six seconds on a 486 DOS machine. By contrast, the EXACT method took 18 seconds.

Output 5.8 *Recidivism Results Using Efron's Approximation*

```
               Testing Global Null Hypothesis: BETA=0

                 Without      With
Criterion       Covariates   Covariates    Model Chi-Square

-2 LOG L          1350.761     1317.495     33.266 with 7 DF (p=0.0001)
Score                .             .        33.529 with 7 DF (p=0.0001)
Wald                 .             .        32.113 with 7 DF (p=0.0001)
```

continued on next page

Output 5.8   continued

```
                  Analysis of Maximum Likelihood Estimates

                    Parameter    Standard    Wald      Pr >      Risk
       Variable DF   Estimate     Error   Chi-Square Chi-Square  Ratio

       FIN      1   -0.379422    0.19138   3.93056    0.0474    0.684
       AGE      1   -0.057438    0.02200   6.81664    0.0090    0.944
       RACE     1    0.313900    0.30799   1.03873    0.3081    1.369
       WEXP     1   -0.149796    0.21222   0.49821    0.4803    0.861
       MAR      1   -0.433704    0.38187   1.28991    0.2561    0.648
       PARO     1   -0.084871    0.19576   0.18797    0.6646    0.919
       PRIO     1    0.091497    0.02865  10.20021    0.0014    1.096
```

If the approximations are so good, why do we need the computationally intensive EXACT method? Farewell and Prentice (1980) showed that the Breslow approximation deteriorates as the number of ties at a particular point in time becomes a large proportion of the number of cases at risk. For the recidivism data in Output 5.6, the number of tied survival times at any given time point is never larger than 2 percent of the number at risk, so it's not surprising that the approximations work well.

Now let's look at an example where the conditions are less favorable. The data consist of 100 simulated job durations, measured from the year of entry into the job until the year that the employee quit. Durations after the fifth year are censored. If the employee was fired before the fifth year, the duration is censored at the end of the last full year in which the employee was working. We know only the year in which the employee quit, so the survival times have values of 1, 2, 3, 4, or 5.

Here's a simple life table for these data:

Duration	Number Quit	Number Censored	Number At Risk	Quit/ At Risk
1	22	7	100	.22
2	18	3	71	.25
3	16	4	50	.32
4	8	1	30	.27
5	4	17	21	.19

The number at risk at each duration is equal to the total number of cases (100) minus the number who quit or were censored at previous durations. Looking at the last column, we see that the ratio of the number quitting to the number at risk is substantial at each of the five points in time. Three covariates were measured at the beginning of the job: years of schooling (ED), salary in thousands of dollars (SALARY), and the prestige of the occupation (PRESTIGE) measured on a scale from 1 to 100.

Output 5.9 displays selected results from using PROC PHREG with the three different methods for handling ties. Breslow's method yields coefficient estimates that are about one-third smaller in magnitude than those using the EXACT method, while the *p*-values (for testing the hypothesis that each coefficient is 0) are substantially higher. In fact, the *p*-value for the SALARY variable is above the .05 level for Breslow's method, but it is only .01 for the EXACT method. Efron's method produces coefficients that are about midway between the other two methods, but the *p*-values are much closer to those of the EXACT method. Clearly, the Breslow approximation is unacceptable for this application. Efron's approximation is not bad for drawing qualitative conclusions, but there is an appreciable loss of accuracy in estimating the magnitudes of the coefficients. With regard to computing time, both approximate methods took 3 seconds on a 486 DOS machine. The EXACT method took 24 seconds.

Output 5.9 *Results for Job Duration Data: Three Methods for Handling Ties*

```
Ties Handling: BRESLOW

                    Parameter   Standard    Wald       Pr >      Risk
    Variable DF     Estimate    Error    Chi-Square Chi-Square   Ratio

    ED        1      0.116453   0.05918    3.87257    0.0491     1.124
    PRESTIGE  1     -0.064278   0.00959   44.93725    0.0001     0.938
    SALARY    1     -0.014957   0.00792    3.56573    0.0590     0.985


Ties Handling: EFRON

                    Parameter   Standard    Wald       Pr >      Risk
    Variable DF     Estimate    Error    Chi-Square Chi-Square   Ratio

    ED        1      0.144044   0.05954    5.85271    0.0156     1.155
    PRESTIGE  1     -0.079807   0.00996   64.20009    0.0001     0.923
    SALARY    1     -0.020159   0.00830    5.90363    0.0151     0.980


Ties Handling: EXACT

                    Parameter   Standard    Wald       Pr >      Risk
    Variable DF     Estimate    Error    Chi-Square Chi-Square   Ratio

    ED        1      0.164332   0.06380    6.63419    0.0100     1.179
    PRESTIGE  1     -0.092019   0.01240   55.10969    0.0001     0.912
    SALARY    1     -0.022545   0.00884    6.50490    0.0108     0.978
```

The DISCRETE Method

The DISCRETE option in PROC PHREG is also an exact method, but one based on a fundamentally different model. In fact, it is not a proportional hazards model at all. The model does fall within the framework of Cox regression, however, since it was proposed by Cox in his original 1972 paper and since the estimation method is a form of partial likelihood. Unlike the EXACT model, which assumes that ties are merely the result of imprecise measurement of time, the DISCRETE model assumes that time is really discrete. When two or more events appear to happen at the same time, there is no underlying ordering—they really happen at the same time.

While most applications of survival analysis involve events that can occur at any moment on the time continuum, there are definitely some events that are best treated as if time were discrete. If the event of interest is a change in the political party occupying the U.S. presidency, that can only occur once every four years. Or suppose the aim is to predict how many months it takes before a new homeowner misses a mortgage payment. Because payments are only due at monthly intervals, a discrete-time model is the natural way to go.

Cox's model for discrete-time data can be described as follows. The time variable t can only take on integer values. Let P_{it} be the conditional probability that individual i has an event at time t, given that an event has not already occurred to that individual. This probability is sometimes called a *discrete-time hazard*. The model says that P_{it} is related to the covariates by a logit-regression equation:

$$\log\left(\frac{P_{it}}{1-P_{it}}\right) = \alpha_t + \beta_1 x_{i1} + \ldots + \beta_k x_{ik}.$$

The expression on the left side of the equation is the logit or log-odds of P_{it}. On the right side, we have a linear function of the covariates, plus a term α_t that plays the same role as $\alpha(t)$ in expression (5.2) for the proportional hazards model. α_t is just a set of constants—one for each time point—that can vary arbitrarily from one time point to another.

This model can be described as a proportional *odds* model, although that term has a different meaning here than it did in Chapter 4 (see the section **The Log-Logistic Model**). The odds that individual i has an event at time t (given that i did not already have an event) is just $O_{it} = P_{it}/(1 - P_{it})$. The model implies that ratio of the odds for any two individuals O_{it}/O_{jt} does *not* depend on time (although it may vary with the covariates).

How can we estimate this model? In Chapter 7, "Analysis of Tied or Discrete Data with the LOGISTIC , PROBIT, and GENMOD Procedures," we will see how to estimate it using standard maximum likelihood methods that yield estimates of both the β coefficients and the α_ts. Using partial likelihood, however, we can treat the α_ts as nuisance parameters and estimate only the βs. If there are J unique times at which events occur, there will be J terms in the partial likelihood function:

$$PL = \prod_{j=1}^{J} L_j$$

where L_j is the partial likelihood of the jth event. Thus, for the job duration data, there are only five terms in the partial likelihood function. But each of those five terms is colossal. Here's why:

At time 1, there were 22 people with events out of 100 who were at risk. To get L_1, we ask the question: given that 22 events occurred, what is the probability that they occurred to these particular 22 people rather than to some different set of 22 people from among the 100 at risk? How many different ways are there of selecting 22 people from among a set of 100? A lot! Specifically, 7.3321×10^{21}. Let's call that number Q, and let q be a running index from 1 to Q, with $q = 1$ denoting the set that actually experienced the events. For a given set q, let ψ_q be the product of the odds for all the individuals in that set. Thus, if the individuals who actually experienced events are labeled $i = 1$ to 22, we have

$$\psi_1 = \prod_{i=1}^{22} O_{i1}.$$

We can then write

$$L_1 = \frac{\psi_1}{\psi_1 + \psi_2 + \ldots + \psi_Q}.$$

This is a simple expression, but there are *trillions* of terms being summed in the denominator. Fortunately, there is a recursive algorithm that makes it practical, even with substantial numbers of ties (Gail et al. 1981). Still, doing this with a large data set with many ties can take a great deal of computer time.

For the job duration data, the DISCRETE method takes only 11 seconds of computer time on a 486 DOS machine as compared with 3 seconds each for the Breslow and Efron approximations and 24 seconds for the EXACT method. But does the discrete-time model make sense for these data? For most jobs it's possible to quit at any point in time, suggesting that the model might not be appropriate. Remember, however, that these are simulated data. Since the simulation is actually based on a discrete-time model, it makes perfectly good sense in this case. Output 5.10 displays the results. Comparing these with the results for the EXACT method in Output 5.9, we see that the chi-square statistics and the *p*-values are similar. However, the coefficients for the DISCRETE method are about one-third larger for ED and PRESTIGE and about

15 percent larger for SALARY. This discrepancy is due largely to the fact that completely different models are being estimated, a hazard model and a logit model. The logit coefficients will usually be larger. For the logit model, $100(e^\beta - 1)$ gives the percent change in the *odds* that an event will occur for a one-unit increase in the covariate. Thus, each additional year of schooling increases the odds of quitting a job by $100(e^{.219} - 1) = 24$ percent.

Output 5.10 *Job Duration Results Using the DISCRETE Method*

```
Ties Handling: DISCRETE

                    Analysis of Maximum Likelihood Estimates

                    Parameter   Standard     Wald       Pr >      Risk
     Variable DF    Estimate      Error   Chi-Square Chi-Square   Ratio

     ED        1    0.219378    0.08480    6.69295    0.0097     1.245
     PRESTIGE  1   -0.120474    0.01776   46.02220    0.0001     0.886
     SALARY    1   -0.026108    0.01020    6.55603    0.0105     0.974
```

Comparison of Methods

Though the job duration coefficients differ for the two exact methods, they are at least in the same ballpark. More generally, it has been shown that if ties result from grouping continuous time data into intervals, the logit model converges to the proportional hazards model as the interval length gets smaller (Thompson 1977). When there are no ties, the partial likelihoods for all four methods (the two exact methods and the two approximations) reduce to the same formula, although PROC PHREG is still slightly faster with the Breslow method.

The examples we've seen so far have been small enough, both in number of observations and numbers of ties, that the computing times for the two exact methods were quite tolerable. Before concluding, let's see what happens as those data sets get larger. I took the 100 observations in the job duration data set and duplicated them to produce data sets of size 200, 400, 800, 1000, and 1200. The models were run on a Power Macintosh 7100/80 using a preproduction version of Release 6.10 SAS/STAT software. Here are the elapsed times, in seconds, for the four methods and seven sample sizes:

	100	200	400	600	800	1000	1200
BRESLOW	3	3	3	3	4	5	5
EFRON	3	3	3	3	4	5	5
EXACT	4	6	18	38	70	129	204
DISCRETE	3	4	6	9	12	19	26

For the two approximate methods, computing time hardly increased at all with the sample size, and the methods had identical times in every case. For the EXACT method, on the other hand, computing time went up much more rapidly than the sample size. Doubling the sample size from 600 to 1200 increased the time by a factor of over five times. I also tried the EXACT method with an additional doubling to 2400 observations, which increased time to 20 minutes, a factor of nearly six times. Computing time for the DISCRETE method rose at about the same rate as the number of observations. On the other hand, the DISCRETE method produced a *floating-point divide error* for anything over 1200 cases. According to a SAS Note, this bug occurs in Release 6.10 whenever the number of ties at any one time point exceeds about 250 (the exact number dependent on the operating system).

What we've learned about the handling of ties can be summarized in six points:

- When there are no ties, all four options in PROC PHREG give identical results.
- When there are few ties, it makes little difference which method is used. But since computing times will also be comparable, you might as well use one of the exact methods.
- When the number of ties is large, relative to the number at risk, the approximate methods tend to yield coefficients that are biased toward 0.
- Both the EXACT and DISCRETE methods produce exact results (i.e., true partial likelihood estimates), but the EXACT method assumes that ties arise from grouping continuous, untied data, while the DISCRETE method assumes that events really occur at the same, discrete times. The choice should be based on substantive grounds, although qualitative results will usually be similar.
- Both of the exact methods need a substantial amount of computer time for large data sets containing many ties. This is especially true for the EXACT method where doubling the sample size increases computing time by at least a factor of 5.
- If the exact methods are too time-consuming, use the Efron approximation, at least for model exploration. It's nearly always better than the Breslow method, with virtually no increase in computer time.

TIME-DEPENDENT COVARIATES

Time-dependent covariates are those that may change in value over the course of observation. While it's simple to modify Cox's model to allow for time-dependent covariates, the computation of the resulting partial likelihood is much more time consuming, and the practical issues surrounding the implementation of the procedure can be quite complex. It's easy to make mistakes without realizing it, so be sure you know what you're doing.

To modify the model in equation (5.2) to include time-dependent covariates, all we need to do is write (t) after the xs that are time dependent. For a model with one fixed covariate and one time-dependent covariate, we have

$$\log h_i(t) = \alpha(t) + \beta_1 x_{i1} + \beta_2 x_{i2}(t).$$

This says that the hazard at time t depends on the value of x_1, and on the value of x_2 at time t. What may not be clear is that $x_2(t)$ can be defined using any information about the individual prior to time t, thereby allowing for lagged or cumulative values of some variables. For example, if we want a model in which the hazard of arrest depends on employment status, we can specify employment as

- whether the person is currently employed
- whether the person was employed in the previous month
- the number of weeks of employment in the preceding three months
- the number of bouts of unemployment in the preceding 12 months.

The use of lagged covariates is often essential for resolving issues of causal ordering (more on that later).

Heart Transplant Example

Constructing appropriate time-dependent covariates frequently requires complex manipulation of the available data. PROC PHREG is particularly good for this kind of work because it provides you with a rich subset of DATA step operators and functions for defining time-dependent covariates. To get some idea of how this works, let's take another look at the Stanford Heart Transplant Data. In **Partial Likelihood: Examples**, we attempted to determine whether a transplant raised or lowered the risk of death by examining the effect of a time-constant covariate TRANS that was equal to 1 if the patient ever had a transplant, and was equal to 0 otherwise. I claimed that those results were completely misleading because patients who died quickly were less likely to get transplants. Now we'll do it right by defining a time-dependent covariate PLANT equal to 1 if the patient has already had a transplant at day t; otherwise, PLANT is equal to 0. Here's how it's done:

```
proc phreg data=stan;
   model surv1*dead(0)=plant surg ageaccpt / ties=exact;
   if wait>surv1 or wait=. then plant=0; else plant=1;
run;
```

Recall that SURV1 is the time in days from acceptance into the program until death or termination of observation; SURG =1 if the patient had previous heart surgery; otherwise SURG=0; AGEACCPT is the patient's age in years at the time of acceptance; and WAIT is the time in days from acceptance until transplant surgery, coded as missing for those who did not receive transplants.

Notice that the new covariate PLANT is listed in the MODEL statement *before* it is defined in the IF statement that follows. At first glance, this IF statement may be puzzling. For patients who were not transplanted, the IF condition will always be true because their WAIT value will be missing. On the other hand, for those who received transplants, it appears that the IF condition will always be false because their waiting time to transplant must be less than their survival time, giving us a fixed covariate rather than a time-dependent covariate. Now it's true that waiting time is always less than survival time for transplanted patients (except for one patient who died on the operating table). But unlike an IF statement in the DATA step, which only operates on a single case at a time, this IF statement compares waiting times for patients who were at risk of a death with survival times for patients who experienced events. Thus, the SURV1 in this statement is not usually the patient's own survival time, but the survival time of some other patient who died. This fact will become clearer (hopefully) in the next subsection when we examine the construction of the partial likelihood.

Results in Output 5.11 indicate that transplantation has no effect on the hazard of death. The effect of age at acceptance is somewhat smaller than it was in Output 5.2, although still statistically significant. However, the effect of prior heart surgery is larger and now significant at the .05 level. Estimation of this model took about twice as much computer time as a comparable model with the fixed version of the transplant variable.

Output 5.11 *Results for Transplant Data with a Time-Dependent Covariate*

Variable	DF	Parameter Estimate	Standard Error	Wald Chi-Square	Pr > Chi-Square	Risk Ratio
PLANT	1	-0.046152	0.30276	0.02324	0.8788	0.955
SURG	1	-0.771454	0.35961	4.60216	0.0319	0.462
AGEACCPT	1	0.031088	0.01391	4.99524	0.0254	1.032

Construction of the Partial Likelihood with Time-Dependent Covariates

With time-dependent covariates, the partial likelihood function has the same form we saw previously in equation (5.4) and equation (5.10). The only thing that changes is that the covariates are now indexed by time. Consider, for example, the 12 selected cases from the Stanford Heart Transplant data shown in Output 5.12. These are all the cases that had death or censoring times between 16 and 38 days, inclusive.

Output 5.12 *Selected Cases from the Stanford Heart Transplant Data*

OBS	SURV1	DEAD	WAIT
19	16	1	4
20	17	1	.
21	20	1	.
22	20	1	.
23	27	1	17
24	29	1	4
25	30	0	.
26	31	1	.
27	34	1	.
28	35	1	.
29	36	1	.
30	38	1	35

On day 16, one death occurred (to case 19). Since 18 people had already died or been censored by day 16, there were 103–18 = 85 people left in the risk set on that day. Let's suppose that we have a single covariate, the time-dependent version of transplant status. The partial likelihood for day 16 is therefore

$$\frac{e^{\beta x_{19}(16)}}{e^{\beta x_{19}(16)} + e^{\beta x_{20}(16)} + e^{\beta x_{21}(16)} + \ldots + e^{\beta x_{103}(16)}} \,.$$

To calculate this quantity, PROC PHREG must compute the value of x on day 16 for each of the 85 people at risk. For cases 19 and 24, a transplant occurred on day 4. Since this was before day 16, we have $x_{19}(16) = 1$ and $x_{24}(16) = 1$. Waiting time is missing for cases 20-22 and cases 25-29, indicating that they never received a transplant. Therefore, $x_{20}(16) = x_{21}(16) = x_{22}(16) = x_{25}(16) = x_{26}(16) = x_{27}(16) = x_{28}(16) = x_{29}(16) = 0$. Case 23 had a transplant on day 17, so on day 16, the patient was still without a transplant and $x_{23}(16) = 0$. Similarly, we have $x_{30}(16) = 0$ because case 30 didn't get a transplant until day 35.

The calculation of the appropriate x values is accomplished by the IF statement discussed earlier in the heart transplant example. At each unique event time, PROC PHREG calculates a term in the partial likelihood function (like the one above) by applying the IF statement to all the cases in the risk set at that time. Again, the value of SURV1 in the IF statement is the event time that PROC PHREG is currently operating on, not the survival time for each individual at risk.

To continue the example, the next term in the partial likelihood function corresponds to the death that occurred to case 20 on day 17:

$$\frac{e^{\beta x_{20}(17)}}{e^{\beta x_{20}(17)} + e^{\beta x_{21}(17)} + e^{\beta x_{22}(17)} + \ldots + e^{\beta x_{103}(17)}}.$$

Of course case 19 no longer shows up in this formula because the patient left the risk set at death. The values of x are all the same as they were for day 16, except for case 23, who had a transplant on day 17. For this case, waiting time is *not* greater than 17, so $x_{23}(17) = 1$. For the data in Output 5.12, there are eight additional terms in the partial likelihood function. For the first five of these, the values of x for cases remaining in the risk set are the same as they were on day 17. On day 35, however, the value of x for case 30 switches from 0 to 1.

The IF statement is evaluated every time a given case appears in a risk set for a particular event time. Thus, those cases with long event (or censoring) times will appear in many different risk sets. For the 103 cases in this data set, there were 63 unique event times. If we sum the size of the risk sets for those 63 times, we get a total of 3,548, which is the number of times that the IF statement must be evaluated. That's just on one iteration. Most partial likelihood programs reconstruct the time-dependent values at each iteration. Since this example requires four iterations, the total number of IF statement evaluations is 14,192. Now you see why time-dependent covariates are more computationally intensive.

PROC PHREG reduces the computational burden by saving the calculated time-dependent values in a temporary data set after the first iteration and re-using them on subsequent iterations. The saved data set can potentially be much larger than the original data set, however, so you may run into trouble if you're short on disk space. To override this feature, specify the MULTIPASS option in the PROC PHREG statement.

Covariates Representing Alternative Time Origins

When I discussed the choice of time origin in Chapter 2, I mentioned that you can include alternative origins as covariates, sometimes as time-dependent covariates. Let's see how this might work with the Stanford Heart Transplant Data. In the analysis just completed, the origin was the date of acceptance into the program, with the time of death or censoring computed from that point. It is certainly plausible, however, that the hazard of death also depends on age or calendar time. We have already included age at acceptance into the program as a time-constant covariate and found that patients who were older at acceptance had a higher hazard of death. But if that's the case, we might also expect that the hazard will continue to increase with age *after* acceptance into the program. A natural way to allow for this possibility is to specify a model with *current* age as a time-dependent covariate. Here's how to do that with PROC PHREG:

```
proc phreg data=stan;
   model surv1*dead(0)=plant surg age / ties=exact;
   if wait>surv1 or wait=. then plant=0; else plant=1;
   age=ageaccpt+surv1;
run;
```

In this program, current age is defined as age at acceptance plus the time to the current event. While this is certainly correct, a surprising thing happens: the results are *exactly* the same as in Output 5.11. Here's why. We can write the time-dependent version of the model as

$$\log h(t) = \alpha(t) + \beta_1 x_1 + \beta_2 x_2(t) + \beta_3 x_3(t) \tag{5.13}$$

where x_1 is the surgery indicator, x_2 is transplant status, and x_3 is current age. We also know that $x_3(t) = x_3(0) + t$, where $x_3(0)$ is age at the time of acceptance. Substituting into equation (5.13), we have

$$\log h(t) = \alpha^*(t) + \beta_1 x_1 + \beta_2 x_2(t) + \beta_3 x_3(0)$$

where $\alpha^*(t) = \alpha(t) + \beta_3 t$. Thus, we have converted a model with a time-dependent version of age to one with a fixed version of age. In the process, the arbitrary function of time changes, but that's of no consequence because it drops out of the estimating equations anyway. The same trick works with calendar time: instead of specifying a model in which the hazard depends on current calendar time, we can estimate a model with calendar time at the point of acceptance and get exactly the same results.

The trick does not work, however, if the model says that the log of the hazard is a *non*linear function of the alternative time origin. For example, suppose we want to estimate the model

$$\log h(t) = \alpha(t) + \beta_1 x_1 + \beta_2 x_2(t) + \beta_3 \log x_3(t)$$

where $x_3(t)$ is again age at time t. Substitution with $x_3(t) = x_3(0) + t$ gets us nowhere in this case because the β_3 coefficient does not distribute across the two components of $x_3(t)$. You must estimate this model with $\log x_3(t)$ as a time-dependent covariate:

```
proc phreg data=stan;
    model surv1*dead(0)=plant surg logage / ties=exact;
    if wait>surv1 or wait=. then plant=0; else plant=1;
    logage=log(ageaccpt+surv1);
run;
```

In sum, if you are willing to forego nonlinear functions of time, you can include any alternative time origin as a fixed covariate, measured at the origin that is actually used in calculating event times.

Time-Dependent Covariates Measured at Regular Intervals

As we saw earlier, calculation of the partial likelihood requires that the values of the covariates be known for every individual who was at risk at each event time. In practice, because we never know in advance when events will occur, we need to know the values of all the time-dependent covariates at every point in time. This requirement was met for the heart transplant data: death times were measured in days, and for each day, we could construct a variable indicating whether a given patient had already had a heart transplant.

Often, however, the information on the covariates is only collected at regular intervals of time that may be longer (or shorter) than the time units used to measure event times. For example, in a study of time to death among AIDS patients, there may be monthly follow-ups in which vital signs and blood measurements are taken. If deaths are reported in days, there is only about a one-in-thirty chance that the time-dependent measurements will be available for a given patient on a particular death day. In such cases, it is necessary to use some ad-hoc method for assigning covariate values to death days. In a moment, I will discuss several issues related to such ad-hoc approaches. First, let's look at an example in which the time intervals for covariate measurement correspond exactly to the intervals in which event times are measured.

For the recidivism example, additional information was available on the employment status of the released convicts over the one-year follow-up period. Specifically, for each of the 52 weeks of follow-up, there was a dummy variable coded 1 if the person was employed full-time during that week; otherwise the variable was coded 0. The data are read as follows:

```
data recid;
   infile 'c:recid.dat';
   input week arrest fin age race wexp mar paro prio emp1-emp52;
run;
```

The important point here is that the 52 values of employment status (EMP1-EMP52) are read in as separate variables on a single input record. The PROC PHREG statements are

```
proc phreg data=recid;
   model week*arrest(0)=fin age race wexp mar paro prio employed
         / ties=efron;
   array emp(*) emp1-emp52;
   do i=1 to 52;
      if week=i then employed=emp(i);
   end;
run;
```

The aim here is to pick out the employment indicator that corresponds to the particular week in which an event occurred and assign that value to the variable EMPLOYED. The ARRAY statement makes it possible to treat the 52 distinct dummy variables as a single subscripted array, thereby greatly facilitating the subsequent manipulations.

The only problem with this code is that the program has to cycle through 52 IF statements to pick out the right value of the employment variable. A more efficient (but somewhat less intuitive) program that directly retrieves the right value is as follows:

```
proc phreg data=recid;
   model week*arrest(0)=fin age race wexp mar paro prio employed
         / ties=efron;
   array emp(*) emp1-emp52;
   employed=emp(week);
run;
```

This program takes about 23 percent less time to run than the DO-IF version. Output 5.13 shows the results (for either version). For the time-constant variables, the coefficients and test statistics are pretty much the same as in Output 5.8. Judging by the chi-square test, however, the new variable EMPLOYED has by far the strongest effect of any variable in the model. The risk ratio of .265 tells us that the risk of arrest for those who were employed full time is a little more than one-fourth the risk for those who were not employed full time.

Output 5.13   *Recidivism Results with a Time-Dependent Covariate*

Variable	DF	Parameter Estimate	Standard Error	Wald Chi-Square	Pr > Chi-Square	Risk Ratio
FIN	1	-0.356722	0.19113	3.48351	0.0620	0.700
AGE	1	-0.046342	0.02174	4.54532	0.0330	0.955
RACE	1	0.338658	0.30960	1.19651	0.2740	1.403
WEXP	1	-0.025553	0.21142	0.01461	0.9038	0.975
MAR	1	-0.293747	0.38303	0.58814	0.4431	0.745
PARO	1	-0.064206	0.19468	0.10876	0.7416	0.938
PRIO	1	0.085139	0.02896	8.64391	0.0033	1.089
EMPLOYED	1	-1.328321	0.25072	28.07006	0.0001	0.265

Unfortunately, these results are undermined by the possibility that arrests affect employment status rather than vice versa. If someone is arrested and incarcerated near the beginning of a particular week, the probability of working full time during the remainder of that week is likely to drop precipitously. This potential reverse causation is a problem that is quite common with time-dependent covariates, especially when event times or covariate times are not measured precisely.

One way to reduce ambiguity in the causal ordering is to *lag* the covariate values. Instead of predicting arrests in a given week by employment status in the same week, we can use employment status in the prior week. This requires only minor modifications in the SAS code:

```
proc phreg;
   where week>1;
   model week*arrest(0)=fin age race wexp mar paro prio employed
        / ties=efron;
   array emp(*) emp1-emp52;
   employed=emp(week-1);
run;
```

One change is to add a WHERE statement to eliminate cases (only one case, in fact) with an arrest in the first week after release. This change is necessary because there were no values of employment status prior to the first week. The other change is to subscript EMP with WEEK–1 rather than with WEEK. With these changes, the coefficient for EMPLOYED drops substantially, from –1.33 to –.79, which implies that the risk of arrest for those who were employed is about 45 percent of the risk of those who were not employed. While this is a much weaker effect than we found using unlagged values of employment status, it is still highly significant with a chi-square value of 13.1. The effects of the other variables remain virtually unchanged.

As this example points out, there are often many different ways of specifying the effect of a time-dependent covariate. Let's consider a couple of the alternatives. Instead of a single lagged version of the employment status indicator, we can have both a one-week and a two-week lag, as shown in the following:

```
proc phreg;
    where week>2;
    model week*arrest(0)=fin age race wexp mar paro prio employ1
        employ2 / ties=efron;
    array emp(*) emp1-emp52;
    employ1=emp(week-1);
    employ2=emp(week-2);
run;
```

Note that because of the two-week lag, it is necessary to eliminate cases with events in either week 1 or week 2. When I tried this variation, I found that *neither* EMPLOY1 nor EMPLOY2 was significant (probably because they are highly correlated), but that the one-week lag was much stronger than the two-week lag. So it looks as though we're better off sticking with the single one-week lag.

Another possibility is that the hazard of arrest may depend on the *cumulative* employment experience after release rather than the employment status in the preceding week. Consider the following SAS code:

```
data recidcum;
    set recid;
    array emp(*) emp1-emp52;
    array cum(*) cum1-cum52;
    cum1=emp1;
    do i=2 to 52;
        cum(i)=cum(i-1) + emp(i);
    end;
    do i=1 to 52;;
        cum(i)=cum(i)/i;
    end;
run;
proc phreg data=recidcum;
    where week>1;
    model week*arrest(0)=fin age race wexp mar paro prio employ
        / ties=efron;
    array cumemp(*) cum1-cum52;
    employ=cumemp(week-1);
run;
```

The DATA step defines a new set of variables CUM1-CUM52 that are the *cumulative proportions of weeks worked* for each of the 52 weeks. The first DO loop creates the cumulative count; the second DO loop changes the counts to proportions. The PROC PHREG statements have the same structure as before, except that the cumulative employment (lagged by one week) has been substituted for the lagged employment indicator. This run produces a marginally significant effect of cumulative employment experience. When I also included the one-week-lagged employment indicator, the effect of the cumulated variable faded to insignificance, while the lagged indicator continued to be a significant predictor. Again, it appears that the one-week lag is a better specification.

You can create the cumulated variable in the PROC PHREG step rather than the DATA step, but it would be unwise to do so. When I tried it that way, the execution time for the DATA step dropped from 17 seconds to 8 seconds, but the PROC step time went from 1.82 minutes to 8.72 minutes. In general, whatever programming *can* be done in the DATA step *should* be done there because the computations only have to be done once. In the PROC PHREG step, on the other hand, the same computations may have to be repeated many times.

Ad-Hoc Estimates of Time Dependent Covariates

It often happens that time-dependent covariates are measured at regular intervals, but the intervals don't correspond to the units in which *event* times are measured. For example, we may know the exact day of death for a sample of cancer patients, but have only monthly measurements of, say, albumin level in the blood. For partial likelihood estimation, we really need daily albumin measurements, so we must somehow impute these from the monthly data. There are often several possible ways to do this, and, unfortunately, none has any formal justification. On the other hand, it's undoubtedly better to use some common-sense method for imputing the missing values rather than discarding the data for the time-dependent covariates.

Let's consider some possible methods and some rough rules of thumb. For the case of monthly albumin measurements and day of death, an obvious method is to use the closest preceding albumin level to impute the level at any given death time. For data over a one-year period, the SAS code might look like this:

```
data blood;
   infile 'blood.dat';
   input deathday status alb1-alb12;
run;

proc phreg;
   model deathday*status(0)=albumin;
   array alb(*) alb1-alb12;
   deathmon=ceil(deathday/30.4);
   albumin=alb(deathmon);
run;
```

Assume that ALB1 is measured at the *beginning* of the first month, and so on. Dividing DEATHDAY by 30.4 converts days into months (including fractions of a month). The CEIL function then takes the smallest integer larger than its argument. Thus, day 40 would be converted to 1.32, which then becomes 2, that is, the second month. This value is then used as a subscript in the ALB array to retrieve the albumin level recorded at the beginning of the second month. (There may be some slippage here because months vary in length. However, if we know the exact day at which each albumin measurement was taken, we can avoid this difficulty by using the methods for irregular intervals described in the next section.)

It may be possible to get better imputations of daily albumin levels by using information on the blood levels in earlier months. If we believe, for example, that albumin levels are likely to worsen (or improve) steadily, it might be sensible to calculate a linear extrapolation based on the most recent *two* months:

```
proc phreg data=blood;
   model deathday*status(0)=albumin;
   array alb(*) alb1-alb12;
   deathmon=deathday/30.4;
   j=ceil(deathmon);
   if j=1 then albumin=alb(1);
   else albumin=alb(j)+(alb(j)-alb(j-1))*(deathmon-j+1);
run;
```

Alternatively, if we believe that albumin levels tend to fluctuate randomly around some average value, we might do better with a weighted average of the most recent value and the mean of all earlier values. Unlike the

linear extrapolation, most of the work for this specification can be done in the
DATA step:

```
data data=blood;
   set;
   array alb(*) alb1-alb12;
   array meanalb(*) mean1-mean12;
   array predalb(*) pred1-pred12;
   pred1=alb1;
   mean1=alb1;
   do i=2 to 12;
      meanalb(i)=(1/i)*alb(i)+(1-1/i)*meanalb(i-1);
      predalb(i)=.7*alb(i)+.3*meanalb(i-1));
   end;
run;

proc phreg;
   model deathday*status(0)=albumin;
   array pred(*) pred1-pred12;
   deathmon=ceil(deathday/30.4);
   albumin=pred(deathmon);
run;
```

This code gives the most recent value an arbitrarily chosen weight
of .7 and the mean of earlier values a weight of .3. Instead of choosing the
weights arbitrarily, they can be estimated by including both the most recent
albumin level and the mean of the earlier level as covariates in the model.

In these examples, we made no use of information on albumin
levels that were recorded *after* the death date. Obviously, we had no other
option for patients who died on that death date. Remember, however, that for
every death date, PROC PHREG retrieves (or constructs) the covariates for all
individuals who were at risk of death on that date, whether or not they died.
For those who did not die on that death date, we could have used the (possibly
weighted) average of the albumin level recorded before the death date and the
level recorded after the death date. I don't recommend this, however. Using
different imputation rules for those who died and those who didn't die is just
asking for artifacts to creep into your results. Even in cases where the
occurrence of the event does *not* stop the measurement of the time-dependent
covariate, it's a dangerous practice to use information recorded after the event
to construct a variable used as a predictor of the event. This method is sensible
only if you are completely confident that the event could not have caused any
changes in the time-dependent covariate. For example, in modeling whether
people will purchase a house, it might be reasonable to use an average of the
local mortgage rates before and after the purchase.

As an alternative to the methods discussed in this subsection, you
may want to consider using PROC EXPAND, a procedure in SAS/ETS software.
PROC EXPAND reads a time series data set, converts it into a continuous-time

function using a variety of interpolation methods, and outputs a new data set with observations at any desired time intervals. It can also impute missing values in a time series. One difficulty is that PROC EXPAND treats data for each time point as a distinct observation, while PROC PHREG expects all of the data for each individual to be contained in a *single* observation. Hence, the data set produced by PROC EXPAND requires some additional DATA step manipulations before you can use it with PROC PHREG.

Time-Dependent Covariates that Change at Irregular Intervals

In the Stanford Heart Transplant example, we had a time-dependent covariate—previous receipt of a transplant—that changed at unpredictable times. No more than one such change could occur for any of the patients. Now we consider the more general situation in which the time-dependent covariate may change at multiple, irregularly spaced points in time.

We'll do this by way of an example. The survival data (hypothetical) in Output 5.14 are for 29 males, ages 50 to 60, who were diagnosed with alcoholic cirrhosis. At diagnosis, they were measured for blood coagulation time (PT). The men were then remeasured at clinic visits that occurred at irregular intervals until they either died or the study was terminated. The maximum number of clinic visits for any patient was 10. The length of the intervals between visits ranged between 3 and 33 months, with a mean interval length of 9.5 months and a standard deviation of 6.0. In Output 5.14, SURV is the time of death or time of censoring, calculated in months since diagnosis. DEAD is coded 1 for a death and is coded 0 if censored. TIME2-TIME10 contain the number of months since diagnosis for each clinic visit. PT1-PT10 contain the measured values of the PT variable at each clinic visit. Variables are recorded as missing if there was no clinic visit.

Output 5.14 *Survival Data for 29 Males with Alcoholic Cirrhosis*

SURV	DEAD	TIME2	TIME3	TIME4	TIME5	TIME6	TIME7	TIME8	TIME9	TIME10	PT1	PT2	PT3	PT4	PT5	PT6	PT7	PT8	PT9	PT10
90	0	7	20	26	35	44	50	56	80	83	23.9	20.8	23.6	23.6	24.0	22.5	24.6	25.1	29.4	27.9
80	0	6	36	42	54	67	78	.	.	.	29.6	15.1	15.4	16.3	13.9	14.6	16.1	.	.	.
36	0	17	28	34	.	.	.	.	.	.	25.9	24.4	24.8	24.3	.	.	.	.	.	.
68	0	15	20	26	32	51	.	.	.	.	26.8	27.9	26.5	26.5	26.8	26.6	.	.	.	.
62	0	22	40	46	.	.	.	.	.	.	23.0	25.2	27.1	27.8	.	.	.	.	.	.
47	0	5	12	24	35	46	.	.	.	.	25.8	26.0	25.2	24.9	26.3	26.6	.	.	.	.
84	0	8	27	31	43	76	.	.	.	.	14.2	11.5	12.9	12.6	12.5	18.6	.	.	.	.
57	0	6	21	27	34	39	45	51	.	.	27.6	27.5	28.0	27.8	29.1	28.2	28.3	28.4	.	.
7	0	4	7	.	.	.	.	.	.	.	25.0	25.1	24.7	.	.	.	.	.	.	.
49	0	16	.	.	.	.	.	.	.	.	25.5	27.4	.	.	.	.	.	.	.	.
55	0	3	9	15	21	33	42	49	.	.	14.8	16.7	16.9	17.7	13.8	13.8	13.7	14.2	.	.
43	0	6	11	18	24	42	.	.	.	.	20.6	19.9	20.3	20.2	19.7	27.1	.	.	.	.
42	0	6	12	18	23	29	35	.	.	.	27.6	27.0	28.1	28.8	29.0	28.4	28.8	.	.	.
11	0	9	.	.	.	.	.	.	.	.	25.3	27.8	.	.	.	.	.	.	.	.
36	1	16	22	28	.	.	.	.	.	.	22.5	22.3	25.2	26.4	.	.	.	.	.	.
36	1	9	26	32	.	.	.	.	.	.	26.9	26.9	24.2	26.2	.	.	.	.	.	.
2	1	.	.	.	.	.	.	.	.	.	19.2	.	.	.	.	.	.	.	.	.
23	1	7	13	.	.	.	.	.	.	.	21.8	20.3	23.8	.	.	.	.	.	.	.
10	1	6	.	.	.	.	.	.	.	.	21.6	22.3	.	.	.	.	.	.	.	.
29	1	21	27	.	.	.	.	.	.	.	18.7	20.2	22.5	.	.	.	.	.	.	.
16	1	6	12	.	.	.	.	.	.	.	28.4	28.7	28.7	.	.	.	.	.	.	.
15	1	7	12	.	.	.	.	.	.	.	17.8	17.7	17.4	.	.	.	.	.	.	.
5	1	3	.	.	.	.	.	.	.	.	20.7	22.6	.	.	.	.	.	.	.	.
15	1	6	.	.	.	.	.	.	.	.	28.0	28.8	.	.	.	.	.	.	.	.
1	1	.	.	.	.	.	.	.	.	.	31.6	.	.	.	.	.	.	.	.	.
13	1	4	10	.	.	.	.	.	.	.	26.0	22.7	25.4	.	.	.	.	.	.	.
39	1	22	35	.	.	.	.	.	.	.	25.5	29.0	29.2	.	.	.	.	.	.	.
20	1	12	.	.	.	.	.	.	.	.	21.3	21.0	.	.	.	.	.	.	.	.
45	1	18	24	38	.	.	.	.	.	.	23.9	28.7	29.5	30.2	.	.	.	.	.	.

Let's estimate a model in which the hazard of death at time *t* depends on the value of PT at time *t*. Since we don't have measures of PT at all death times, we'll use the closest preceding measurement. The SAS code for accomplishing this is as follows:

```
proc phreg data=alco;
   model surv*dead(0)=pt;
   time1=0;
   array time(*) time1-time10;
   array p(*) pt1-pt10;
   do j=1 to 10;
   if surv ge time(j) and time(j) ne . then pt=p(j);
   end;
run;
```

For a given death time, the DO loop cycles through all 10 possible clinic visits. If the death time is greater than the time of *j*th visit, the value of PT is reassigned to be the value observed at visit *j*. PROC PHREG keeps doing this until it either

- encounters a missing value of the TIME variable (no clinic visit)
- encounters a TIME value that is greater than the death time
- goes through all 10 possible visits.

Hence, PROC PHREG always stops at the most recent clinic visit and assigns the value of PT recorded at that visit.

When I ran this model, I got a coefficient for PT of .083 with a nonsignificant likelihood-ratio chi-square value of 1.87, suggesting that the blood measurement is of little predictive value. But suppose the hazard depends on the *change* in PT relative to the patient's initial measurement rather than upon the absolute level. You can implement this idea by changing the IF statement above to read as follows:

```
if surv ge time(j) and time(j) ne . then pt=p(j)-pt1;
```

With this minor change in specification, the coefficient of PT increased in magnitude to .352 with a chi-square of 6.97, which is significant at beyond the .01 level.

In general, the only additional requirement for handling irregular intervals between measurements of some covariate is data on the timing of the measurement. The variables containing the times of the measurements must always be in the same metric as the event-time variable. A DO loop like the one above can then retrieve the appropriate measurement for each event time.

Covariates that are Undefined in Some Intervals

In the heart transplant example, we estimated the effect of a heart transplant on the hazard of death. Earlier in the chapter (Output 5.3), after eliminating the patients who did not receive a transplant, we also examined the effects of several covariates that were defined only for those who received transplants: date of transplant, age at transplant, waiting time until transplant, and three measures of tissue matching. We could combine these two analyses into a single model if we could figure out what to do with the covariates that are undefined for patients who have not yet received transplants. One way to do it is to treat the transplant-specific variables as time-dependent covariates that have values of 0 before a transplant occurred. The SAS code to do that is as follows:

```
proc phreg data=stan;
    model surv1*dead(0)=surg ageaccpt plant m1td m2td m3td
        waittd dottd / ties=exact;
    if wait>surv1 or wait=. then plant=0; else plant=1;
    if plant=1 then do;
        m1td=m1;
        m2td=m2;
        m3td=m3;
        waittd=wait;
        dottd=dot;
    end;
    else do;
        m1td=0;
        m2td=0;
        m3td=0;
        waittd=0;
        dottd=0;
    end;
run;
```

This program defines the time-dependent transplant indicator PLANT as in the heart transplant example. Then whenever PLANT=1 (i.e., the patient has received a transplant), the time-dependent versions of five variables are defined equal to their values measured at the time of the transplant. When PLANT=0, these variables are set to 0.

The results in Output 5.15 are similar to those in the earlier, separate analyses. There is a significant effect of age at acceptance, although the magnitude and significance level are both attenuated from what we saw in Output 5.2. We also see a coefficient for the M3 measure that approaches statistical significance. Notice, however, that in contrast to Output 5.2, age at transplant is not included in the model. That's because age at transplant is equal to age at acceptance plus waiting time for those who received a transplant. (This does not prevent estimation of a model with all three variables because not everyone received a transplant. However, a model with three variables can produce estimates that are not interpretable.)

You can interpret the coefficient for PLANT as the effect of a transplant when all the other time-dependent covariates are equal to 0. This is not substantively meaningful, however, because a date of transplant of 0 is not possible with these data. Instead, the model should be interpreted in the following way: the effect of a transplant depends on the levels of the transplant-specific variables. More specifically, the effect of a transplant for any given individual is a linear function of those five variables, with coefficients given in Output 5.15. The coefficient of PLANT is the intercept in that linear function.

Output 5.15 *Heart Transplant Results with Several Time-Dependent Covariates*

Variable	DF	Parameter Estimate	Standard Error	Wald Chi-Square	Pr > Chi-Square	Risk Ratio
SURG	1	-0.663841	0.38647	2.95051	0.0859	0.515
AGEACCPT	1	0.029589	0.01445	4.19147	0.0406	1.030
PLANT	1	0.788753	1.20651	0.42738	0.5133	2.201
M1TD	1	-0.226452	0.19339	1.37110	0.2416	0.797
M2TD	1	0.164605	0.44867	0.13460	0.7137	1.179
M3TD	1	0.600854	0.33729	3.17337	0.0748	1.824
WAITTD	1	0.004256	0.00530	0.64515	0.4219	1.004
DOTTD	1	-0.000298	0.0002993	0.98940	0.3199	1.000

COX MODELS WITH NONPROPORTIONAL HAZARDS

Earlier, I mentioned that the Cox model can be easily extended to allow for nonproportional hazards. In fact, we've just finished a lengthy discussion of one class of nonproportional models. Whenever you introduce time-dependent covariates into a Cox regression model, it's no longer accurate to call it a proportional hazards (PH) model. Why? Because the time-dependent covariates will change at different rates for different individuals, so the ratios of their hazards cannot remain constant. As we've seen, however, that creates no real problem for the partial likelihood estimation method.

But suppose you don't have any time-dependent covariates. How do you know if your data satisfy the PH assumption, and what happens if the assumption is violated? Although these are legitimate questions, I personally believe that concern about the PH assumption is often excessive. Every model embodies many assumptions, some more questionable or consequential than others. The reason people focus so much attention on the PH assumption is that the model is *named* for that property. At the same time, they often ignore such critical questions as: Are all the relevant covariates included? Is the censoring mechanism noninformative? Is measurement error in the covariates acceptably low? (As in ordinary linear regression, measurement error in the covariates tends to attenuate coefficients (Nakamura 1992)).

To put this issue in perspective, you need to understand that violations of the PH assumption are equivalent to interactions between one or more covariates and time. That is, the PH model assumes that the effect of each covariate is the same at all points in time. If the effect of a variable varies with time, the PH assumption is violated for that variable. It's unlikely that the PH assumption is ever exactly satisfied, but that's true of nearly all statistical assumptions. If we estimate a PH model when the assumption is violated for some variable (thereby suppressing the interaction), then the coefficient we estimate for that variable is a sort of *average* effect over the range of times observed in the data. Is this so terrible? In fact, researchers suppress interactions all the time when they estimate regression models. In models with even a moderately large number of variables, no one tests for all the possible 2-way interactions—there are just too many of them.

In some cases, however, we may have reason to believe that the interactions with time are so strong that it would be misleading to suppress them. In other situations, we might have a strong theoretical interest in those interactions, even when they are not very strong. For those cases, we need to examine methods for testing and modeling nonproportional hazards. In this section, we'll look at one method that explicitly incorporates the interactions into the model and at a second method, called *stratification*, that subsumes the interactions into the arbitrary function of time. Later in the chapter (see the section **Covariate-Wise Residuals**), we'll see a third method based on residuals.

Interactions with Time as Time-Dependent Covariates

A common way of representing interaction between two variables in a linear regression model is to include a new variable that is the product of the two variables in question. To represent the interaction between a covariate x and time in a Cox model, we can write

$$\log h(t) = \alpha(t) + \beta_1 x + \beta_2 x t .$$

Factoring out the x, we can rewrite this as

$$\log h(t) = \alpha(t) + (\beta_1 + \beta_2 t) x .$$

In this equation, the effect of x is $\beta_1 + \beta_2 t$. If β_2 is positive, then the effect of x increases linearly with time; if it's negative, the effect decreases linearly with time. β_1 can be interpreted as the effect of x at time 0, the origin of the process.

You can easily estimate this model by defining a time-dependent covariate $z=xt$. Here's an example. Recall that the main goal of the recidivism study was to determine whether those who received financial aid had lower arrest rates than those who did not. But the aid was only given during the first 13 weeks of the one-year observation period. The data also show that the proportion of convicts who were working full time increased steadily over the one-year period. So it's plausible that the effect of financial aid was greatest during the earlier weeks when the treatment was being delivered and financial need was most pressing. To test that hypothesis, we can run the following SAS code, which yields the results in Output 5.16:

```
proc phreg data=recid;
   model week*arrest(0)=fin age race wexp mar paro prio fintime
        / ties=efron;
   fintime=fin*week;
run;
```

The first thing to notice in Output 5.16 is that the coefficient for FINTIME, the product of FIN and WEEK, is *far* from statistically significant. Thus, there is *no* evidence here that the effect of financial aid varies across the one-year interval.

Output 5.16 *A Model for Recidivism with Time by Financial Aid Interaction*

Variable	DF	Parameter Estimate	Standard Error	Wald Chi-Square	Pr > Chi-Square	Risk Ratio
FIN	1	-0.343492	0.42503	0.65313	0.4190	0.709
AGE	1	-0.057431	0.02200	6.81337	0.0090	0.944
RACE	1	0.313922	0.30799	1.03888	0.3081	1.369
WEXP	1	-0.149658	0.21224	0.49722	0.4807	0.861
MAR	1	-0.433790	0.38188	1.29032	0.2560	0.648
PARO	1	-0.084970	0.19576	0.18839	0.6643	0.919
PRIO	1	0.091606	0.02868	10.20168	0.0014	1.096
FINTIME	1	-0.001250	0.01321	0.00895	0.9246	0.999

Perhaps we have simply not specified the appropriate form of the interaction. Since financial aid ended after 13 weeks, it's possible that the effect of the aid was constant for those 13 weeks, but then dropped precipitously for the remaining 39 weeks. To represent this, we can dichotomize the time variable before forming the product with FIN:

```
proc phreg data=recid;
   model week*arrest(0)=fin age race wexp mar paro prio fintime
         / ties=efron;
   fintime=fin*(week>13);
run;
```

Results (not shown) include a coefficient of −.19 for FIN and −.23 for FINTIME, both with *p*-values over .50. So again, we have no evidence that the effect of financial aid changes over the one-year period. In fact, the direction of the estimated change is the opposite of what we expected. The −.19 coefficient for FIN can be interpreted as the effect of financial aid in the first 13 weeks. To get the estimated effect for the last 39 weeks, we add the coefficients for FIN and FINTIME:

$$-.19+(-.23)= -.42$$

Thus, we find a *stronger* effect in the later period.

As these runs show, there are usually a variety of ways to specify the interaction of a covariate and time. Some textbooks recommend forming the product of the covariate and the *logarithm* of time, possibly to avoid numerical overflows. But there is no theoretical reason to prefer this specification, and the algorithm used by PROC PHREG is robust to such numerical problems. Instead of dichotomizing time, you can trichotomize it by creating indicator variables for two out of three periods and forming the product of each indicator and the variable of interest. It's also straightforward to include interactions between time and time-dependent covariates. Then, not only do the covariates change over time, but also the *effects* of those variables change with time.

To sum up, we now have a way to test for violations of the PH assumption: For any suspected covariate, simply add to the model a time-dependent covariate representing the interaction of the original covariate and time. If the interaction covariate does not have a significant coefficient, then we may conclude that the PH assumption is not violated *for that variable*. On the other hand, if the interaction variable does have a significant coefficient, we have evidence for nonproportionality. Of course, we also have a model that incorporates the nonproportionality. So the method of diagnosis is also the cure.

Nonproportionality Via Stratification

Another approach to nonproportionality is *stratification*, a technique that is most useful when the covariate that interacts with time is both categorical and not of direct interest. Consider the myelomatosis data described in Chapter 2 and analyzed in Chapter 3. For that data, the primary interest was in the effect of the treatment indicator TREAT. There was also a covariate called RENAL, an indicator of whether renal functioning was impaired at the time of randomization to treatment. In Chapter 3, we found that RENAL was strongly related to survival time, but the effect of TREAT was not significant. Suppose we believe (or suspect) that the effect of RENAL varies with time since randomization. Alternatively, we can say that the shape of the hazard function is different for those with and without impaired renal functioning. Letting x represent the treatment indicator and z the renal functioning indicator, we can represent this idea by postulating separate models for the two renal functioning groups:

Impaired   Not Impaired
$$\log h_i(t) = \alpha_0(t) + \beta x_i. \qquad \log h_i(t) = \alpha_1(t) + \beta x_i.$$

Notice that the coefficient of x is the same in both equations, but the arbitrary function of time is allowed to differ. We can combine the two equations into a single equation by writing

$$\log h_i(t) = \alpha_z(t) + \beta x_i.$$

You can easily estimate this model by the method of partial likelihood using these steps:

1. Construct separate partial likelihood functions for each of the two renal functioning groups.
2. Multiply those two functions together.
3. Choose values of β that maximize this function.

PROC PHREG does this automatically if you include a STRATA statement:

```
proc phreg data=myel;
   model dur*stat(0)=treat / ties=exact;
   strata renal;
run;
```

Output 5.17 shows the results. PROC PHREG first reports some simple statistics for each of the strata, then it reports the usual output for the regression model. In contrast to the PROC LIFETEST results of Chapter 3, we now find a statistically significant effect of the treatment. Notice, however, that there is no estimated coefficient for RENAL. Whatever effects this variable may have, they are entirely absorbed into the two arbitrary functions of time.

Output 5.17 *Myelomatosis Data with Stratified Cox Regression*

```
Summary of the Number of Event and Censored Values

                                                          Percent
     Stratum    RENAL          Total     Event   Censored  Censored

         1      0                18        10        8      44.44
         2      1                 7         7        0       0.00
         ------------------------------------------------------------
       Total                     25        17        8      32.00

             Testing Global Null Hypothesis: BETA=0

               Without        With
Criterion     Covariates    Covariates    Model Chi-Square

-2 LOG L        66.342        60.268       6.074 with 1 DF (p=0.0137)
Score              .             .         5.791 with 1 DF (p=0.0161)
Wald               .             .         4.925 with 1 DF (p=0.0265)

             Analysis of Maximum Likelihood Estimates

                 Parameter    Standard    Wald        Pr >       Risk
Variable  DF     Estimate      Error    Chi-Square  Chi-Square   Ratio

TREAT      1     1.463986     0.65965    4.92549     0.0265      4.323
```

For comparison purposes, I also estimated three other PROC PHREG models:

- a model with TREAT as the only covariate and no stratification. The coefficient was .56, with a *p*-value (based on the Wald chi-square test) of .27, which is approximately the same as the *p*-value for the log-rank test reported in Chapter 3.
- a model with both TREAT and RENAL as covariates. The coefficient of TREAT was 1.22, with a *p*-value of .04.
- a model that included TREAT, RENAL, and the (time-varying) product of RENAL and DUR. The coefficient of TREAT was 1.34, with a *p*-value of .05. The interaction term was not significant.

Based on these results, it is clearly essential to control for RENAL in order to obtain good estimates of the treatment effect, but whether you do it by stratification or by including RENAL as a covariate doesn't seem to make much difference. Note that you cannot stratify by a variable and also include it as a covariate. These are alternative ways of controlling for the variable.

Compared with the explicit interaction method of the previous section, the method of stratification has two main advantages:

- The interaction method requires that you choose a particular form for the interaction, but stratification allows for any kind of change in the effect of a variable over time. For example, including the product of RENAL and DUR as a covariate forces the effect of RENAL to either increase linearly or decrease linearly with time. Stratification by RENAL allows for reversals (possibly more than one) in the relationship between time and the effect of RENAL.

- Stratification is easier to set up, and takes much less computation time. This can be important in working with large samples.

But there are also important disadvantages of stratification:

- No estimates are obtained for the effect of the stratifying variable. As a result, stratification only makes sense for nuisance variables whose effects have little or no intrinsic interest.

- There is no way to test for either the main effect of the stratifying variable or its interaction with time. In particular, it is *not* legitimate to compare the log-likelihoods for models with and without a stratifying variable.

- If the form of the interaction with time is correctly specified, the explicit interaction method should yield more efficient estimates of the coefficients of the other covariates. Again, there is a trade-off between robustness and efficiency.

Now for some complications. In the example we've just been considering, the stratifying variable had only two values. If a variable with more than two values is listed in the STRATA statement, PROC PHREG sets up a separate stratum for each value. The stratifying variable can be either character or numeric, with no restrictions on the possible values. If more than one variable is listed in the STRATA statement, PROC PHREG creates a separate stratum for every observed combination of values. Obviously you must exercise some care in using this option as you can easily end up with strata that have only one observation. For stratifying variables that are numeric, it is also easy to specify a limited number of strata that correspond to cutpoints on the variable. See SAS Technical Report P-229, *SAS/STAT Software, Changes and Enhancements, Release 6.07* for details.

In my view, the most useful application of stratification is for samples involving some kind of clustering or multi-level grouping. Examples include animals within litters, children within schools, patients within hospitals, and so on. In all of these situations, it is reasonable to expect that observations within a cluster will not be truly independent, thereby violating one of the standard assumptions used in constructing the likelihood function. The result is likely to be standard error estimates that are biased downward and test statistics that are biased upward. A highly effective solution is to treat each cluster as a distinct stratum. You can accomplish this by giving every cluster a unique identification number, and then stratifying on the variable containing that number. This method assumes that observations are *conditionally* independent within clusters, and that the coefficients of the covariates are the same across clusters. (The conditional independence assumption will be violated if, for example, the death of one patient had a deleterious effect on the risk of death for other patients in the same hospital.)

LEFT TRUNCATION AND LATE ENTRY INTO THE RISK SET

In standard treatments of partial likelihood, it is assumed that every individual is at risk of an event at time 0 and continues to be at risk until either the event of interest occurs or the observation is censored. At that point the individual is removed from the risk set, never to return. It doesn't have to be this way, however. If there are periods of time when it is known that a particular individual is not at risk for some reason, the partial likelihood method allows for the individual to be removed from the risk set and then to be returned at some later point in time. Unfortunately, the vast majority of partial likelihood programs are not set up to handle this possibility.

The most common situation is *left truncation* or *late entry to the risk set*. This situation often arises without the investigator even realizing it. Here are three examples:

■ Patients are recruited into a study at varying lengths of time after diagnosis with some disease. The investigator wishes to specify a model in which the hazard of death depends on the time since diagnosis. But by the design of the study, it is impossible for the patients to die between diagnosis and recruitment. If they had died, they would not have been available for recruitment.

■ At a specific point in time, all employees in a firm are interviewed and asked how long they have been working for the firm. Then, they are followed forward to determine how long they stay with the firm. The investigator estimates a model in which the hazard of termination depends on the length of employment with the firm. But again, it is impossible for these employees to have terminated before the initial interview. If they had terminated, they would not have been present for that interview.

- High school girls are recruited into a study of teen pregnancy. The desired model expresses the hazard of pregnancy as a function of age. But girls were not included in the study if they had become pregnant before the study began. Thus, the girls in the study were not *observationally* at risk of pregnancy at ages prior to the initial interview. Obviously, they were at risk during those ages, but the design of the study makes it impossible to observe pregnancies that occurred prior to the initial interview.

In all three cases, the solution is to remove the individual from the risk set between the point of origin and the time of the initial contact, which you can easily accomplish using PROC PHREG. In Release 6.10 and later, the method is straightforward and is explicitly described in the documentation. In earlier versions, it is necessary to trick the program by defining a time-dependent covariate whose values are missing at times when the individual is not in the risk set.

To illustrate these methods, let's specify a model for the Stanford Heart Transplant Data in which the hazard is expressed as a function of patient age rather than time since acceptance into the program. To do this, we must first convert the death time variable into patient age (in years):

```
data stan2;
   set stan;
   agels=(dls-dob)/365.25;
run;
```

Recall that DLS is date last seen and DOB is date of birth. Then AGELS is age at which the patient was last seen, which may be either a death time or a censoring time. Our problem is that, by design, patients were not at risk of an observable death before they were accepted into the program.

In Release 6.10, we can specify a model in the following way:

```
proc phreg data=stan2;
   model (ageaccpt,agels)*dead(0)=surg ageaccpt / ties=exact;
run;
```

Although this syntax is similar to the PROC LIFEREG syntax for interval-censored data, the intent is completely different. (AGEACCPT, AGELS) represents an interval of time during which the individual was continuously at risk of the event. Thus, AGEACCPT is time of entry into the risk set and AGELS is the time of departure. Note that AGEACCPT can also be included as a covariate.

An additional complication is that the risk interval specified by this syntax is *open on the left*, meaning that the entry point is not actually included in the interval. That makes little difference for this example where age is measured to the nearest day, but it can make a big difference if only the month or year of age are known. In that case, people can end up being excluded from risk sets in which they were actually at risk. An easy fix is to subtract some small number from the entry-time variable in the DATA step, for example, as in the following statement:

```
ageaccpt=ageaccpt-.0027;
```

This lowers the age of acceptance by about one day.

In earlier releases of PROC PHREG, left truncation can be accommodated by specifying the model in the following way:

```
proc phreg data=stan2;
   model agels*dead(0)=surgtd ageaccpt / ties=exact;
   if agels<ageaccpt then surgtd=.;
   else surgtd=surg;
run;
```

This code takes the time-constant variable SURG and turns it into a time dependent covariate SURGTD, which has missing values at all ages less than the age at acceptance. When PROC PHREG is constructing the risk set for a particular death time and it encounters a missing value for any time-dependent covariate, it excludes the observation from the risk set for that death time but leaves it in other risk sets where it is not missing. When there is more than one time-constant covariate, any one of the variables can be chosen for this special treatment. (You can also use this approach in Release 6.10 if desired, but it is less computationally efficient).

When there is a time-dependent covariate in the model, it is the natural choice for setting its values equal to missing for times when the individual is not at risk. For example, if we include transplant status in the model, we can write the following program:

```
proc phreg data=stan2;
   model agels*dead(0)=surg ageaccpt plant / ties=exact;
   if agels<agetrans or agetrans=. then plant=0;
   else plant=1;
   if agels<ageaccpt then plant=.;
run;
```

Compare the results in Output 5.18 with those in Output 5.11, which had the same covariates but specified the principal time axis as time since acceptance. In this analysis, all the coefficients are larger in magnitude than they were in Output 5.11 and the *p*-values are smaller. The dramatic increase in the effect of age at acceptance is a direct consequence of specifying age as the time axis. With age held constant (every risk set consists of people who are all the same age), age at acceptance is an exact linear function of time since acceptance. In the earlier analysis, any effects of time since acceptance were part of the baseline hazard function and were, therefore, not visible in the estimated coefficients.

Output 5.18 *Results for Transplant Data with Age as the Principal Time Axis*

Variable	DF	Parameter Estimate	Standard Error	Wald Chi-Square	Pr > Chi-Square	Risk Ratio
SURG	1	-0.930188	0.42201	4.85852	0.0275	0.394
PLANT	1	-0.470765	0.37269	1.59560	0.2065	0.625
AGEACCPT	1	1.000121	0.28297	12.49134	0.0004	2.719

So far, I have explained how to handle situations in which individuals who are *not* in the risk set at time 0 enter the risk set at some later point in time and then remain in the risk set until an event occurs. Now let's consider situations in which individuals temporarily leave the risk set for some reason and then return at a later point in time. Suppose, for example, that a sample of children is followed for a period of five years to detect any occurrences of parental abuse. If some children are placed in foster homes for temporary periods, it may be desirable to remove them from the risk set for those periods. The missing data method just described can be extended in a straightforward way: whenever an individual is out of the risk set, we set a time-dependent covariate equal to the missing value code. Again, if there are no time-dependent covariates, we convert one of the time-constant covariates to a time dependent covariate.

Release 6.10 software has an equivalent method with a very different set-up. A separate record is created for each interval during which the individual was continuously at risk. Thus, for a child who had one temporary period in a foster home, the first record corresponds to the interval from time 0 (however defined) to the time of entry into the foster home. This record is coded as censored since the event of interest did not occur. The second record is for the interval from the time of exit from the foster home to the last time of observation, coded as censored if no event occurred at the termination of observation. The MODEL statement then has the form

MODEL (*start,finish*)*CENSOR(0)=X1 X2;

Here, *start* is the time at which the interval begins (measured from the origin) and *finish* is the time at which the interval ends. The extension to multiple time outs should be straightforward.

ESTIMATING SURVIVOR FUNCTIONS

As we have seen, the form of the dependence of the hazard on time is left unspecified in the proportional hazards model. Furthermore, the partial likelihood method discards that portion of the likelihood function that contains information about the dependence of the hazard on time. Nevertheless, it is still possible to get nonparametric estimates of the survivor function based on a fitted proportional hazards model.

When there are no time-dependent covariates, the Cox model can be written as

$$S(t) = [S_0(t)]^{\exp(\beta x)}$$

where $S(t)$ is the survival probability at time t for an individual with covariate values $\mathbf{x}$, and $S_0(t)$ is the *baseline survivor function*, that is, the survivor function for an individual whose covariate values are all 0. After estimating β by partial likelihood, you can get an estimate of $S_0(t)$ by a nonparametric maximum likelihood method. With that estimate in hand, you can generate the estimated survivor function for any set of covariate values by substitution in the equation above.

In PROC PHREG, you accomplish this with the BASELINE statement. The easiest task is to get the survivor function for $\mathbf{x} = \bar{\mathbf{x}}$, the vector of sample means. For the recidivism data set, the SAS code for accomplishing this task is as follows:

```
proc phreg data=recid;
   model week*arrest(0)=fin age prio
         / ties=efron;
   baseline out=a survival=s logsurv=ls loglogs=lls;
run;

proc print data=a;
run;
```

(Only statistically significant covariates are included in this run so that the width of an output record does not exceed the printed page). The OUT=A option requests that SAS put the survival estimates in a temporary data set named A. SURVIVAL=S asks that the survival probabilities be stored in a variable named S. You can interpret these probabilities as estimates of the survivor function, *controlling for the effects of the covariates.* LOGSURV requests the logarithm of the survival probabilities, also known as the cumulative hazard function. LOGLOGS requests $\log[-\log S(t)]$. These logarithmic transformations of the survivor functions were discussed in more detail in Chapters 2, 3, and 4.

Data set A is printed in Output 5.19. There are fifty records, corresponding to the 49 unique weeks in which arrests were observed to occur, plus an initial record for time 0. Each record gives the mean value for each of the three covariates. The S column gives the estimated survival probabilities. The last two columns are the two logarithmic transforms.

Output 5.19   *Survivor Function Estimates for Recidivism Data at Sample Means*

OBS	FIN	AGE	PRIO	WEEK	S	LS	LLS
1	0.5	24.5972	2.98380	0	1.00000	0.00000	.
2	0.5	24.5972	2.98380	1	0.99801	-0.00200	-6.21670
3	0.5	24.5972	2.98380	2	0.99601	-0.00399	-5.52280
4	0.5	24.5972	2.98380	3	0.99402	-0.00600	-5.11671
5	0.5	24.5972	2.98380	4	0.99203	-0.00800	-4.82813
6	0.5	24.5972	2.98380	5	0.99004	-0.01001	-4.60378
7	0.5	24.5972	2.98380	6	0.98804	-0.01203	-4.41998
8	0.5	24.5972	2.98380	7	0.98604	-0.01406	-4.26428
9	0.5	24.5972	2.98380	8	0.97601	-0.02428	-3.71816
10	0.5	24.5972	2.98380	9	0.97200	-0.02840	-3.56145
11	0.5	24.5972	2.98380	10	0.96999	-0.03047	-3.49104
12	0.5	24.5972	2.98380	11	0.96593	-0.03467	-3.36193
13	0.5	24.5972	2.98380	12	0.96184	-0.03891	-3.24646
14	0.5	24.5972	2.98380	13	0.95979	-0.04104	-3.19320
15	0.5	24.5972	2.98380	14	0.95363	-0.04748	-3.04744
16	0.5	24.5972	2.98380	15	0.94951	-0.05181	-2.96010
17	0.5	24.5972	2.98380	16	0.94538	-0.05616	-2.87948
18	0.5	24.5972	2.98380	17	0.93918	-0.06275	-2.76859
19	0.5	24.5972	2.98380	18	0.93293	-0.06942	-2.66754
20	0.5	24.5972	2.98380	19	0.92876	-0.07391	-2.60492
21	0.5	24.5972	2.98380	20	0.91831	-0.08522	-2.46257
22	0.5	24.5972	2.98380	21	0.91414	-0.08977	-2.41050
23	0.5	24.5972	2.98380	22	0.91205	-0.09206	-2.38534
24	0.5	24.5972	2.98380	23	0.90996	-0.09435	-2.36070
25	0.5	24.5972	2.98380	24	0.90160	-0.10358	-2.26738
26	0.5	24.5972	2.98380	25	0.89528	-0.11061	-2.20170
27	0.5	24.5972	2.98380	26	0.88891	-0.11775	-2.13915

continued on next page

Output 5.19   continued

28	0.5	24.5972	2.98380	27	0.88467	-0.12254	-2.09928
29	0.5	24.5972	2.98380	28	0.88041	-0.12737	-2.06068
30	0.5	24.5972	2.98380	30	0.87614	-0.13223	-2.02324
31	0.5	24.5972	2.98380	31	0.87400	-0.13467	-2.00493
32	0.5	24.5972	2.98380	32	0.86972	-0.13958	-1.96909
33	0.5	24.5972	2.98380	33	0.86542	-0.14455	-1.93416
34	0.5	24.5972	2.98380	34	0.86109	-0.14956	-1.90008
35	0.5	24.5972	2.98380	35	0.85242	-0.15968	-1.83458
36	0.5	24.5972	2.98380	36	0.84590	-0.16736	-1.78763
37	0.5	24.5972	2.98380	37	0.83719	-0.17771	-1.72761
38	0.5	24.5972	2.98380	38	0.83500	-0.18032	-1.71303
39	0.5	24.5972	2.98380	39	0.83063	-0.18557	-1.68434
40	0.5	24.5972	2.98380	40	0.82186	-0.19618	-1.62870
41	0.5	24.5972	2.98380	42	0.81746	-0.20155	-1.60173
42	0.5	24.5972	2.98380	43	0.80863	-0.21241	-1.54922
43	0.5	24.5972	2.98380	44	0.80418	-0.21793	-1.52360
44	0.5	24.5972	2.98380	45	0.79972	-0.22349	-1.49840
45	0.5	24.5972	2.98380	46	0.79078	-0.23473	-1.44932
46	0.5	24.5972	2.98380	47	0.78855	-0.23756	-1.43733
47	0.5	24.5972	2.98380	48	0.78406	-0.24326	-1.41361
48	0.5	24.5972	2.98380	49	0.77284	-0.25769	-1.35601
49	0.5	24.5972	2.98380	50	0.76607	-0.26648	-1.32247
50	0.5	24.5972	2.98380	52	0.75703	-0.27836	-1.27885

Of what use are these estimated functions? If you have hypotheses about the shape of the hazard function, the estimates can provide some helpful evidence, as we saw in Chapter 3. In particular, a constant hazard function implies a cumulative hazard function that increases as a straight line. If a graph of the log-survivor function curves upward, it is evidence for an increasing hazard. On the other hand, if the log-survivor function bends below a straight line, it suggests that the hazard is decreasing with time. For this purpose, it really doesn't matter at what covariate values the survivor function is calculated.

A graph of the negative log-survivor (cumulative hazard) function, shown in Output 5.20, is produced by the following statements:

```
data b;
   set a;
   ls=-ls;
run;

proc gplot data=b;
   symbol1 value=none interpol=join;
   plot ls*week;
run;
```

The curve appears to bend slightly upward, suggesting a hazard that increases with time. That's consistent with what we found in Chapters 3 and 4.

Output 5.20 *Graph of the Cumulative Hazard Function for Recidivism Data*

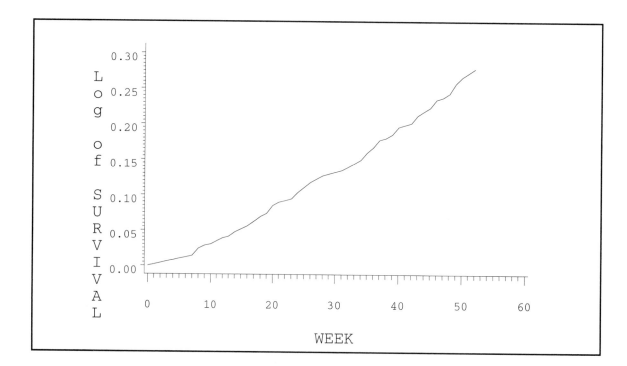

By combining the BASELINE statement with stratification, we can also produce graphs that are helpful in evaluating the proportional hazards assumption. Suppose we take financial aid (FIN) as the stratifying variable for the recidivism data. That might seem self-defeating since FIN is the variable of greatest interest and stratifying on it means that no tests or estimates of its effect are produced. But after stratifying, we can graph the baseline hazard function for the two financial aid groups using the following code:

```
proc phreg data=recid;
   model week*arrest(0)=age prio / ties=efron;
   strata fin;
   baseline out=a loglogs=lls survival=s;
run;

proc gplot data=a;
   plot lls*week=fin;
   symbol1 interpol=join color=black line=1;
   symbol2 interpol=join color=black line=2;
run;
```

The resulting graph in Output 5.21 shows the log-log survivor functions for each of the two financial aid groups, evaluated at the means of the covariates. If the hazards are proportional, the log-log survivor functions should be parallel. Here's why. If two hazard functions, $h_1(t)$ and $h_2(t)$, are proportional, we can write

$$h_1(t) = \gamma h_2(t)$$

where γ is the constant of proportionality. Substituting this into equation (2.6), it's easily shown that

$$S_1(t) = [S_2(t)]^{\gamma}.$$

Taking the logarithm, multiplying by –1, and taking the logarithm a second time yields

$$\log[-\log S_1(t)] = \log \gamma + \log[-\log S_2(t)]$$

which says that the two log-log survival curves differ by a constant amount, $\log \gamma$. Examining Output 5.21, we see that the two curves are approximately the same shape, but also farther apart in some regions than others.

Output 5.21   *Log-Log Survivor Plots for the Two Financial Aid Groups*

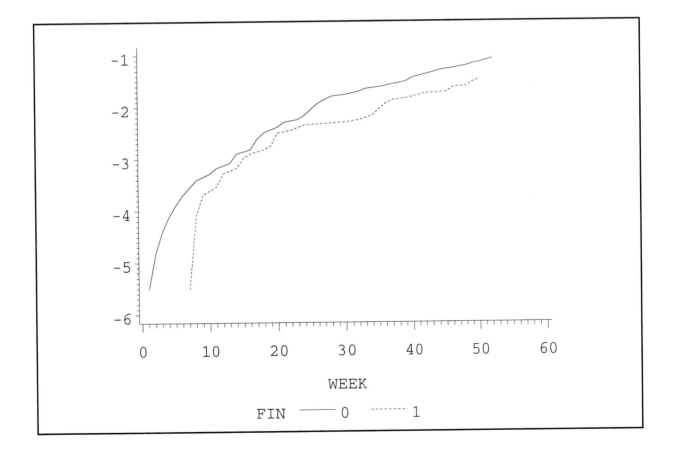

The differences are more dramatic if we compare the smoothed hazard functions produced with the SMOOTH macro that was introduced in Chapter 3 and that is described in detail in Appendix 1, "Macro Programs." After producing baseline data set A, which contains the survivor function estimates, the macro is invoked by submitting the following statement, which gives the graph in Output 5.22.

```
%smooth(data=a,time=week,survival=s)
```

Here we see evidence that the hazard of arrest is almost identical during the earlier weeks, but it rapidly diverges after week 15 or thereabouts, reaching a maximum difference around week 25. (Group 2 received aid, Group 1 did not). This evidence suggests that it takes awhile for the financial aid to have its desired effect, but that the effect eventually wears off after the aid is terminated.

Output 5.22   *Smoothed Hazard Functions for Two Financial Aid Groups*

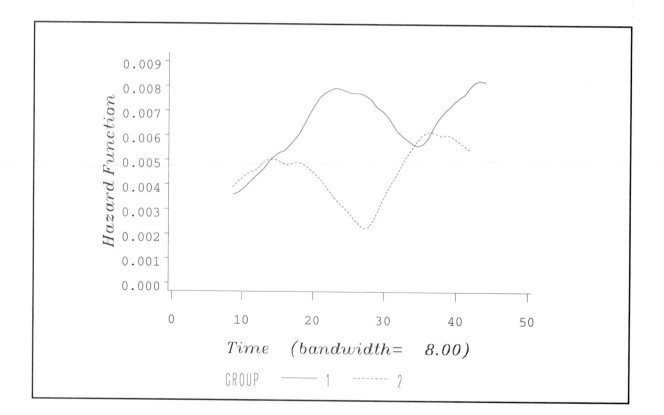

This graph suggests a different specification for the interaction between financial aid and time that we investigated earlier (see **Interactions with Time as Time-Dependent Covariates**). Specifically, let's construct a dummy variable that is coded as 1 when time is between 20 and 30 weeks and is coded as 0 elsewhere. Then, we include the product of that variable and FIN in the Cox regression model:

```
proc phreg data=recid;
   model week*arrest(0)=fin finmid age prio / ties=efron;
   mid=(20<week<30);
   finmid=fin*mid;
run;
```

Results in Output 5.23 show that the interaction is significant at the .03 level. During this middle period, the arrest rate for those who did not receive financial aid is more than five times larger than the rate for those who did receive aid. The *p*-value is perhaps an underestimate, however, since the unusual specification is dependent on the graphical analysis rather than some a priori hypothesis.

Output 5.23 *Cox Regression with the Nonproportional Effect of Financial Aid*

Analysis of Maximum Likelihood Estimates						
Variable	DF	Parameter Estimate	Standard Error	Wald Chi-Square	Pr > Chi-Square	Risk Ratio
FIN	1	-0.158078	0.20504	0.59435	0.4407	0.854
FINMID	1	-1.455933	0.66475	4.79696	0.0285	0.233
AGE	1	-0.066964	0.02084	10.32821	0.0013	0.935
PRIO	1	0.096731	0.02727	12.58657	0.0004	1.102

Another major use of the baseline survivor function is to obtain predictions about survival time for particular sets of covariate values. These covariate values need not be ones that appear in the data set being analyzed. For the recidivism data, for example, we may want to say something about arrest times for 40-year-olds with three prior convictions who did not receive financial aid. The mechanics of doing this are a bit awkward. You must create a new data set containing the values of the covariates for which you want predictions and then pass the name of that data set to PROC PHREG:

```
data covals;
   input fin age prio;
   cards;
0 40 3
run;
```

```
proc phreg data=recid;
   model week*arrest(0)=fin age prio /
         ties=efron;
   baseline out=a covariates=covals survival=s lower=lcl
         upper=ucl / nomean;
run;

proc print data=a;
run;
```

The advantage of doing it this way is that predictions can easily be generated for many different sets of covariate values just by including more input lines in the data set COVALS. Each input line produces a complete set of survivor estimates, but all estimates are output to a single data set. The NOMEAN option suppresses the output of survivor estimates evaluated at the mean values of the covariates, which are otherwise included by default. The LOWER= and UPPER= options (available in Release 6.10 and later) give 95-percent confidence intervals around the survival probability.

Output 5.24 displays a portion of the data set generated by the BASELINE statement above. In generating predictions, it's typical to focus on a single summary measure rather than the entire distribution. The median survival time is easily obtained by finding the smallest value of t such that $S(t) \leq .50$. That won't work for the recidivism data, however, because the data are censored long before a .50 probability is reached. For these data, it's probably more useful to pick a fixed point in time and calculate survival probabilities at that time under varying conditions. For the covariate values in Output 5.24, the six-month (26 week) survival probability is .95, with a 95 percent confidence interval of .92 to .99.

Output 5.24   *Portion of Survivor Function Estimate for Recidivism Data*

OBS	FIN	AGE	PRIO	WEEK	S	LCL	UCL
19	0	40	3	18	0.97101	0.94823	0.99434
20	0	40	3	19	0.96916	0.94510	0.99384
21	0	40	3	20	0.96453	0.93728	0.99258
22	0	40	3	21	0.96267	0.93415	0.99207
23	0	40	3	22	0.96174	0.93257	0.99182
24	0	40	3	23	0.96080	0.93100	0.99156
25	0	40	3	24	0.95705	0.92471	0.99053
26	0	40	3	25	0.95421	0.91996	0.98973
27	0	40	3	26	0.95132	0.91514	0.98894
28	0	40	3	27	0.94939	0.91192	0.98841
29	0	40	3	28	0.94746	0.90869	0.98788

continued on next page

Output 5.24   continued

30	0	40	3	30	0.94551	0.90544	0.98734
31	0	40	3	31	0.94453	0.90382	0.98707
32	0	40	3	32	0.94256	0.90056	0.98653
33	0	40	3	33	0.94058	0.89728	0.98598
34	0	40	3	34	0.93859	0.89399	0.98542
35	0	40	3	35	0.93457	0.88737	0.98428
36	0	40	3	36	0.93154	0.88239	0.98342

Release 6.10 and later lets you choose between two alternative methods (labeled PL for product limit and CH for cumulative hazard) for calculating the survivor function and its transformations, but there are no strong reasons for preferring one or the other. PL is the default. These two methods produce identical results (apart from rounding error) when there is only one censoring time for all cases, as with the recidivism data. Note, finally, that the BASELINE statement will not produce any output when there are time-dependent covariates.

RESIDUALS AND INFLUENCE STATISTICS

In earlier releases of PROC PHREG, the OUTPUT statement could produce a data set containing eight different diagnostic statistics for each individual. An additional six statistics are available in Release 6.10. While there isn't space to discuss all of them, I'll concentrate on those that I think are most useful and interpretable. As with the BASELINE statement, OUTPUT will not produce a data set if there are any time-dependent covariates.

Individual Residuals

All releases of PROC PHREG have options for three different residual statistics that are computed for each individual in the sample: Cox-Snell residuals (LOGSURV), martingale residuals (RESMART), and deviance residuals (RESDEV). (For a detailed discussion of these residuals, see Collett (1994, p. 150)). Martingale residuals are obtained by transforming Cox-Snell residuals, and deviance residuals are a further transformation of martingale residuals. For most purposes, you can ignore the Cox-Snell and martingale residuals. While Cox-Snell residuals were useful for assessing the fit of the parametric models in Chapter 4, they are not very informative for Cox models estimated by partial likelihood.

Deviance residuals behave much like residuals from OLS regression: they are symmetrically distributed around 0 and have an approximate standard deviation of 1.0. They are negative for observations that have longer survival times than expected and positive for observations with survival times that are smaller than expected. Deviance residuals can also be used like residuals from OLS regression. Very high or very low values suggest that the observation may be an outlier in need of special attention. You can plot the residuals against the covariates, and any unusual patterns may suggest features of the data that have not been adequately fitted by the model. Be aware, however, that censoring can produce striking patterns that don't necessarily imply any problem with the model.

Here's an example in which deviance residuals for the recidivism data are plotted against AGE:

```
proc phreg data=recid;
   model week*arrest(0)=fin age prio / ties=efron;
   output out=c resdev=dev;
run;

proc gplot data=c;
   symbol1 value=dot h=.2;
    plot dev*age;
run;
```

These statements produce the graph in Output 5.25.

Clearly, there is a disjunction between two groups of observations. The elongated cluster of points in the lower portion of the graph are all the censored observations, while the more widely dispersed points in the upper portion of the graph are the uncensored observations. Note also the rise in the censored observations with increasing age. That's because age is associated with longer times to arrest, yet all censored observations are censored at the same point in time. With increasing age, survival to one year becomes more consistent with the model's predictions. Some of the residuals exceed 3, which is large enough to warrant concern.

Output 5.25 *Graph of Deviance Residuals by Age for Recidivism Data*

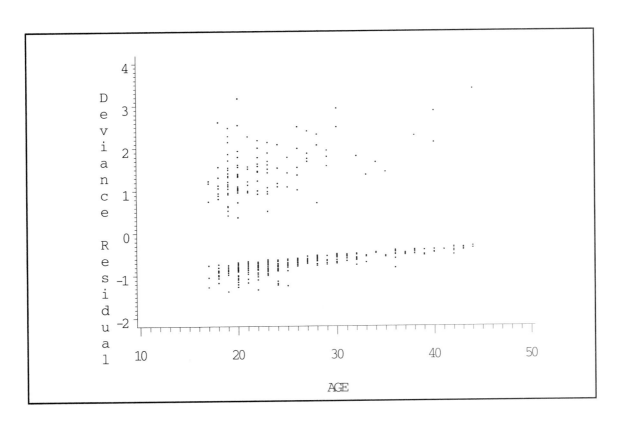

Covariate-Wise Residuals

Release 6.10 and later can also produce Schoenfeld residuals (RESSCH), weighted Schoenfeld residuals (WTRESSCH), and score residuals (RESSCO). All three share a rather unusual property: instead of a single residual for each individual, there is a separate residual for each covariate for each individual. They also sum to 0 (approximately) in the sample. A major difference among them is that the score residuals are defined for all observations, while the Schoenfeld residuals (both weighted and unweighted) are not defined for censored observations (they are missing in the output data set).

My experience in examining graphs of these three residuals is that they all behave much the same. Since the Schoenfeld residuals are better known and easier to explain, I'll concentrate on them. Here's how they work. Suppose that individual i dies at time t_i, and at that time there were 30 people at risk of death, indexed by $j = 1,\ldots,30$. For each of those 30 people, the estimated Cox model implies a certain probability of dying at that time, denoted by p_j. Imagine randomly selecting one of these 30 people, with probability p_j. For each covariate x_k, we can calculate its expected value for a randomly selected person (from that risk set) as

$$\bar{x}_k = \sum_{j=1}^{30} x_{kj} p_j \, .$$

The Schoenfeld residual is then defined as the covariate value for the person who *actually* died, x_{ik}, minus the expected value.

The main function of these residuals is to detect possible departures from the proportional hazards assumption. Since Schoenfeld residuals are, in principle, independent of time, a plot that shows a relationship with time is evidence against that assumption. For the recidivism data, I produced a data set containing the Schoenfeld residuals using these statements:

```
proc phreg data=recid;
   model week*arrest(0)=fin age prio /
         ties=efron;
   output out=b ressch=schfin schage schprio;
run;

proc print data=b;
run;
```

Note that the key word RESSCH is followed by three arbitrarily chosen variable names corresponding to the three covariates in the model. These variables contain the Schoenfeld residuals in the output data set. Output 5.26 displays the 18 observations with the lowest arrest times in the data set.

Output 5.26 *Portion of the Output Data Set with Schoenfeld Residuals*

WEEK	ARREST	FIN	SCHFIN	AGE	SCHAGE	PRIO	SCHPRIO
12	1	1	0.58848	27	4.3964	0	-3.9624
11	1	0	-0.40653	19	-3.5396	18	13.8255
11	1	1	0.59347	19	-3.5396	2	-2.1745
10	1	0	-0.40284	21	-1.5256	14	9.7362
9	1	1	0.59574	26	3.4613	0	-4.2572
9	1	1	0.59574	30	7.4613	3	-1.2572
8	1	1	0.59318	21	-1.5440	4	-0.2909
8	1	0	-0.40682	28	5.4560	4	-0.2909
8	1	1	0.59318	20	-2.5440	11	6.7091
8	1	0	-0.40682	23	0.4560	5	0.7091
8	1	1	0.59318	40	17.4560	1	-3.2909
7	1	1	0.59193	20	-2.5387	2	-2.2861
6	1	0	-0.40616	19	-3.5221	6	1.7059
5	1	0	-0.40475	19	-3.5098	3	-1.2896

continued on next page

Output 5.26 continued

4	1	0	−0.40351	18	−4.4960	1	−3.2795
3	1	0	−0.40284	30	7.4915	3	−1.2774
2	1	0	−0.40260	44	21.4789	2	−2.2760
1	1	0	−0.40163	20	−2.5150	0	−4.2657

Consider the person who was arrested in week 12. He was 27 years old which, according to the Schoenfeld residual, was about 4.4 years older than the model predicts. He had no prior convictions, but the model predicts that a person arrested at that time should have about 4 prior convictions (SCHPRIO=−3.96). He also received financial aid, although the model predicts a probability of only .41 that a person arrested in week 12 would be receiving aid (SCHFIN=.59). These are not especially large numbers compared with others in Output 5.26. The person arrested in week 2, for example, was 21 years older than predicted.

The next step is to plot the residuals for each covariate against time:

```
proc gplot data=b;
   plot schfin*week schprio*week schage*week;
   symbol1 value=dot h=.02;
run;
```

Output 5.27 shows the graphs produced by this code.

Output 5.27 *Graphs of Schoenfeld Residuals Versus Time, Recidivism Data*

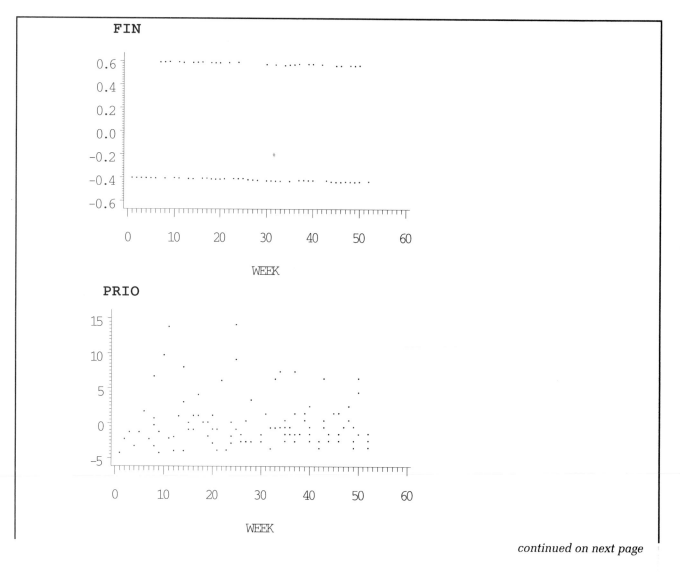

continued on next page

Output 5.27 continued

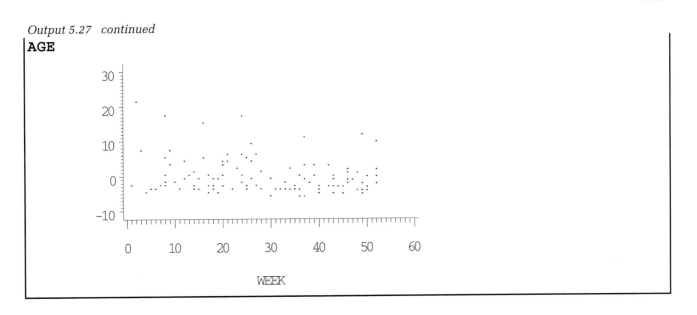

The graph for the FIN residuals is not very informative, which is typical of graphs for dichotomous covariates. For PRIO, the residuals have a fairly random scatter. For AGE, there appears to be a slight tendency for the residuals to decline with time since release. To get a less subjective assessment (but still ad hoc), I did an OLS regression of the residuals for each variable on WEEK. The *p*-values for FIN and PRIO were .93 and .53, respectively, while the *p*-value for AGE was .02, suggesting that there may be some departure from proportionality for that variable.

Influence Diagnostics

Most OLS regression packages nowadays can compute various influence statistics that measure how much the results would change if a particular observation is removed from the analysis. Such statistics can also be computed for Cox regression models (Collett 1994, p. 169), and several are now available with PROC PHREG in Release 6.10 and later. The likelihood displacement (LD) statistic measures influence on the model as whole. This statistic tells you (approximately) how much the log-likelihood (multiplied by 2) will change if the individual is removed from the sample. The DFBETA statistics tell you how much each coefficient will change by removal of a single observation. These are also approximations. (There is also an LMAX statistic that measures overall influence, but its interpretation is rather esoteric. LMAX is preferable to LD for plots against covariates, however.)

For the 25 cases in the myelomatosis data set that was analyzed in Chapter 3, I used the following PROC PHREG statements to fit a model and produce the influence statistics:

```
proc phreg data=myel;
   model dur*status(0)=treat renal;
   id id;
   output out=c ld=ldmyel dfbeta=dtreat drenal;
run;
```

The estimated coefficients were 4.11 for RENAL and 1.24 for TREAT. The OUTPUT statement creates a new data set C with the variables LDMYEL, DTREAT and DRENAL, as well as with all the variables in the MODEL statement. The ID statement is necessary to put the ID variable in the new data set. Data set C is displayed in Output 5.28.

Output 5.28 *Influence Statistics for Myelomatosis Data*

ID	DUR	STATUS	RENAL	TREAT	DFRENAL	DFTREAT	LDMYEL
1	8	1	1	1	-0.08058	-0.21768	0.13393
2	180	1	0	2	0.11234	0.04908	0.01232
3	632	1	0	2	0.08879	0.00971	0.00587
4	852	0	0	1	0.07526	0.08582	0.02097
5	52	1	1	1	0.18409	0.08899	0.03600
6	2240	0	0	2	0.01587	-0.11223	0.04067
7	220	1	0	1	-0.09357	-0.19650	0.10797
8	63	1	1	1	0.04170	0.09916	0.02762
9	195	1	0	2	0.11180	0.04819	0.01207
10	76	1	0	2	0.11273	0.04974	0.01250
11	70	1	0	2	0.11303	0.05023	0.01263
12	8	1	0	1	-1.44585	-0.46469	1.71233
13	13	1	1	2	0.02970	0.01809	0.00120
14	1990	0	0	2	0.01587	-0.11223	0.04067
15	1976	0	0	1	0.08603	0.10383	0.03048
16	18	1	1	2	0.01759	0.00851	0.00033
17	700	1	0	2	0.08717	0.00699	0.00575
18	1296	0	0	1	0.08603	0.10383	0.03048
19	1460	0	0	1	0.08603	0.10383	0.030484
20	210	1	0	2	0.11106	0.04694	0.011744
21	63	1	1	1	0.04170	0.09916	0.027625
22	1328	0	0	1	0.08603	0.10383	0.030484
23	1296	1	0	2	0.07554	-0.01244	0.006041
24	365	0	0	1	0.05943	0.05934	0.010271
25	23	1	1	2	-0.01780	-0.01950	0.001089

The signs of the DFBETA statistics are the reverse of what you might expect—a negative sign means that the coefficient *increases* when the observation is removed. Most of the observations have rather small values for the influence statistics, but observation 12 has exceptionally large values for all three. In particular, the value −1.45 for DRENAL indicates that if observation 12 is removed, the RENAL coefficient will increase to approximately 4.11+1.45 = 5.56, an increase of 35 percent. Why is this observation so influential? It turns out that if you actually reestimate the model without this observation, the algorithm does not converge. The only indication of this, unfortunately, is that even though the coefficient of RENAL is large (over 19), the estimated standard error is gigantic (1471). Why no convergence? If you look closely at Output 5.28, you'll see that all the durations when RENAL=1 (renal impairment) are smaller than all the durations when RENAL=0 (no impairment) *with one exception*. You guessed it, observation 12 had no impairment, but it did have an early death. In general, convergence does not occur when there is no overlap in the duration times for the two values of a dichotomous covariate. The coefficient for the covariate gets larger in magnitude with every iteration of the Newton-Raphson algorithm. In this example, observation 12 is the crucial observation that prevents this from happening.

What should be done here? When some observations are found to be unusually influential, a common strategy is to make sure that the data for those observations is correct. Often, such observations are found to contain recording or coding errors. (Of course, there's a danger in selectively targeting some observations for error checking.) When no errors are detected, the researcher needs to be up front about the possible sensitivity of the model to one or to a small number of observations. For this example, the removal of observation 12 makes a strong effect even stronger (so strong that the algorithm does not converge), so there was no danger of drawing a misleading qualitative conclusion. The other question to ask is whether the model needs to be modified or elaborated to take the peculiar features of the influential observations into account. Perhaps there are other covariates that ought to be included, or perhaps there is some nonlinearity that is inadequately modeled.

TESTING LINEAR HYPOTHESES WITH THE TEST STATEMENT

Most of what I said in Chapter 4 (see the section **Hypothesis Tests**) about hypothesis testing in AFT models also applies to Cox regression models. There are a couple of exceptions, however. First, there is no CLASS statement in PROC PHREG, so you don't automatically get a global test of the null hypothesis that all the coefficients corresponding to a categorical covariate are equal to 0. On the other hand, PROC PHREG has a TEST statement that makes it easy to test any linear hypothesis about sets of coefficients. If you already know how to use the TEST statement in PROC REG or PROC LOGISTIC, then you don't need to read any more in this section. The syntax and usage of TEST in all three procedures is identical.

The most common use of the TEST statement is to test hypotheses about sets of dummy (indicator) variables that correspond to a single categorical variable. For the recidivism data set, the EDUC variable has values 2 through 6 (see **Categorical Variables and the CLASS Statement** in Chapter 4 for details). Instead of treating EDUC as a quantitative variable, let's create a set of four dummy variables and include them as covariates in the Cox model:

```
data recid2;
   set recid;
   ed3=(educ=3);
   ed4=(educ=4);
   ed5=(educ=5);
   ed6=(educ=6);
run;

proc phreg data=recid2;
   model week*arrest(0)=fin age prio ed3-ed6 / ties=efron;
   No_Educ: test ed3,ed4,ed5,ed6;
   Ed3_Ed6: test ed3=ed6;
   Ed4_Ed6: test ed4=ed6;
run;
```

The first TEST statement, labeled No_Educ, tests the null hypothesis that the coefficients for all the dummy variables are 0. The statement labeled Ed3_Ed6 tests the null hypothesis that the coefficients for Ed3 and Ed6 are equal to each other. The next statement does the same for Ed4 and Ed6. The labels aren't strictly necessary, but if you have more than one TEST statement, you really need them to tell the tests apart in the output.

Output 5.29 displays the results. Looking first at the individual coefficients and their associated chi-square statistics, we see that none of the four dummy variables is significantly different from 0. Remember, however, that each of these coefficients is a comparison with the omitted category of education (which corresponds to sixth grade or less). Since there are only 24 cases in this category, it is not surprising that none of the other categories differs significantly from it. More useful is the global test reported for No_Educ, which has a Wald chi-square statistic of 4.55 with 4 degrees of freedom, again not significant at the .05 level. The magnitude of this statistic is invariant to the choice of the omitted category. The two pairwise tests are also far below the critical value. Obviously, there are four other pairwise tests that could be performed, but given these results it is unlikely that any of them would show up as statistically significant. (Many would argue that with a null result for the global test, the pairwise tests shouldn't even be performed).

Output 5.29   *Results from Using the TEST Statement for the Recidivism Data*

Variable	DF	Parameter Estimate	Standard Error	Wald Chi-Square	Pr > Chi-Square	Risk Ratio
FIN	1	-0.363827	0.19129	3.61730	0.0572	0.695
AGE	1	-0.060054	0.02096	8.20843	0.0042	0.942
PRIO	1	0.083822	0.02839	8.71525	0.0032	1.087
ED3	1	0.547664	0.51868	1.11487	0.2910	1.729
ED4	1	0.315671	0.54082	0.34070	0.5594	1.371
ED5	1	-0.180876	0.67309	0.07221	0.7881	0.835
ED6	1	-0.463956	1.12150	0.17114	0.6791	0.629

Linear Hypotheses Testing

Label	Wald Chi-Square	DF	Pr > Chi-Square
NO_EDUC	4.5519	4	0.3364
ED3_ED6	1.0013	1	0.3170
ED4_ED6	0.5836	1	0.4449

CONCLUSION

It's no accident that Cox regression has become the overwhelmingly favored method for doing regression analysis of survival data. It makes no assumptions about the shape of the distribution of survival times; it allows for time-dependent covariates; it is appropriate for both discrete-time and continuous-time data; it easily handles left truncation; it can stratify on categorical control variables; and it can be extended to nonproportional hazards. The principal *disadvantage* is that you lose the ability to test hypotheses about the shape of the hazard function. As we'll see in Chapter 8, however, the hazard function is often so confounded with unobserved heterogeneity that it's difficult to draw any *substantive* conclusion from the shape of the observed hazard function. So the loss may not be as great as it seems.

PROC PHREG goes further than most Cox regression programs in realizing the full potential of this method. In this chapter, I have particularly stressed those features of PROC PHREG that most distinguish it from other Cox regression programs, namely, its extremely general capabilities for time-dependent covariates, its exact methods for tied data, and its ability to handle left truncation. If you already have some familiarity with PROC PHREG, you may have noticed that I said nothing about its several variable selection methods. I confess that I have never used them. While I am not totally opposed to such automated model-building methods, I think they should be reserved for those cases in which there are a large number of potential covariates, little theoretical guidance for choosing among them, and a goal that emphasizes prediction rather than hypothesis testing. If you find yourself in this situation, you may want to consider the best subset selection method that uses the SELECTION=SCORE and BEST= options. This method is computationally efficient because no parameters are estimated. Yet, it gives you lots of useful information.

We still haven't finished with PROC PHREG. Chapter 6, "Competing Risks," shows how to use it for competing risks models in which there is more than one kind of event. Chapter 8, "Heterogeneity, Repeated Events, and Other Topics," considers PROC PHREG's capabilities for handling repeated events.

CHAPTER **6**

Competing Risks

p.185 *Introduction*

p.186 *Type-Specific Hazards*

p.189 *Time in Power for Leaders of Countries: Example*

p.190 *Estimates and Tests without Covariates*

p.195 *Covariate Effects via Cox Models*

p.200 *Accelerated Failure Time Models*

p.206 *An Alternative Approach to Multiple Event Types*

p.208 *Conclusion*

INTRODUCTION

In the previous chapters, all the events in each analysis were treated as though they were identical: all deaths were the same, all job terminations were the same, and all arrests were the same. In many cases, this is a perfectly acceptable way to proceed. But more often than not, it is essential—or at least desirable—to distinguish different kinds of events and treat them differently in the analysis. To evaluate the efficacy of heart transplants, you will certainly want to treat deaths due to heart failure differently from deaths due to accident or cancer. Job terminations that occur when an employee quits are likely to have quite different determinants than those that occur when the employee is fired. And financial aid to released convicts will more plausibly reduce arrests for theft or burglary than for rape or assault.

In this chapter, we consider the method of competing risks for handling these kinds of situations. What is most characteristic of competing risk situations is that the occurrence of one type of event removes the individual from risk of all the other event types. People who die of heart disease are no longer at risk of dying of cancer. Employees who quit can no longer be fired.

Because competing risk analysis requires no new SAS procedures, this chapter will be short. With only minor changes in the SAS statements, you can estimate competing risks models with the LIFETEST, LIFEREG, or PHREG procedures. All that's necessary is to change the code that specifies which observations are censored and which are not. After considering a bit of the theory of competing risks, most of the chapter will be devoted to examples. At the end, however, I also discuss an alternative to competing risks analysis that may be more appropriate for some situations and is equally easy to implement.

Despite the practical importance of methods for handling multiple kinds of events, textbooks often give them minimal coverage. For example Collett's (1994) otherwise excellent survey of survival analysis only discusses competing risks in a footnote. Lawless (1982) has seven pages on competing risks out of a total of 570. Lee (1992) doesn't even mention the topic. In this chapter, I have relied heavily on Kalbfleisch and Prentice (1980) and Cox and Oakes (1984).

TYPE-SPECIFIC HAZARDS

The classification of events into different types is often somewhat arbitrary and may vary according to the specific goals of the analysis. I'll have more to say about that later. For now, let's suppose that the events we are interested in are deaths, and we have classified them into five types according to cause: heart disease, cancer, stroke, accident, and a residual category that we'll call *other*. Let's assign the numbers 1 through 5, respectively, to these death types. For each type of death, we are going to define a separate hazard function that we'll call a type-specific or cause-specific hazard.

As before, let T_i be a random variable denoting the time of death for person i. Now let J_i be a random variable denoting the type of death that occurred to person i. Thus, $J_5=2$ means that person 5 died of cancer. We now define $h_{ij}(t)$, the hazard for death type j at time t for person i, as follows:

$$h_{ij}(t) = \lim_{\Delta t \to 0} \frac{\Pr\{t \le T_i < t + \Delta t, J_i = j \mid T_i \ge t\}}{\Delta t}, \quad j = 1, \ldots, 5. \tag{6.1}$$

Comparing this with the definition of the hazard in equation (2.2), we see that the only difference is the appearance of $J_i = j$. Thus, the conditional probability in equation (6.1) is the probability that death occurs between t and $t+\Delta t$, *and* the death is of type j, given that the person had not already died by time t. The overall hazard of death is just the sum of all the type-specific hazards, that is,

$$h_i(t) = \sum_j h_{ij}(t). \tag{6.2}$$

You can interpret type-specific hazards in much the same way as ordinary hazards. Their metric is the number of events per unit interval of time, except now the events are of a specific type. The reciprocal of the hazard is the expected length of time until an event of that type occurs, assuming that the hazard stays constant.

Based on the type-specific hazards, we can also define type-specific survival functions:

$$S_j(t) = \exp\left\{-\int_0^t h_j(u)du\right\}.$$ (6.3)

The interpretation of these functions is somewhat controversial, however. Lawless (1982, p. 485) claims that they don't refer to any well-defined random variable and that they are useful only as a way of examining hypotheses about the hazard. On the other hand, we can define the hypothetical variable T_{ij} as the time at which the jth event type either occurred to the ith person *or would have occurred if other event types had not preceded it*. In other words, we suppose that a person who dies of cancer at time T_2 would have later died of heart disease at time T_1 if the cancer death had not occurred. For a given set of T_{ij}s, we only observe the one that is smallest. If we further assume that the T_{ij}s are independent across event types, we can say that

$$S_{ij}(t) = \Pr\{T_{ij} \geq t\}.$$ (6.4)

That is, the type-specific survival function gives the probability that an event of type j occurs later than time t. You can see why people might want to forgo this interpretation, but I personally find it helpful.

Now that we have the type-specific hazards, we can proceed to formulate models for their dependence on covariates. Any of the models that we have considered so far—both proportional hazards models and accelerated failure-time models—are possible candidates. For example, we can specify general proportional hazards models for all five death types:

$$\log h_{ij}(t) = \alpha_j(t) + \boldsymbol{\beta}_j \mathbf{x}_i(t), \qquad j = 1,\ldots,5$$ (6.5)

where $\mathbf{x}_i(t)$ is a vector of covariates, some of which may vary with time. Note that the coefficient vector $\boldsymbol{\beta}$ is subscripted to indicate that the effects of the covariates may be different for different death types. In particular, some coefficients may be set to 0, thereby excluding the covariate for a specific death type. If $\boldsymbol{\beta}_j$ is the same for all j, then the model reduces to the proportional hazards model of Chapter 5, "Estimating Cox Regression Models with PROC PHREG," where no distinction is made among event types. The $\alpha(t)$ function is also subscripted to allow the dependence of the hazard on time to vary across death types.

Although it is a bit unusual, there is nothing to prevent you from choosing, say, a log-normal model for heart disease, a gamma model for cancer, and a proportional hazards model for strokes. What makes this possible is that *the models may be estimated separately for each event type, with no loss of statistical precision*. This is, perhaps, the most important principle of competing risks analysis. More technically, the likelihood function for all event types taken together can be factored into a separate likelihood function for each event type. The likelihood function for each event type treats all other events as though the individual were censored at the time when the event occurred.

There are a few computer programs, like RATE (Tuma 1984), that estimate models for competing risks simultaneously, but their only advantage is to reduce the number of statements needed to specify the models. This advantage must be balanced against the disadvantage of having to specify the same functional form and the same set of covariates for all event types.

The only time you need to estimate models for two or more events simultaneously is when there are parameter restrictions that cross event types. For example, Kalbfleisch and Prentice (1980, p. 170) consider a model that imposes the restriction $\alpha_j(t) = \alpha_j + \alpha_0(t)$ on equation (6.3). This restriction says that the baseline hazard function for each event type is proportional to a common baseline hazard function. Later in the chapter, we'll see how to test this restriction (see **Estimates and Tests Without Covariates**).

A further implication is that you don't need to estimate models for all event types unless you really want to. If you're only interested in the effects of covariates on deaths from heart disease, then just estimate a single model for heart disease, treating all other death types as censoring. Besides reducing the amount of computation, this fact also makes it unnecessary to do an exhaustive classification of death types. You only need to distinguish the event type of interest from all other types of event.

Since we are treating events other than those of immediate interest as a form of censoring, it's natural to ask what assumptions must be made about the censoring mechanism. In Chapter 2, "Basic Concepts of Survival Analysis," we saw that censoring must be *noninformative* if the estimates are to be unbiased. We must make exactly the same assumption in the case of competing risks. That is, we must assume that, conditional on the covariates, those who are at particularly high (or low) risk of one event type are no more (or less) likely to experience other kinds of events. Inversely, if we know that someone died of heart disease at age 50, that should give us no information (beyond what we know from the covariates) about his risk of dying of cancer at that age. *Noninformativeness* is implied by the somewhat stronger assumption that the hypothetical T_{ij}s (discussed above) are independent across j. Unfortunately, as we saw in Chapter 2 with censoring, it is impossible to test whether competing events are actually noninformative. I'll discuss this issue further in the conclusion to this chapter.

TIME IN POWER FOR LEADERS OF COUNTRIES: EXAMPLE

The main data set that I will use to illustrate competing risks analysis was constructed by Bienen and van de Walle (1991). They identified a fairly exhaustive set of primary leaders of all countries world-wide over the past 100 years or so. For each leader, they determined the number of years in power and the manner by which he or she lost power. Each period of leadership is called a *spell*. The mode of exit for a leader from a position of power was classified into three categories:

- death from natural causes
- constitutional means
- nonconstitutional means (including assassination).

Clearly, it is unreasonable to treat all three types as equivalent. While constitutional and nonconstitutional exits might have similar determinants, death from natural causes is clearly a distinct phenomenon.

The data set included the following variables:

YEARS	Number of years in power, integer valued. Leaders in power less than one year were coded 0.
LOST	0=still in power in 1987; 1=exit by constitutional means; 2=death by natural causes; and 3=nonconstitutional exit.
MANNER	How the leader reached power: 0=constitutional means; 1=nonconstitutional means.
START	Year of entry into power.
MILITARY	Background of the leader: 1=military; 0=civilian.
AGE	Age of the leader, in years, at the time of entry into power.
CONFLICT	Level of ethnic conflict: 1=medium or high; 0=low.
LOGINC	Natural logarithm of GNP per capita (dollar equivalent) in 1973.
GROWTH	Average annual rate of per capita GNP growth between 1965-1983.
POP	Population, in millions (year not indicated).
LAND	Land area, in thousands of square kilometers.
LITERACY	Literacy rate (year not indicated).
REGION	0=Middle East; 1=Africa; 2=Asia; 3=Latin America; 4=North America, Europe, and Australia.

In the analysis to follow, I restrict the leadership spells to

- ■ countries outside of Europe, North America, and Australia
- ■ spells that began in 1960 or later
- ■ only the first leadership spell for those leaders with multiple spells.

This leaves a total of 472 spells, of which 115 were still in progress at the time observation was terminated in 1987. Of the remaining spells, 27 ended when the leader died of natural causes, 165 were terminated by constitutional procedures, and 165 were terminated by nonconstitutional means. The restriction to starting years greater than 1960 was made so that the variables describing countries (income, growth, population, and literacy) would be reasonably concurrent with the exposure to risk.

ESTIMATES AND TESTS WITHOUT COVARIATES

The simplest question we might ask about the multiple event types is whether the type-specific hazard functions are the same for all event types, that is, $h_j(t) = h(t)$ for all j. For the leader data, just looking at the frequencies of the three event types suggests that deaths due to natural causes ($n=27$) are much less likely to occur than the other two types, which have identical frequencies ($n=165$). In fact, we can easily obtain a formal test of the null hypothesis from these three frequencies. If the null hypothesis of equal hazards is correct, the expected frequencies of the three event types should be equal in any time interval. Thus, we have an expected frequency of $119=(472 - 115)/3$ for each of the three types. Calculating Pearson's chi-square test (by hand) yields a value of 88.9 with 2 d.f. So we can certainly conclude that the hazard for naturally occurring deaths is lower than for the other two exit modes.

Although the hazards are not equal, it's still possible that they might be proportional (in a different sense than that of Chapter 5); that is, if the hazard for death changes with time, the hazards for constitutional and nonconstitutional exits may also change by a proportionate amount. We can write this hypothesis as

$$h_j(t) = \omega_j h(t) \qquad j = 1, ..., 3$$

(6.6)

where the ω_js are constants of proportionality.

We can obtain a graphic examination of this hypothesis by using PROC LIFETEST to estimate log-log survivor functions for each of the three event types. If the hazards are proportional, the log-log survivor functions should be parallel, as explained in Chapter 5 (see the section **Estimating Survivor Functions**). Here's the SAS code to do it:

```
proc lifetest data=leaders notable outsurv=a;
   time years*lost(0,2,3);
run;

proc lifetest data=leaders notable outsurv=b;
   time years*lost(0,1,3);
run;

proc lifetest data=leaders notable outsurv=c;
   time years*lost(0,1,2);
run;

data combined;
   set a b c;
   retain outcome 0;
   if years=0 and survival=1 then outcome=outcome+1;
   lls=log(-log(survival));
run;

proc gplot data=combined;
   where _censor_=0;
   symbol1 interpol=join color=black v=none line=1;
   symbol2 interpol=join color=black v=none line=2;
   symbol3 interpol=join color=black v=none line=8;
   plot lls*years=outcome;
run;
```

For each type of exit, we estimate the survivor curve by treating the other types as censoring. The DATA step concatenates the three data sets, creates a variable called OUTCOME (with values of 1, 2, or 3 corresponding to constitutional exits, natural deaths, and nonconstitutional exits) and computes the log-log survivor function. Finally the three curves are plotted on a single graph.

Output 6.1   *Log-Log Survival Plot for Three Types of Exits, Leaders Data*

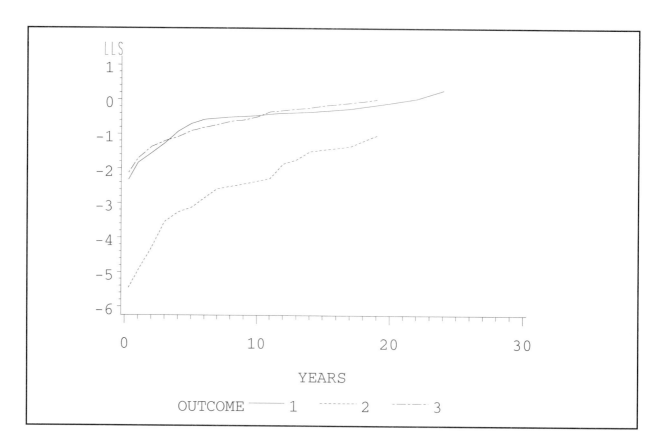

Output 6.1 shows the log-log survivor curves for the three event types. The curves for constitutional and nonconstitutional exits are virtually indistinguishable. Not surprisingly, the curve for natural deaths is much lower than the other two curves. There is also some tendency for the natural death curve to move closer to the other two in later years, which is evidence of nonproportionality.

We can also examine smoothed hazard plots using the SMOOTH macro described in Appendix 1, "Macro Programs." In this case, we can invoke the macro with this statement, which produces the plot in Output 6.2:

```
%smooth(data=combined,time=years,width=4)
```

Here, we see more dramatic differences between the plots for constitutional and nonconstitutional exits. The hazard for constitutional exits drops much more rapidly at first, but then rises again after year 15. By contrast, the hazard for nonconstitutional exit declines rather slowly. In interpreting these curves, it's important to keep in mind that for both constitutional and nonconstitutional exits, more than 80 percent of the exits occurred before the seventh year. Consequently, the hazard estimates for later years are based on a relatively small number of observations and may be unreliable.

Output 6.2 *Smoothed Hazard Functions for Three Types of Exits*

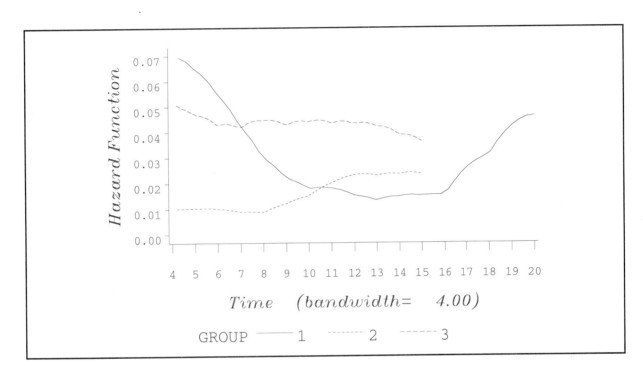

Cox and Oakes (1984) proposed a parametric test of the proportional hazards hypothesis in equation (6.6). Consider the model

$$\log h_j(t) = \alpha_0(t) + \alpha_j + \beta_j t \qquad j = 1, 2, \dots \tag{6.7}$$

If $\beta_j = \beta$ for all j, then the proportional hazards hypothesis is satisfied. Otherwise this model says that the log-hazards for any two event types diverge linearly with time. Cox and Oakes showed that if there are two event types, equation (6.7) implies a logistic regression model for type of event, with time of the event as an independent variable. Under the proportional hazards hypothesis, the coefficient for time will be 0.

For more than two event types, equation (6.7) implies a *multinomial* logit model for event type. Here's how to estimate that model with PROC CATMOD:

```
proc catmod data=leaders;
   where lost ne 0;
   direct years;
   model lost=years / noprofile;
run;
```

Notice that leadership spells that are still in progress (LOST=0) when the observation is terminated are excluded from the analysis. The DIRECT statement tells CATMOD to treat YEARS as a quantitative rather than a categorical variable. Output 6.3 shows selected portions of the analysis.

Output 6.3 *Test of Proportionality with PROC CATMOD*

```
             MAXIMUM-LIKELIHOOD ANALYSIS-OF-VARIANCE TABLE
Source                    DF    Chi-Square      Prob

         INTERCEPT               2           69.33     0.0000
         YEARS                   2           17.89     0.0001

         LIKELIHOOD RATIO       42           68.45     0.0061



              ANALYSIS OF MAXIMUM-LIKELIHOOD ESTIMATES

                                            Standard    Chi-
         Effect          Parameter  Estimate   Error    Square    Prob

         INTERCEPT           1       0.0134    0.1432     0.01    0.9253
                             2      -2.5393    0.3140    65.40    0.0000
         YEARS               3      -0.00391   0.0267     0.02    0.8834
                             4       0.1394    0.0359    15.10    0.0001
```

Looking first at the ANOVA table, we see that the effect of YEARS is highly significant, indicating a rejection of the proportionality hypothesis. The coefficients in the lower half of the output tell us which hazard functions are proportional and which are not. Parameter 3 is the β coefficient for the contrast between type 1 (constitutional exit) and type 3 (nonconstitutional exit). The chi-square statistic is minuscule, indicating that proportionality cannot be rejected for these two hazard types. Moreover, the fact that parameter 1 is also near 0 suggests that the hazard functions for these two event types are nearly identical. On the other hand, parameter 4 is highly significant. This coefficient is a contrast between the type 2 hazard (death from natural causes) and the type 3 hazard (nonconstitutional exit). Its value tells us that the hazard for natural death increases much more rapidly with time than the hazard for nonconstitutional exit; specifically, their ratio increases by about 15 percent each year (calculated as $100(e^{.1394}-1)$).

COVARIATE EFFECTS VIA COX MODELS

We have just seen evidence that the hazard for natural death is lower than that for the other two exit types, but that it increases more rapidly with time. On the other hand, the hazard functions for constitutional and nonconstitutional exits are nearly indistinguishable (despite the apparent differences in Output 6.2). We now look at whether the effects of covariates are the same or different across event types by fitting a Cox model to each type. The SAS program for doing this is as follows:

```
proc phreg data=leaders;
   model years*lost(0)=manner start military age conflict
        loginc growth pop land literacy / ties=efron;
   strata region;
run;

proc phreg data=leaders;
   model years*lost(0,1,2)=manner start military age conflict
        loginc growth pop land literacy / ties=efron;
   strata region;
run;

proc phreg data=leaders;
   model years*lost(0,1,3)=manner start military age conflict
        loginc growth pop land literacy / ties=efron;
   strata region;
run;

proc phreg data=leaders;
   model years*lost(0,2,3)=manner start military age conflict
        loginc growth pop land literacy / ties=efron;
   strata region;
run;
```

The first model treats all event types the same. I've included that model for comparison, as well as for some hypothesis tests that we'll look at shortly. The second model focuses on type 3 by treating types 1 and 2 as censoring. That's followed by a models for type 2, treating types 1 and 3 as censoring, and a model for type 1, treating types 2 and 3 as censoring. Notice that I have stratified by region. Alternatively, I could have created three dummy variables to represent the four regions and included them in the model. However, stratification is easier to specify and less restrictive (it allows for interactions between region and time).

In Output 6.4 we see what happens when no distinction is made among the different kinds of exits. Four variables are statistically significant by conventional criteria. The strongest effect is age at entry into power, with each additional year of age associated with a 2.3 percent increase in the risk of leaving power. Recall from Chapter 5, moreover, that if age at origin is a covariate in a Cox model, its coefficient may actually be interpreted as the effect of age as a time-dependent covariate. We also see that

- leaders who attained power by nonconstitutional means (MANNER=1) have a 47 percent greater risk of leaving power
- leaders in countries with higher per capita GNP (LOGINC) have a lower risk of exit
- the risk of exit declined by about 2 percent per year (START) since 1960.

The coefficient for the logarithm of GNP (–.1822) needs a little explanation. If both the hazard and a covariate in a regression model are logged, we can interpret the coefficient (without transformation) as the percent change in the hazard for a 1-*percent* increase in the covariate (in its original metric). Thus, we conclude that a 1-percent increase in per capita GNP yields a .18 percent decrease in the risk of exit.

Output 6.4 *PROC PHREG Analysis for Exits by Any Means*

```
                     Testing Global Null Hypothesis: BETA=0

                   Without        With
    Criterion     Covariates    Covariates     Model Chi-Square

    -2 LOG L       2596.320      2561.077       35.243 with 10 DF (p=0.0001)
    Score             .             .           34.829 with 10 DF (p=0.0001)
    Wald              .             .           34.628 with 10 DF (p=0.0001)
                   Analysis of Maximum Likelihood Estimates
                     Parameter    Standard       Wald        Pr >       Risk
    Variable   DF    Estimate      Error     Chi-Square   Chi-Square    Ratio

    MANNER      1     0.382797     0.15520      6.08355     0.0136      1.466
    AGE         1     0.022743     0.00556     16.73312     0.0001      1.023
    START       1    -0.017531     0.00814      4.63251     0.0314      0.983
    MILITARY    1    -0.231220     0.16342      2.00180     0.1571      0.794
    CONFLICT    1     0.127089     0.13131      0.93667     0.3331      1.136
    LOGINC      1    -0.182206     0.08259      4.86652     0.0274      0.833
    GROWTH      1    -0.002041     0.02138      0.00912     0.9239      0.998
    LAND        1   0.000010945   0.0000480     0.05194     0.8197      1.000
    POP         1  -0.000063245   0.0006373     0.00985     0.9210      1.000
    LITERACY    1     0.000702     0.00321      0.04785     0.8268      1.001
```

The picture changes somewhat when we focus on the hazard for nonconstitutional exits in Output 6.5. Leaders who acquired power by nonconstitutional means are 2.5 times as likely as other leaders to exit by nonconstitutional means. Income also has a stronger effect: a 1-percent increase in per capita GNP now yields a .43 percent decrease in the risk of nonconstitutional exit. Age is no longer important, but we still see a reduction in the hazard over time since 1960. In addition, we find that leaders in countries with ethnic conflict have a 66 percent greater chance of nonconstitutional exit.

Constitutional exits show a different pattern (Output 6.6). Manner of acquiring power is not important, nor is income or conflict. Age shows up again, however, and we also see an effect of literacy. Each one-percentage-point increase in the literacy rate is associated with a 1.4-percent reduction in the risk of a constitutional exit.

Output 6.5 *PROC PHREG Analysis for Nonconstitutional Exits*

Variable	DF	Parameter Estimate	Standard Error	Wald Chi-Square	Pr > Chi-Square	Risk Ratio
MANNER	1	0.928161	0.22047	17.72317	0.0001	2.530
AGE	1	0.008973	0.00845	1.12869	0.2881	1.009
START	1	-0.033498	0.01221	7.53257	0.0061	0.967
MILITARY	1	-0.413794	0.22757	3.30625	0.0690	0.661
CONFLICT	1	0.504451	0.20335	6.15408	0.0131	1.656
LOGINC	1	-0.433399	0.14135	9.40072	0.0022	0.648
GROWTH	1	-0.048583	0.03112	2.43758	0.1185	0.953
LAND	1	0.000020113	0.0000802	0.06286	0.8020	1.000
POP	1	-0.001027	0.00154	0.44253	0.5059	0.999
LITERACY	1	-0.005693	0.00452	1.58425	0.2081	0.994

Output 6.6 *PROC PHREG Analysis for Constitutional Exits*

Variable	DF	Parameter Estimate	Standard Error	Wald Chi-Square	Pr > Chi-Square	Risk Ratio
MANNER	1	-0.308283	0.25750	1.43333	0.2312	0.735
AGE	1	0.023977	0.00862	7.73043	0.0054	1.024
START	1	0.002392	0.01201	0.03969	0.8421	1.002
MILITARY	1	-0.012040	0.26053	0.00214	0.9631	0.988
CONFLICT	1	-0.029853	0.20372	0.02147	0.8835	0.971
LOGINC	1	-0.130681	0.11939	1.19812	0.2737	0.877
GROWTH	1	0.033905	0.03453	0.96398	0.3262	1.034
LAND	1	-0.000026111	0.0000703	0.13792	0.7104	1.000
POP	1	0.000412	0.0008461	0.23656	0.6267	1.000
LITERACY	1	0.013688	0.00561	5.95030	0.0147	1.014

For deaths from natural causes (Output 6.7), it is not terribly surprising that age is the only significant variable. Each one-year increase in age is associated with an 8.3 percent increase in the hazard of death.

Output 6.7 *Deaths from Natural Causes*

Variable	DF	Parameter Estimate	Standard Error	Wald Chi-Square	Pr > Chi-Square	Risk Ratio
MANNER	1	0.302690	0.70202	0.18591	0.6663	1.353
AGE	1	0.079380	0.02038	15.17644	0.0001	1.083
START	1	-0.058506	0.03530	2.74749	0.0974	0.943
MILITARY	1	-0.299045	0.78251	0.14605	0.7023	0.742
CONFLICT	1	-0.553633	0.50851	1.18536	0.2763	0.575
LOGINC	1	0.194861	0.28309	0.47381	0.4912	1.215
GROWTH	1	0.092281	0.08538	1.16806	0.2798	1.097
LAND	1	0.000034665	0.0001797	0.03720	0.8471	1.000
POP	1	0.000956	0.00220	0.18847	0.6642	1.001
LITERACY	1	-0.012390	0.01361	0.82909	0.3625	0.988

We see, then, that the coefficients can differ greatly across different event types. But perhaps these differences are merely the result of random variation. What we need is a test of the null hypothesis that $\beta_j = \beta$ for all j, where β_j is the vector of coefficients for event type j. A test statistic is readily constructed from output given by PROC PHREG. For each model, PROC PHREG reports $-2 \times$ log-likelihood (for the model with covariates). For the four models we just estimated, the values are

All types combined	2561.08
Nonconstitutional	1202.04
Constitutional	1139.41
Natural Death	155.38

To construct the test, we sum the values for the three specific death types, yielding a total of 2496.83. We then subtract that from the value for all types combined, for a difference of 64.25. This is a likelihood-ratio chi-square statistic for the null hypothesis. How many degrees of freedom? Well, when we estimated separate models for the three event types, we got a total of 30 coefficients. When we collapsed them all together, we only estimated 10. The difference of 20 is the degrees of freedom. Since the chi-square statistic is significant at well beyond the .01 level, we may reject the hypothesis that the coefficients are all equal across event types.

That result is not terribly surprising because deaths from natural causes are unlikely to have the same determinants as constitutional and nonconstitutional exits. A more interesting question is whether the covariates for the latter two event types have identical coefficients. We can obtain a test statistic for that null hypothesis by estimating a model that combines constitutional and nonconstitutional exits and that treats natural deaths as censoring. For that model, $-2 \times$ log-likelihood=2392. If we sum the values for the two separate models (given above), we get 2341.45. The difference of 50.55

has 10 degrees of freedom (the difference in the number of estimated parameters) for a *p*-value less than .0001. So again, we may conclude that different models are required for constitutional and nonconstitutional exits.

If we had concluded, instead, that corresponding coefficients were equal across all event types, a natural next step would be to test whether they were all equal to 0. No special computations are needed for that test, however. Just estimate the model without distinguishing among the event types, and examine the global statistics for the null hypothesis that all coefficients are equal to 0. In Output 6.4, all three chi-square statistics (Wald, score, and likelihood ratio) have values of about 35 with 10 d.f., giving strong evidence against that null hypothesis. Note that this is a conditional test, the condition being that the coefficients are equal. To test the hypothesis that corresponding coefficients are equal *and* that they are equal to 0, simply add this conditional chi-square statistic to the chi-square statistic for testing equality, and then add the degrees of freedom as well. Thus, for this example, the likelihood-ratio statistic is 35.23+64.25=99.48 with 40 d.f.

We can also construct test statistics for hypotheses about coefficients for specific covariates, using only the coefficients and their standard errors (Lagakos 1978). The coefficient for CONFLICT for nonconstitutional exits was .5044 with a standard error of .2034. By contrast, the coefficient for CONFLICT for constitutional exits was −.02985 with a standard error of .2037. The first coefficient is significantly different from 0; the second is not. But is there a significant difference between them? A 1-degree-of-freedom Wald chi-square statistic for testing the null hypothesis that $\beta_1 = \beta_2$ is easily calculated by the following formula:

$$\frac{(b_1 - b_2)^2}{[s.e.(b_1)]^2 + [s.e.(b_2)]^2} \tag{6.8}$$

where b_1 is the estimate of β_1 and $s.e.(.)$ means estimated standard error. For our particular question, we have

$$\frac{(.5044 - [-.02985])^2}{[.2034]^2 + [.2037]^2} = 3.44.$$

Since that does not exceed the .05 criterion, we have insufficient statistical justification for concluding that the two coefficients are different.

This particular statistic, in one form or another, is widely used to test for differences in parameter estimates across two independent groups. Here, however, we do not have independent groups because the same set of 472 leaders is used to estimate models for both constitutional and nonconstitutional exits, suggesting that we may need a covariance term in the denominator of the statistic. In fact, we do not. What justifies this statistic is the fact that the likelihood function factors into a distinct likelihood for each event type. It follows that the parameter estimates for each event type are asymptotically independent of the parameter estimates for all other event types. This only holds for mutually exclusive event types, however. We cannot use this statistic to test for the difference between a coefficient for constitutional exits and the corresponding coefficient for all types of exits.

Since we found no reason to reject the hypothesis that the two coefficients for CONFLICT are equal, we may want to go further and test whether they are 0. This is easily accomplished by taking the reported chi-square statistics for CONFLICT, for both constitutional and nonconstitutional exits, and summing them: .021+6.15=6.27 with 2 d.f. This is just barely significant at the .05 level.

The tests for a single covariate can be generalized to more than two event types. For a given covariate, let b_j be its coefficient for event type j; let s_j^2 be the squared, estimated standard error of b_j, and let $X_j^2 = b_j^2/s_j^2$ be the reported Wald chi-square statistic for testing that $\beta_j = 0$. To test the hypothesis that all the coefficients for the chosen covariate are 0, we sum the Wald chi-square statistics

$$Q = \sum_j X_j^2$$

(6.9)

which has degrees of freedom equal to the number of event types. To test the hypothesis that all coefficients are equal to each other, we calculate

$$Q - \frac{\left(\sum_j \dfrac{b_j}{s_j^2}\right)^2}{\sum_j \left(\dfrac{1}{s_j^2}\right)}$$

(6.10)

which has degrees of freedom equal to one less than the number of event types.

ACCELERATED FAILURE TIME MODELS

Competing risks analysis with accelerated failure time models is basically the same as with Cox models. As before, the key point is to treat all events as censoring except the one that you're focusing on. There are, however, some complications that arise in constructing tests of equality of coefficients across event types. There are also some special characteristics of the leader data that require slightly different treatment with AFT models.

One of those characteristics is the presence of zeros in the YEARS variable. Recall that any leaders who served less than one year were assigned a time value of 0. Of the 472 leaders, 172 fell in this category. This poses no problem for PROC PHREG, which is only concerned with the rank order of the time variable. PROC LIFEREG, on the other hand, excludes any observations with times of 0 or less because it must take the logarithm of the event time. But we certainly don't want to exclude 36 percent of the cases. One approach is to assign some arbitrarily chosen number between 0 and 1. A more elegant solution is to treat such cases as though they were left censored at time 1. We discussed how to do this in some detail in the section **Left Censoring and Interval Censoring** in Chapter 4, "Estimating Parametric Regression Models with PROC LIFEREG." For the leaders data, we need a short DATA step to create LOWER and UPPER variables that are appropriately coded:

```
data leaders2;
   set leaders;
   lower=years;
   upper=years;
   if years=0 then do;
      lower=.;
      upper=1;
   end;
   if lost in (0,1,2) then upper=.;
run;

proc lifereg data=leaders2;
   model (lower,upper)= / d=exponential;
run;
```

This program fits an exponential model with no covariates for nonconstitutional exits (LOST=3). For uncensored observations, LOWER and UPPER have the same value. For observations with YEARS=0, we set LOWER=. and UPPER=1. For right-censored observations (including those with events other than the one of interest), UPPER=. and LOWER=YEARS. To fit the model for the other two types of exit, we simply change the second IF statement so that the numbers in parentheses include all outcomes to be treated as right censored.

Another minor problem concerns the variable REGION, which indexes four different regions of the world. In the PROC PHREG analysis, I simply stratified on this variable. Since there is no stratification option in PROC LIFEREG, I treated REGION as a CLASS variable. I also excluded from the models all variables that are not statistically significant in any of the PROC PHREG models, namely, POP, GROWTH, and LAND.

For each of the three event types, I estimated all five of the AFT models discussed in Chapter 4. The models and their log-likelihoods are shown below:

	Nonconstitutional	Constitutional	Natural Death
Exponential	-383.39	-337.30	-87.17
Weibull	-372.51	-336.46	-82.48
Log-normal	-377.04	-338.09	-83.60
Gamma	-372.47	-336.14	(-81.36)
Log-logistic	-374.95	-335.88	-82.78

(In fitting the gamma model to natural deaths, PROC LIFEREG reported a "domain error" after 23 iterations. I've given the log-likelihood at the last iteration).

For the nonconstitutional exits, we can certainly reject the hypothesis that the hazard is constant over time. The chi-square statistic for comparing the exponential model with the generalized gamma model is 21.84 with 2 d.f., yielding a *p*-value of .00002. The log-normal model must also be rejected (*p*=.003). The Weibull model, on the other hand, is only trivially different from the gamma model.

Output 6.8 shows the parameter estimates for the Weibull model. Consider first the scale estimate of 1.41, which can tell us whether the hazard is increasing or decreasing. Using the transformation 1/1.41−1=−.29, we get the coefficient of log *t* in the equivalent proportional hazards model. This result indicates that the hazard of a nonconstitutional exit *decreases* with time since entry into power. The *p*-values for the covariates are quite similar to those in Output 6.5 for the Cox model, but naturally the coefficients are all reversed in sign. To directly compare the magnitudes of the coefficients with those of the Cox model, each must be divided by the scale estimate of 1.41. After this adjustment, the values are remarkably similar. We also see major differences among the regions, something that was hidden in the Cox analysis. Specifically, expected time until a nonconstitutional exit is more than seven times greater (exp(2.036)) in Asia (REGION=2) than it is in Latin America (REGION=3), and it is nearly four times greater (exp(1.36)) in Africa (REGION=1).

Output 6.8 *Weibull Model for Nonconstitutional Exits*

```
Variable  DF    Estimate  Std Err  ChiSquare  Pr>Chi  Label/Value

INTERCPT   1  -40.613628  17.19016  5.581921  0.0181  Intercept
MANNER     1   -1.3805637  0.314275  19.2971   0.0001
AGE        1   -0.0124068  0.011424  1.179367  0.2775
START      1    0.0409823  0.017753  5.328748  0.0210
MILITARY   1    0.65101314 0.313507  4.31207   0.0378
```

continued on next page

Output 6.8 continued

CONFLICT	1	-0.7198897	0.284319	6.410939	0.0113	
LOGINC	1	0.67502886	0.207258	10.60776	0.0011	
LITERACY	1	0.00717186	0.006329	1.283939	0.2572	
REGION	3			20.27154	0.0001	
	1	0.90367671	0.445726	4.110452	0.0426	0
	1	1.3636263	0.392624	12.06248	0.0005	1
	1	2.03618418	0.469196	18.83329	0.0001	2
	0	0	0	.	.	3
SCALE	1	1.40636388	0.112069		Extreme value scale parameter	

For constitutional exits, the picture is rather different. All the
models have similar log-likelihoods, and even the exponential model is not
significantly worse than the Weibull or gamma models. Invoking parsimony,
we might as well stick with the exponential model, which is displayed in
Output 6.9. The Lagrange multiplier test at the bottom of the output shows,
again, that the exponential model cannot be rejected. As with the
nonconstitutional exits, the results are quite similar to those of the Cox model
in Output 6.6. Apart from the region differences, the only significant variables
are AGE and LITERACY. Except for the reversal of sign, the coefficients are
directly comparable to those of the Cox model. Again, we see that Latin
America has the shortest expected time until a constitutional exit, but the
longest expected time is now in Africa rather than Asia.

Output 6.9 *Exponential Model for Constitutional Exits*

Variable	DF	Estimate	Std Err	ChiSquare	Pr>Chi	Label/Value	
INTERCPT	1	12.4138487	11.75998	1.114294	0.2912	Intercept	
MANNER	1	0.31121992	0.262383	1.406902	0.2356		
AGE	1	-0.0316866	0.008315	14.52052	0.0001		
START	1	-0.0091941	0.012045	0.58262	0.4453		
MILITARY	1	0.02842144	0.252641	0.012656	0.9104		
CONFLICT	1	0.15729162	0.198299	0.629171	0.4277		
LOGINC	1	0.13661152	0.11349	1.448965	0.2287		
LITERACY	1	-0.0113363	0.005606	4.088443	0.0432		
REGION	3			22.22296	0.0001		
	1	0.54130357	0.332609	2.648582	0.1036		0
	1	1.70321651	0.370201	21.16728	0.0001		1
	1	0.53356446	0.218025	5.989092	0.0144		2
	0	0	0	.	.		3
SCALE	0	1	0		Extreme value scale parameter		

Lagrange Multiplier ChiSquare for Scale 1.470416 Pr>Chi is 0.2253.

For deaths due to natural causes, the only model that is clearly rejectable is the exponential model. Of the remaining models, the Weibull model again appears to be the best choice because its log-likelihood is only trivially different from that of the gamma model. The Weibull estimates are reported in Output 6.10.

As in the Cox model, there is a strong effect of age at entry, with older leaders having shorter times until death.

Output 6.10 *Weibull Estimates for Natural Deaths*

Variable	DF	Estimate	Std Err	ChiSquare	Pr>Chi	Label/Value
INTERCPT	1	-23.147601	20.05743	1.331868	0.2485	Intercept
MANNER	1	-0.2216481	0.390909	0.321496	0.5707	
AGE	1	-0.045097	0.010756	17.57777	0.0001	
START	1	0.03021782	0.020888	2.092815	0.1480	
MILITARY	1	0.22103044	0.415786	0.282595	0.5950	
CONFLICT	1	0.07358984	0.280434	0.068861	0.7930	
LOGINC	1	-0.151372	0.156287	0.938096	0.3328	
LITERACY	1	0.00302367	0.007256	0.17367	0.6769	
REGION	3			4.308315	0.2300	
	1	0.35965592	0.447182	0.646853	0.4212	0
	1	0.76721078	0.449127	2.918033	0.0876	1
	1	0.637755	0.374528	2.899605	0.0886	2
	0	0	0	.	.	3
SCALE	1	0.59938852	0.08855			Extreme value scale parameter

The next logical step is to construct tests of hypotheses about equality of coefficients across different event types. For tests about individual covariates, the chi-square statistics in equations (6.8) – (6.10) will do just fine. Unfortunately, we cannot use the method employed for Cox models to construct a global test of whether all the coefficients for one event type are equal to the corresponding coefficients for another event type. For the AFT models, fitting a model to all events without distinction involves a different likelihood than constraining parameters to be equal across the separate likelihoods. As a result, if you try to calculate the statistics described in the previous section, you're likely to get negative chi-square statistics.

In general, there's no easy way around this problem. For Weibull models (actually for any parametric proportional hazards model), the likelihood test can be corrected by a function of the number of events of each type at each point in time (Narendranathan and Stewart 1991). Here, I consider an alternative test for Weibull models that I think is more easily performed. It also yields a test for each covariate as a by-product. It is, in fact, a simple generalization of the test for proportional hazards discussed earlier in this chapter (see **Time in Power for Leaders of Countries: Example**).

Suppose we believe that constitutional and nonconstitutional exits are both governed by Weibull models, but with different parameters. We can write the two models as

$$\log h_j(t) = \alpha_j \log t + \beta_{0j} + \beta_{1j}x_1 + \ldots + \beta_{kj}x_k \tag{6.9}$$

with $j=1$ for constitutional exits and $j=2$ for nonconstitutional exits. Now consider the following question: Given that an exit (other than a natural death) occurs at time t, what determines whether it is a constitutional or a nonconstitutional exit? Equation (6.9) implies that this question is answered by a logit model:

$$\log \frac{\Pr(J=1 \mid T=t)}{\Pr(J=2 \mid T=t)} = (\alpha_1 - \alpha_2)\log t + (\beta_{01} - \beta_{02}) + (\beta_{11} - \beta_{12})x_1 + \ldots + (\beta_{k1} - \beta_{k2})x_k.$$

Four SAS procedures will estimate this model: PROC LOGISTIC, PROC PROBIT, PROC GENMOD, and PROC CATMOD. I used PROC PROBIT because it is easy to set up and has a CLASS statement. The SAS code is as follows:

```
data leaders3;
   set leaders;
   lyears=log(years+.5);
run;

proc probit data=leaders3;
   where lost=1 or lost=3;
   class lost region;
   model lost=lyears manner age start military conflict loginc
         literacy region / d=logistic;
run;
```

The DATA step is needed so that the log of time can be included in the model (0.5 was added to avoid problems with times of 0). The WHERE statement eliminates the censored cases and those who died of natural causes.

Output 6.11 shows the results. We can interpret each of the coefficients in this table as an estimate of the difference between corresponding coefficients in the two Weibull models. We see that there are highly significant differences in the coefficients for MANNER and LITERACY but only marginally significant differences between the coefficients for AGE, START, and LYEARS. The test for LYEARS is equivalent to a test of whether the scale parameters are the same in the AFT version of the model.

The null hypothesis that *all* the corresponding coefficients are equal in the two Weibull models is equivalent to the hypothesis that all the coefficients in the implied logit model are 0. To test that hypothesis, we can reestimate the model without any covariates and take twice the positive difference in the log-likelihoods for the models with and without covariates. In this case, the chi-square statistic is 170.9 with 11 degrees of freedom, a highly significant result. This approach can easily be generalized to more than two event types by fitting a multinomial logit model with PROC CATMOD.

Output 6.11 *Logit Model Comparing Constitutional and Nonconstitutional Exits*

Variable	DF	Estimate	Std Err	ChiSquare	Pr>Chi	Label/Value
INTERCPT	1	-42.92625	20.72742	4.288995	0.0384	Intercept
LYEARS	1	0.27487372	0.142439	3.724008	0.0536	
MANNER	1	-1.3251809	0.380053	12.15802	0.0005	
AGE	1	0.02770364	0.014376	3.713684	0.0540	
START	1	0.040657	0.021427	3.600388	0.0578	
MILITARY	1	0.06982074	0.394855	0.031268	0.8596	
CONFLICT	1	-0.2432904	0.342547	0.504439	0.4776	
LOGINC	1	0.0581073	0.2502	0.053937	0.8163	
LITERACY	1	0.03338248	0.008947	13.92021	0.0002	
REGION	3			5.535861	0.1365	
	1	0.11108729	0.506247	0.048151	0.8263	0
	1	-0.6683864	0.50343	1.762696	0.1843	1
	1	0.47374632	0.456832	1.07542	0.2997	2
	0	0	0	.	.	3

AN ALTERNATIVE APPROACH TO MULTIPLE EVENT TYPES

The competing risks approach presumes that each event type has its own hazard model that governs both the occurrence and timing of events of that type. The appropriate imagery is one of independent causal mechanisms operating in parallel. Whichever type of event happens first, the individual is then no longer at risk of the other types.

This is clearly a defensible way of thinking about deaths due to natural causes, on the one hand, and forcible removal from power, on the other. It may not be so sensible, however, for the distinction between constitutional exits and nonconstitutional exits. We might imagine that a leader will stay in power as long as his popularity with key groups stays sufficiently high. When that popularity drops below a certain point, pressures will build for his removal. *How* he is removed is another question, and the answer depends on such things as the constitutional mechanisms that are available and the cultural traditions of the country. In this way of thinking about things, we have one mechanism governing the timing of events and another distinct mechanism that determines the type of event, given that an event occurs.

For an even more blatant example, consider the event *buying a personal computer*, and suppose we subdivide this event into two types: buying a Macintosh computer and buying an IBM-compatible computer. Now it would be absurd to suppose that there are two parallel processes here and that we merely observe whichever produces an event first. Rather, we have one process that governs the decision to buy a computer at all and another that governs which type is purchased. These kinds of situations arise most commonly when the different event types are alternative means for achieving some goal.

If we adopt this point of view, a natural way to proceed is to estimate one model for the timing of events (without distinguishing among event types) and a second model for the type of event (restricting the analysis to those individuals who experienced an event). For the timing of events, any of the models that we have considered so far are possible contenders. For the type of event, a binomial or multinomial logit model is a natural choice, although there are certainly alternatives.

We have already estimated a logit model for constitutional versus nonconstitutional exits, with the results displayed in Output 6.11. There we interpreted the coefficients as differences in coefficients in the underlying hazard models. Now I am suggesting that we interpret these coefficients directly as determinants of whether a loss of power was by constitutional or nonconstitutional means, given that an exit from power occurred. We see, for example, that those who obtained power by nonconstitutional means are about four times as likely to lose power in the same way. On the other hand, each additional percentage point of literacy increases the odds that the exit will be constitutional rather than nonconstitutional by about 3 percent. Although the effects are only marginally significant, there are consistently positive effects of *time* on constitutional rather than nonconstitutional changes: older leaders, more recently installed leaders, and leaders who have been in power longer are all more likely to exit via constitutional mechanisms.

We still need a model for timing of exits from power, treating deaths from natural causes as censoring. Output 6.12 shows the results of estimating a Cox model, with the statements:

```
proc phreg data=leaders;
   model years*lost(0,2)=manner age start military conflict
      loginc literacy / ties=efron;
   strata region;
run;
```

Since nearly half of the exits occurred at 0 or 1 year, I also re-estimated the model with the TIES=EXACT option. It took about 35 seconds to estimate (on a 486 machine), and it produced results that were nearly identical to those in Output 6.12.

Output 6.12 *Cox Model for Timing of Constitutional and Nonconstitutional Exits*

Variable	DF	Parameter Estimate	Standard Error	Wald Chi-Square	Pr > Chi-Square	Risk Ratio
MANNER	1	0.373259	0.15841	5.55217	0.0185	1.452
AGE	1	0.017054	0.00572	8.88029	0.0029	1.017
START	1	-0.014880	0.00837	3.15885	0.0755	0.985
MILITARY	1	-0.207177	0.16368	1.60204	0.2056	0.813
CONFLICT	1	0.169923	0.13564	1.56932	0.2103	1.185
LOGINC	1	-0.240164	0.08843	7.37649	0.0066	0.786
LITERACY	1	0.001862	0.00330	0.31750	0.5731	1.002

Three results stand out in Output 6.12:

- Those who acquired power by nonconstitutional means had about a 45 percent higher risk of losing power (by means other than natural death).
- Each additional year of age increased the risk of exit by about 1.7 percent.
- A 1-percent increase in GNP per capita yielded about a .24 percent decrease in the risk of exit.

In my judgment, of all the analyses done in this chapter, Output 6.11 and Output 6.12 give the most meaningful representation of the processes governing the removal of leaders from power. To that, we may also wish to add Output 6.7, which shows that only age is associated with the risk of a death from natural causes.

CONCLUSION

As we have seen, competing risks analysis is easily accomplished with conventional software by doing a separate analysis for each event type, treating other events as censoring. The biggest drawback of competing risks analysis is the requirement that times for different event types be independent, or at least that each event be noninformative for the others. This requirement is exactly equivalent to the requirement for random censoring discussed in Chapter 2. In either case, violations can lead to substantially biased coefficient estimates.

The seriousness of this problem depends greatly on the particular application. For the leaders data set, I argued that death due to natural causes is likely to be noninformative for the risk of either a constitutional or a nonconstitutional exit. For the latter two types, however, the presumption of noninformativeness may be unreasonable. In thinking about this issue, it is helpful to ask the question, "Are there unmeasured variables that may affect more than one event type?" If the answer is yes, then there should be a presumption of dependence.

Unfortunately, there's not a lot that can be done about the problem. It's possible to formulate models that incorporate dependence among event types but, for any such model, there's an independence model that does an equally good job of fitting the data. Dependence models typically impose parametric restrictions on the shape of the hazard functions, and the results may be heavily dependent on those restrictions. Heckman and Honoré (1989) showed that you can identify nonparametric dependence models, so long as there is at least one continuous covariate with different coefficients for different event types (along with some other mild conditions), but the practical implications of their theorem have yet to be explored. Just because you can do something doesn't mean you can do it well.

So for all practical purposes, we have little choice but to use a method that rests on assumptions that may be implausible and cannot be tested. In Chapter 8, "Heterogeneity, Repeated Events, and Other Topics," I describe a sensitivity analysis for informative censoring that may also be useful for competing risks. Basically, this method amounts to redoing the analysis under two worst-case scenarios and hoping that the qualitative conclusions don't change. The other thing to remember is that you can reduce the problem of dependence by measuring and including those covariates that are likely to affect more than one type of event. For example, a diet that is high in saturated fat is thought to be a common risk factor for both heart disease and cancer. If a measure of dietary fat intake is included in the regression model, it can partially alleviate concerns about possible dependence among these two event types.

CHAPTER **7**

Analysis of Tied or Discrete Data with the LOGISTIC, PROBIT, and GENMOD Procedures

p.211 *Introduction*

p.212 *The Logit Model for Discrete Time*

p.216 *The Complementary Log-Log Model for Continuous-Time Processes*

p.219 *Data with Time-Dependent Covariates*

p.223 *Issues and Extensions*

p.231 *Conclusion*

INTRODUCTION

This chapter shows how to use the LOGISTIC, PROBIT and GENMOD procedures to analyze data in which many events occur at the same points in time. In Chapter 5, "Estimating Cox regression Models with PROC PHREG," we looked at several different methods for handling tied data with PROC PHREG. There we saw that Breslow's method—the standard formula for partial likelihood estimation with tied data—is often a poor approximation when there are many ties. This problem was remedied by two exact methods, one that assumed that ties result from imprecise measurement and another that assumed that events really occur at the same (discrete) time. Unfortunately, both of these methods are computationally demanding for large data sets with many ties. We also looked at tied data in Chapter 4, "Estimating Parametric Regression Models with PROC LIFEREG," under the heading of interval censoring. While PROC LIFEREG is adept at estimating parametric models with interval censoring, it cannot incorporate time-dependent covariates.

The maximum likelihood methods described in this chapter do not suffer from these limitations. They do not rely on approximations; the computations are quite manageable even with large data sets; and they are particularly good at handling large numbers of time-dependent covariates. In addition, the methods make it easy to test hypotheses about the dependence of the hazard on time.

The basic idea is simple. Each individual's survival history is broken down into a set of discrete time units that are treated as distinct observations. After pooling these observations, the next step is to estimate a binary regression model predicting whether an event did or did not occur in each time unit. Covariates are allowed to vary over time from one time unit to another.

This general approach has two versions, depending on the form of the binary regression model. By specifying a logit link, you get estimates of the discrete-time proportional odds model proposed by Cox. This method is directly analogous to the TIES=DISCRETE option in PROC PHREG. Alternatively, by specifying a complementary log-log link, you get estimates of an underlying proportional hazards model in continuous time. This is analogous to the TIES=EXACT option in PROC PHREG.

The mechanics of this approach are similar to those of the piecewise exponential model described in Chapter 4. The main difference is that the piecewise exponential model assumes that you know the exact time of the event within a given interval. By contrast, the procedures in this chapter presume that you know only that an event occurred within a given interval. That difference aside, the two approaches have the same advantages and disadvantages, and many of the same issues arise in implementation. For these reasons, anyone who wants to use the piecewise exponential model can benefit from reading this chapter.

THE LOGIT MODEL FOR DISCRETE TIME

We begin with the logit version of the model because it is more widely used and because logit regression is already familiar to many readers. In Chapter 5 (see **The DISCRETE Method**), we considered Cox's model for discrete-time data. In brief, we let P_{it} be the conditional probability that individual i has an event at time t, given that an event has not already occurred to that individual. The model says that P_{it} is related to the covariates by a logistic regression equation:

$$\log\left(\frac{P_{it}}{1 - P_{it}}\right) = \alpha_t + \beta_1 x_{it1} + \ldots + \beta_k x_{itk} \tag{7.1}$$

where t =1, 2, 3,.... This model is most appropriate when events can only occur at regular, discrete points in time, but it has also been frequently employed when ties arise from grouping continuous-time data into intervals.

In Chapter 5, we saw how to estimate this model by the method of partial likelihood, thereby discarding any information about the α_ts. Now we are going to estimate the same model by *maximum* likelihood, so that we get explicit estimates of the α_ts. The procedure is best explained by way of an example. As in Chapter 5, we'll estimate the model for 100 simulated job durations, measured from the year of entry into the job until the year that the employee quit. Durations after the fifth year are censored. We know only the year in which the employee quit, so the survival times have values of 1, 2, 3, 4, or 5. These values are contained in a variable called DUR, while the variable EVENT is coded 1 if the employee quit; otherwise, it is coded 0. Covariates are ED (years of education), PRESTIGE (a measure of the prestige of the occupation), and SALARY in the first year of the job. None of these covariates are time dependent.

The first task is to take the original data set (JOBDUR) with one record per person and create a new data set (JOBYRS) with one record for each year that each person was observed. Thus, someone who quit in the third year gets three observations, while someone who still had not quit after five years on the job gets five observations. The following DATA step accomplishes this task:

```
data jobyrs;
   set jobdur;
   do year=1 to dur;
      if year=dur and event=1 then quit=1;
      else quit=2;
      output;
   end;
run;
```

The DO loop creates 272 person-years that are written to the output data set. The IF statement defines the dependent variable QUIT, which equals 1 if the employee quit in that particular person-year; otherwise, QUIT equals 2. (I use 2 rather than 0 for nonevents because the default in PROC LOGISTIC and PROC PROBIT is to predict the probability of the *smaller* value of a binary variable. You can change the default in PROC LOGISTIC with the DESCENDING option.) Thus, if a person quit in the fifth year, QUIT is coded 2 for the first four records and 1 in the last record. For people who don't quit during any of the five years, QUIT is coded 2 for all five records.

Output 7.1 shows the first 20 records produced by this DATA statement. Observation 1 is for a person who quit in the first year of the job. Observations 2 through 5 correspond to a person who quit in the fourth year. QUIT is coded 2 for the first three years and 1 for the fourth. Observations 6 through 10 correspond to a person who still held the job at the end of the fifth year.

Output 7.1   *First 20 Cases of Person-Year Data Set for Job Durations*

OBS	DUR	EVENT	QUIT	YEAR	ED	PRESTIGE	SALARY
1	1	1	1	1	7	3	19
2	4	1	2	1	14	62	17
3	4	1	2	2	14	62	17
4	4	1	2	3	14	62	17
5	4	1	1	4	14	62	17
6	5	0	2	1	16	70	18
7	5	0	2	2	16	70	18
8	5	0	2	3	16	70	18
9	5	0	2	4	16	70	18
10	5	0	2	5	16	70	18
11	2	1	2	1	12	43	135
12	2	1	1	2	12	43	135
13	3	1	2	1	9	18	12
14	3	1	2	2	9	18	12
15	3	1	1	3	9	18	12
16	1	1	1	1	11	31	12
17	1	1	1	1	13	26	6
18	1	1	1	1	10	1	4
19	2	1	2	1	12	28	17
20	2	1	1	2	12	28	17

Now we're ready to estimate a logistic regression model for these data. We can use any of the three procedures discussed in this chapter, but let's start with PROC PROBIT. (Despite the name, PROC PROBIT can optionally estimate logistic regression models). The following PROC PROBIT statements accomplish this task:

```
proc probit data=jobyrs;
   class year quit;
   model quit=ed prestige salary year / d=logistic;
run;
```

By specifying YEAR as a CLASS variable, we tell PROC PROBIT to create a set of four indicator (dummy) variables, with the reference category being YEAR=5 (the highest value). Output 7.2 shows the results. Comparing these estimates with the partial likelihood estimates in Output 5.10, we see that the coefficients of ED, PRESTIGE, and SALARY are similar, as are the chi-square statistics. Again, this is not surprising since they are simply alternative ways of estimating the same model. Despite the similarity in results, however, PROC PHREG (using the TIES=DISCRETE option) took six times as long to estimate the model as PROC PROBIT did.

Output 7.2 *ML Estimates of Discrete-Time Logistic Model for Job Duration Data*

```
Weighted Frequency Counts for the Ordered Response Categories

                          Level      Count
                            1          68
                            2         204

Log Likelihood for LOGISTIC -99.68329834

    Variable  DF   Estimate  Std Err  ChiSquare  Pr>Chi  Label/Value

    INTERCPT   1  3.44431429 1.182107  8.489692  0.0036  Intercept
    ED         1  0.22485581  0.08598  6.839274  0.0089
    PRESTIGE   1 -0.1235217  0.018099 46.57946   0.0001
    SALARY     1 -0.0268422  0.010386  6.679172  0.0098

    YEAR       4                      23.25297   0.0001
               1 -2.6874898 0.832656 10.41748   0.0012            1
               1 -1.4475238 0.767124  3.560574  0.0592            2
               1 -0.0129973 0.727165  0.000319  0.9857            3
               1  0.23547505 0.777895 0.091632  0.7621            4
               0       0        0        .        .               5
```

Unlike partial likelihood, the maximum likelihood method also gives us estimates for the effect of time on the odds of quitting, as reflected in the α_ts in equation (7.1). INTERCPT, in Output 7.2, is an estimate of α_5, the log-odds of quitting in year 5 for a person with values of 0 on all covariates. For level j of the YEAR variable, the coefficient is an estimate of $\alpha_j - \alpha_5$, that is, the difference in the log-odds of quitting in year j and the log-odds of quitting in year 5 (controlling for the covariates). We see that the log-odds is lowest in the first year of the job, rises steadily to year 3, and then stays roughly constant for the next two years. Overall, the effect of YEAR is highly significant with a Wald chi-square statistic of 23.25 with 4 d.f.

When the model in equation (7.1) is estimated by partial likelihood, there can be no restrictions on the α_ts. With the ML method of this chapter, however, we can readily estimate restricted versions of the model. In fact, because time (in this case YEAR) is just another variable in the regression model, we can specify the dependence of the hazard on time as any function that SAS allows in the DATA statement. For example, if we remove YEAR from the CLASS statement but keep it in the MODEL statement, we constrain the effect of YEAR to be linear on the log-odds of quitting. Alternatively, we can take the logarithm of YEAR before putting it in the model, or we can fit a quadratic model with YEAR and YEAR squared. The log-likelihoods for these models are

Unrestricted	−99.68
Linear	−103.14
Logarithmic	−100.99
Quadratic	−100.01

Taking twice the positive difference between the linear and unrestricted log-likelihoods, we get a chi-square statistic of 6.92 with 3 d.f., for a *p*-value of .07. (The three degrees of freedom correspond to the three additional parameters estimated in the unrestricted model). While this is marginally acceptable, the logarithmic and quadratic models fit much better with *p*-values of .45 and .72, respectively. And since the logarithmic model has one fewer coefficient than the quadratic model, it has the edge in parsimony. The coefficients for ED, PRESTIGE, and SALARY in the logarithmic model (not shown) hardly change at all from the unrestricted model. The coefficient for the logarithm of YEAR is 2.00, indicating that a 1-percent increase in time in the job produces a 2-percent increase in the odds of quitting.

THE COMPLEMENTARY LOG-LOG MODEL FOR CONTINUOUS-TIME PROCESSES

As already noted, the logit model presumes that events can only occur at discrete points in time. For most applications, however, ties occur because event times are measured coarsely even though events can actually occur at any point in time. Aside from the implausibility of the logit model for such data, the model suffers from a lack of invariance to the length of the time interval. In other words, switching from person-months to person-years changes the *model* in a fundamental way, so that coefficients are not directly comparable across intervals of different length.

To avoid these difficulties, we can first specify a model for continuous-time data and from that derive a model for data grouped into intervals. (In essence, that's how the EXACT method was developed for PROC PHREG). Suppose that the intervals are of equal length beginning at the origin. We'll index them by *t*=1, 2, 3, ... As before, let P_{it} be the probability that an event occurs to individual *i* in interval *t*, given that the individual did not have events in any of the earlier intervals. If we now assume that events are generated by Cox's proportional hazards model, it follows (Prentice and Gloeckler 1978) that

$$\log[-\log(1 - P_{it})] = \alpha_t + \beta_1 x_{it1} + \ldots + \beta_k x_{itk}. \tag{7.2}$$

The transformation on the left side is called *the complementary log-log function*, which is also what we call the model.

Like the logit function, the complementary log-log function takes a quantity that varies between 0 and 1 and changes it to a something that varies between minus and plus infinity. Unlike the logit function, however, the complementary log-log function is *asymmetrical*. For example, after taking the logit transformation, a change in probability from .25 to .50 is the same as from

.50 to .75. On the complementary log-log scale, however, the difference between probabilities of .25 and .50 is larger than the difference between .50 and .75. This difference has an important practical implication. In the logit model, switching the values of the binary dependent variable merely changes the signs of the coefficients. In the complementary log-log model, on the other hand, switching the values produces completely different coefficient estimates, and it can even result in nonconvergence of the ML algorithm. It's essential, then, that model be set up to predict the probability of an *event*.

Another important point about the model in equation (7.2) is that the β coefficients are identical to the coefficients in the underlying proportional hazards model. That doesn't mean that the estimates you get from grouped data will be the same as those from the original ungrouped data. What it does mean is that both are estimating the same underlying parameters and are directly comparable to each other. It also means that the complementary log-log coefficients have a relative risk interpretation, just like Cox model coefficients, and that the *model* (not the estimates) is invariant to interval length.

Originally, people preferred the logit model because there was little software for the complementary log-log model. Now there's no excuse. Several popular packages have complementary log-log options, and SAS makes it available in the LOGISTIC, PROBIT and GENMOD procedures. In PROC LOGISTIC and PROC GENMOD, you specify it with the LINK=CLOGLOG option in the MODEL statement. In PROC PROBIT, you specify D=GOMPERTZ as an option in the MODEL statement. (D=GOMPERTZ is a misnomer. The correct name of the distribution function corresponding to the complementary log-log is *Gumbel*, not Gompertz.)

To estimate the complementary log-log model for the job duration data, we can use exactly the same SAS statements that we used for the logit model, but with D=GOMPERTZ instead of D=LOGISTIC. Alternatively, let's see how to do it with PROC GENMOD:

```
data jobyrs2;
   quit=2-quit;
   n=1;
run;

proc genmod data=jobyrs2;
   class year;
   model quit/n=ed prestige salary year / d=binomial
         link=cloglog type3;
run;
```

The DATA step recodes QUIT to the more familiar 1-0 coding. The N variable is necessary because PROC GENMOD assumes that the data are grouped—we need to specify that each group has only one member. The MODEL statement uses the grouped data syntax (QUIT/N) for the dependent variable. D=BINOMIAL (which can be abbreviated D=B) tells PROC GENMOD that the dependent variable has a binomial distribution. The TYPE3 option requests likelihood-ratio statistics for all hypothesis tests.

Output 7.3   *ML Estimates of the Complementary Log-Log Model for Job Duration Data*

Parameter		DF	Estimate	Std Err	ChiSquare	Pr>Chi
INTERCEPT		1	2.1955	0.8814	6.2050	0.0127
ED		1	0.1655	0.0634	6.8171	0.0090
PRESTIGE		1	-0.0926	0.0123	56.5157	0.0001
SALARY		1	-0.0229	0.0088	6.7346	0.0095
YEAR	1	1	-2.0954	0.6563	10.1941	0.0014
YEAR	2	1	-1.1098	0.6103	3.3070	0.0690
YEAR	3	1	0.0489	0.5790	0.0071	0.9327
YEAR	4	1	0.2131	0.6214	0.1176	0.7317
YEAR	5	0	0.0000	0.0000	.	.
SCALE		0	1.0000	0.0000	.	.

LR Statistics For Type 3 Analysis

Source	DF	ChiSquare	Pr>Chi
ED	1	6.8211	0.0090
PRESTIGE	1	84.1978	0.0001
SALARY	1	9.8945	0.0017
YEAR	4	30.9055	0.0001

The coefficients in Output 7.3 are directly comparable to those in Output 5.9 for the EXACT method in PROC PHREG. Indeed, they are very similar—much closer to each other than either is to the two approximate methods in Output 5.9. On the other hand, the EXACT method took over seven times as much computer time as the complementary log-log method, even though the latter was based on nearly three times as many observations.

We can interpret the coefficients just as if this were a proportional hazards model. A one-year increase in education produces a 100(exp(.1655)-1)=18 percent increase in the hazard of quitting. A one-unit increase in prestige yields a 100(exp(-.0926)−1)=−9 percent change in the hazard of quitting. For a thousand-dollar increase in salary, we get a 100(exp(-0.0229)−1)=−2 percent change in the hazard of quitting.

Again, we see a strong effect of YEAR, with approximately the same pattern as in the logit model. As with that model, we can easily estimate constrained effects of YEAR by including the appropriate transformed variable as a covariate. Some of these constrained models have familiar names. If the logarithm of YEAR is a covariate, then we are estimating a Weibull model. If we just include YEAR itself (without the CLASS statement), we have the Gompertz model described briefly in Chapter 2, "Basic Concepts of Survival Analysis," but not otherwise available in SAS.

Comparing the results in Output 7.3 with those for the logit model in Output 7.2, we see that the coefficients are somewhat larger for the logit model but the chi-square statistics and *p*-values are similar. This is the usual pattern. Only rarely do the two methods lead to different qualitative conclusions.

The GENMOD procedure has a couple of features that make it an attractive alternative to PROC LOGISTIC and PROC PROBIT. First, as already noted, you can get likelihood-ratio chi-square statistics in addition to the usual Wald chi-square statistics. In Output 7.3, the chi-square statistics reported in the upper table are the standard Wald chi-square statistics calculated by squaring the ratio of the coefficient to its standard error. The likelihood-ratio chi-square statistics are given below. As I've mentioned in earlier chapters, there is some evidence that likelihood-ratio statistics more closely approximate a true chi-square distribution in small to moderate-sized samples. In this example, the likelihood-ratio chi-square statistics for SALARY and PRESTIGE are noticeably larger than the Wald chi-square statistics, although the reverse can easily happen.

A second major advantage of PROC GENMOD is the ability to specify interactions in the MODEL statement (as in PROC GLM) rather than having to create the appropriate variables in a DATA step. For example, suppose we want to know if the effect of SALARY varies by YEAR. We can accomplish that by specifying the following:

```
model quit/n=ed prestige salary year salary*year
      / d=binomial link=cloglog type3;
```

The resulting chi-square statistic for the interaction is 8.19 with 4 d.f., for a *p*-value of .08. There is insufficient evidence, then, to conclude that the effect of salary varies by year.

DATA WITH TIME-DEPENDENT COVARIATES

Since the maximum likelihood method is particularly effective at handling time-dependent covariates, let's look at another example with three covariates that change over time. The sample consists of 301 male biochemists who received their doctorates in 1956 or 1963. At some point in their careers, all of these biochemists had jobs as assistant professors at graduate departments in the U.S. The event of interest is a promotion to associate professor. The biochemists were followed for a maximum of 10 years after beginning their assistant professorships. For a complete description of the data and its sources, see Long, Allison, and McGinnis (1993). That article focuses on comparisons of men and women, but here I look only at men in order to simplify the analysis. The data set includes the following variables:

DUR   years from beginning of job to promotion or censoring.

EVENT   has a value of 1 if the person was promoted; otherwise, EVENT has a value of 0.

UNDGRAD   *selectivity* of undergraduate institution (ranges from 1 to 7).

PHDMED   has a value of 1 if the person received his Ph.D. from a medical school; otherwise, PHMED has a value of 0.

PHDPREST   a measure of prestige of the person's Ph.D. institution (ranges from 0.92 to 4.62).

ART1-ART10   the cumulative number of articles the person published in each of the 10 years.

CIT1-CIT10   the number of citations in each of the 10 years to all previous articles.

PREST1   a measure of prestige of the person's first employing institution (ranges from 0.65 to 4.6).

PREST2   prestige of the person's second employing institution (coded as missing for those who did not change employers). No one had more than two employers during the period of observation.

JOBTIME   year of employer change, measured from start of assistant professorship (coded as missing for those who did not change employers).

The covariates describing the biochemists' graduate and undergraduate institutions are fixed over time, but article counts, citation counts, and employer prestige all vary with time. The citation counts, taken from *Science Citation Index* (Institute for Scientific Information), are sometimes interpreted as a measure of the *quality* of a scientist's published work, but it may be more appropriate to regard them as a measure of *impact* on the work of other scientists.

The first and most complicated step is to convert the file of 301 persons into a file of person-years. The following DATA step accomplishes that task:

```
data rankyrs;
   infile 'c:rank.dat';
   input dur event undgrad phdmed phdprest art1-art10
         cit1-cit10 prest1 prest2 jobtime;
   array arts(*) art1-art10;
   array cits(*) cit1-cit10;
```

```
    if jobtime=. then jobtime=11;
    do year=1 to dur;
        if year=dur and event=1 then promo=1;
            else promo=0;
        if year ge jobtime then prestige=prest2;
            else prestige=prest1;
        articles=arts(year);
        citation=cits(year);
        year2=year*year;
        output;
    end;
  run;
```

This DATA step has the same basic structure as the one for the job duration data. The DO loop creates and outputs a record for each person-year, for a total of 1,741 person-years. Within the DO loop, the dependent variable (PROMO) has a value of 1 if a promotion occurred in that person-year; otherwise, PROMO has a value of 0.

What's new is that the multiple values of each time-dependent covariate must be read into a single variable for each of the person-years. For the article and citation variables, which change every year, we create arrays that enable us to refer to, say, articles in year 3 as ARTS(3). For the two job prestige variables, we must test to see whether the current year (in the DO loop) is greater than or equal to the year in which a change occurred. If it is, we assign the later value to the variable PRESTIGE; otherwise, PRESTIGE is assigned the earlier value. Note that for this to work, we recode the JOBTIME variable so that missing values (for people who didn't have a second employer) are recoded as 11. That way the DO loop index, which has a maximum value of 10, never equals or exceeds this value. Finally, we define YEAR2 equal to YEAR squared so that we can fit a quadratic function of time.

Now we can proceed to estimate regression models. For academic promotions, which usually take effect at the beginning of an academic year, it makes sense to think of time as being truly discrete. A logit model, then, seems entirely appropriate. Using PROC LOGISTIC, we specify the model as follows:

```
  proc logistic descending data=rankyrs;
      model promo=undgrad phdmed phdprest articles citation
            prestige year year2;
  run;
```

The DESCENDING option in the PROC LOGISTIC statement forces PROC LOGISTIC to model the probability of a 1 rather than the probability of a 0.

Output 7.4 *Estimates of Logit Model for Academic Promotions*

Variable	DF	Parameter Estimate	Standard Error	Wald Chi-Square	Pr > Chi-Square	Standardized Estimate	Odds Ratio
INTERCPT	1	-8.4767	0.7758	119.3807	0.0001	.	0.000
UNDGRAD	1	0.1947	0.0636	9.3785	0.0022	0.146561	1.215
PHDMED	1	-0.2355	0.1718	1.8804	0.1703	-0.062241	0.790
PHDPREST	1	0.0270	0.0931	0.0841	0.7719	0.014524	1.027
ARTICLES	1	0.0734	0.0181	16.3590	0.0001	0.242278	1.076
CITATION	1	0.00013	0.00131	0.0098	0.9212	0.005878	1.000
PRESTIGE	1	-0.2569	0.1139	5.0888	0.0241	-0.111086	0.773
YEAR	1	2.0811	0.2337	79.2863	0.0001	2.583886	8.013
YEAR2	1	-0.1585	0.0203	60.9980	0.0001	-1.879202	0.853

Output 7.4 shows the results. Not surprisingly, there is a strong effect of number of years as an assistant professor. The odds of a promotion increases rapidly with time, but at a decreasing rate; there is actually some evidence of a reversal after seven years. I also estimated a model with a set of 10 dummy variables for years as an assistant professor, but a likelihood-ratio chi-square test showed no significant difference between that model and the more restricted version shown here. Higher-order polynomials also failed to produce a significant improvement. On the other hand, the chi-square test for comparing the model in Output 7.4 and a model that excluded both YEAR and YEAR2 was 178.98 with 2 d.f.

Article counts had the next largest effect (as measured by the Wald chi-square test): each additional published article is associated with an increase of 7.6 percent in the odds of a promotion. But there is no evidence of any effect of citations, suggesting that it's the quantity of publications that matters in promotions, not the importance or impact of the published work.

Somewhat surprisingly, while there is no effect of the prestige of the institution where a biochemist got his doctorate, there is a substantial effect of the selectivity of his undergraduate institution. Each 1-point increase on the 7-point selectivity scale is associated with a 21-percent increase in the odds of a promotion, controlling for other covariates. There is also a slightly *negative* effect of the prestige of the current employer, suggesting that it may be harder to get promoted at a more prestigious department.

Notice that once the person-year data set is created, the time-dependent covariates are treated just like fixed covariates. Thus, many models can be estimated with the saved data set without additional data manipulations, making it especially convenient to estimate models with large numbers of time dependent covariates. By contrast, in PROC PHREG the time-dependent covariates must be recalculated whenever a new model is estimated.

ISSUES AND EXTENSIONS

In this section, we look at a number of complications and concerns that arise in the analysis of tied data using maximum likelihood methods.

Dependence among the Observations?

A common reaction to the methods described in this chapter is that there must be something wrong. In general, when multiple observations are created for a single individual, it's reasonable to suppose that those observations are not independent, thereby violating a basic assumption used to construct the likelihood function. The consequence is thought to be biased standard error estimates and inflated test statistics. Even worse, there are different numbers of observations for different individuals, so some appear to get more weight than others.

While concern about dependence is often legitimate, it is not applicable here. In this case, the creation of multiple observations is not an ad-hoc method; rather, it follows directly from factoring the likelihood function for the data (Allison 1982). The basic idea is this. In its original form, the likelihood for data with no censoring can be written as a product of probabilities over all n observations,

$$\prod_{i=1}^{n} \Pr(T_i = t_i) \tag{7.3}$$

where T_i is the random variable and t_i is the particular value observed for individual i. Each of the probabilities in equation (7.3) can be factored in the following way. If $t_i = 5$, we have

$$\Pr(T_i = 5) \ = \ P_{i5}(1 - P_{i4})(1 - P_{i3})(1 - P_{i2})(1 - P_{i1}) \tag{7.4}$$

where, again, P_{it} is the conditional probability of an event at time t, given that an event has not already occurred. This factorization follows immediately from the definition of conditional probability. Each of the five terms in equation (7.4) may be treated as though it came from a distinct, independent observation.

For those who may still be unconvinced, a comparison of the standard errors in Output 5.10 with those in Output 7.2 should be reassuring. They are virtually identical, despite the fact that the partial likelihood estimates in Output 5.10 are based on 100 persons, while the maximum likelihood estimates in Output 7.2 are based on 272 person-years.

This lack of dependence holds only when no individual has more than one event. When events are repeatable, as discussed in Chapter 8, "Heterogeneity, Repeated Events, and Other Topics," there is a real problem of dependence. But the problem is neither more nor less serious than it is for other methods of survival analysis.

Handling Large Numbers of Observations

Although the creation of multiple observations for each individual does not violate any assumptions about independence, it may cause practical problems when the number of individuals is large and the time intervals are small. For example, if you have a sample of 1,000 persons observed at monthly intervals over a five-year period, you could end up with a working data set of nearly 60,000 person-months. While this is not an impossibly large number, it can certainly increase the time you spend waiting for results, thereby inhibiting exploratory data analysis.

If you find yourself in this situation, there are several options you may want to consider:

- First, you should ask yourself if you really need to work with such small time intervals. If the time-dependent covariates are only changing annually, you might as well switch from person-months to person-years. True, there will be some loss of precision in the estimates, but this is usually minimal. And by switching to the piecewise exponential model described in Chapter 4 (which has a similar data structure), you can even avoid the loss of precision. On the other hand, if the time-dependent covariates *are* changing at monthly intervals, you really should stick to that level of analysis.

- Second, if your covariates are all categorical or they at least have a small number of levels, you can achieve great computational economy by estimating the models from data that are grouped by covariate values. You can achieve this economy by using PROC SUMMARY to create a grouped data set and then using the grouped data syntax in PROC LOGISTIC, PROC PROBIT, or PROC GENMOD. Alternatively, PROC CATMOD will automatically group the data when you specify a logit model, and you can save the grouped data set for further analysis.

- Third, if you are estimating logit models, you may want to sample on the dependent variable, at least for exploratory analysis. Typically, the data sets created for the methods in this chapter have a dichotomous dependent variable with an extreme split—the number of nonevents will be many times larger than the number of events. What you can do is take *all* the observations with events and a random subsample of the observations without events, so that the two groups are approximately equal. Is this legitimate? Well, it is for the logit model (but not for the complementary log-log model). It is now fairly well known that random sampling on the dependent variable in a logit analysis does not bias coefficient estimates (Prentice and Pike 1979).

■ Fourth, you may want to consider abandoning the maximum likelihood approach and using partial likelihood with Efron's approximation. If the time intervals are small, then the data will probably not have a large number of ties, and the Efron approximation should work well. Of course, you lose the ability to test hypotheses about the dependence of the hazard on time.

Unequal Intervals

To this point, we have assumed that the time intervals giving rise to tied survival times are all of equal length. It's not uncommon, however, for some intervals to be longer than others, either by design or by accident. For example, a study of deaths following surgery may have weekly follow-ups soon after the surgery when the risk of death is highest and then switch to monthly follow-ups later on. Some national panel studies, like the Panel Survey of Income Dynamics, were conducted annually in most years, but not in all. As a result, some intervals are two years long instead of one. Even if the intervals are equal by design, it often happens that some individuals cannot be reached on some follow-ups.

Regardless of the reason, it should be obvious that, other things being equal, the probability of an event will increase with the length of the interval. And if time-dependent covariates are associated with interval length, the result can be biased coefficient estimates. The solution to this problem depends on the pattern of unequal intervals and the model being estimated.

There is one case in which no special treatment is needed. If you are estimating the models in equation (7.1) or equation (7.2), which place no restrictions on the effect of time, *and* if the data are structured so that every individual's interval at time *t* is the same length as every other individual's interval at time *t*, then the separate parameters that are estimated for every time interval automatically adjust for differences in interval length. This situation is not as common as you might think, however. Even when intervals at the same *calendar* time have the same length, intervals at the same *event* time will have different lengths whenever individuals have different origin points.

In all other cases, an ad-hoc solution will usually suffice: simply include the length of the interval as a covariate in the model. If there are only two distinct interval lengths, a single dummy variable will work. If there are a small number of distinct lengths, construct a set of dummy variables. If there are many different lengths, you will probably need to treat length as a continuous variable but include a squared term in the model to adjust for nonlinearity.

Empty Intervals

In some data sets, there are time intervals in which no individual experiences an event. For example, in the leader data that we analyzed in Chapter 6, "Competing Risks," none of the 472 leaders lost power in the 22nd year of rule. Naturally, this is most likely to occur when the number of time intervals is large and the number of individuals is small. Whenever there are *empty* intervals, if you try to estimate a model with an unrestricted effect of time, as in equation (7.1) or equation (7.2), the ML algorithm will not converge. This result is a consequence of the following general principle. For any dichotomous covariate, consider the 2×2 contingency table formed by that covariate and the dichotomous dependent variable. If any of the four cells in that table has a frequency of 0, the result is nonconvergence.

An easy solution is to fit a model with restrictions on the time effect. The quadratic function that was estimated in Output 7.4, for example, will not suffer from this problem. Alternatively, if you don't want to lose the flexibility of the unrestricted model, you can constrain the coefficient for any empty interval to be the same as that of an adjacent interval. The simplest way to do this is to recode the variable containing the interval values so that the adjacent intervals have the same value. For the leader data, this requires a DATA step with the following statement:

```
if year=22 then year=21;
```

Then specify YEAR as a CLASS variable in PROC PROBIT or PROC GENMOD. Instead of separate dummy (indicator) variables for years 21 and 22, this code produces one dummy variable equal to 1 if an event time was equal to either of those two years; otherwise, the variable is equal to 0.

Left Truncation

In Chapter 5, we discussed a problem known as left truncation, in which individuals are not at risk of an event until some time after the origin time. This commonly occurs when "survivors" are recruited into a study at varying points in time. We saw how this problem can be easily corrected with the partial likelihood method using PROC PHREG. The solution is equally easy for the maximum likelihood methods discussed in this chapter, although quite different in form. In creating the multiple observations for each individuals, you simply delete any time units in which the individual is known not to be at risk of an event. For example, if patients are recruited into a study at various times since diagnosis, no observational units are created for time intervals that occurred prior to recruitment. We can still include time since diagnosis as a covariate, however.

This method also works for temporary withdrawals from the risk set. If your goal is to predict migration of people from Mexico to the U.S., you will probably want to remove anyone from the risk set when he or she was in prison, in the military, and so on. Again, you simply exclude any time units in which the individual is definitely not at risk.

Competing Risks

In Chapter 6, we saw that the likelihood function for data arising from multiple event types can be factored into a separate likelihood function for each event type, treating other event types as censoring. Strictly speaking, this result only holds when time is continuous and measured precisely, so that there are no ties. When time is discrete or when continuous-time data are grouped into intervals, the likelihood function does *not* factor. If you want full-information maximum likelihood estimates, you must estimate a model for all events simultaneously. On the other hand, it's also possible to do separate analyses for each event type without biasing the parameter estimates and with only slight loss of precision.

These points are most readily explained for the logit model for competing risks. Let P_{ijt} be the conditional probability that an event of type j occurs to person i at time t, given that no event occurs prior to time t. The natural extension of the logit model to multiple event types is the multinomial logit model:

$$P_{ijt} = \frac{\exp\{\beta_j x_{it}\}}{1 + \sum_k \exp\{\beta_k x_{it}\}},$$

or, equivalently

$$\log\left(\frac{P_{ijt}}{P_{i0t}}\right) = \beta_j x_{it},$$

where P_{i0t} is the probability that no event occurs at time t to individual i. As in the case of a single event type, the likelihood for data arising from this model can be manipulated so that each discrete-time point for each individual appears as a separate observation. If there are, say, three event types, these individual time units can have a dependent variable coded 1, 2, or 3 if an event occurred and coded 4 if no event occurred. We can then use PROC CATMOD to estimate the model simultaneously for all event types.

For the job-duration data analyzed earlier in this chapter, suppose that there are actually two event types, quitting (EVENT=1) and being fired

(EVENT=2). The following statements produce a person-year data set with a dependent variable called OUTCOME, which is coded 1 for quit, 2 for fired, and 3 for neither:

```
data jobyrs2;
   set jobdur;
   do year=1 to dur;
      if year=dur and event=1 then outcome=1;
      else if year=dur and event=2 then outcome=2;
      else outcome=3;
      output;
   end;
run;
```

We can use PROC CATMOD to estimate the multinomial logit model:

```
proc catmod data=jobyrs2;
   direct ed prestige salary year;
   model outcome=ed prestige salary year / noprofile noiter;
run;
```

The DIRECT statement forces the four covariates to be treated as quantitative variables rather than categorical variables. NOPROFILE and NOITER merely suppress unneeded output.

Output 7.5 displays the results. The analysis-of-variance table gives statistics for testing the null hypothesis that *both* coefficients for each covariate are 0, a hypothesis that is resoundingly rejected for ED, PRESTIGE, and YEAR. The effect of SALARY is less dramatic, but still significant at the .03 level. The lower portion of the table gives the coefficient estimates and their respective test statistics. The odd-numbered parameters all pertain to the contrast between type 1 (quit) and no event, while the even-numbered parameters all pertain to the contrast between type 2 (fired) and no event. (PROC CATMOD treats no event as the reference category because it has the largest coded value, 3). We see that education increases the odds of quitting but reduces the odds of being fired, with both coefficients highly significant. Prestige of the job, on the other hand, reduces the risk of quitting while increasing the risk of being fired. Again, both coefficients are highly significant. Finally, the odds of quitting increase markedly with each year, but the odds of being fired hardly change at all.

Output 7.5 *PROC CATMOD Results for Competing Risks Analysis of Job Data*

```
        MAXIMUM-LIKELIHOOD ANALYSIS-OF-VARIANCE TABLE

        Source                DF    Chi-Square     Prob

        ------------------------------------------------
        INTERCEPT              2         1.03     0.5965
        ED                    2        21.07     0.0000
        PRESTIGE              2        66.56     0.0000
        SALARY                2         6.75     0.0342
        YEAR                  2        19.56     0.0001


        LIKELIHOOD RATIO     534       269.58     1.0000



           ANALYSIS OF MAXIMUM-LIKELIHOOD ESTIMATES

                                        Standard   Chi-
        Effect        Parameter  Estimate   Error   Square    Prob

        ---------------------------------------------------------
        INTERCEPT          1      0.3286   0.8196    0.16   0.6885
                           2     -1.5491   1.6921    0.84   0.3599
        ED                 3      0.1921   0.0836    5.28   0.0216
                           4     -0.7941   0.2011   15.59   0.0001
        PRESTIGE           5     -0.1128   0.0169   44.47   0.0000
                           6      0.1311   0.0274   22.82   0.0000
        SALARY             7     -0.0255   0.0103    6.17   0.0130
                           8      0.0110   0.0150    0.53   0.4652
        YEAR               9      0.7725   0.1748   19.54   0.0000
                          10     -0.00962  0.2976    0.00   0.9742
```

Now, we'll redo the analysis with separate runs for each event type. For this, we rely on a well-known result from multinomial logit analysis (Begg and Gray 1984). To estimate a model for event type 1, simply eliminate from the sample all the person-years in which events of type 2 occurred. Then, do a binomial logit analysis for type 1 versus no event. To estimate a model for event type 2, eliminate all the person-years in which events of type 1 occurred. Then, do a binomial logit analysis for type 2 versus no event. Here's the SAS code that accomplishes these tasks:

```
proc logistic data=jobyrs2;
   where outcome ne 2;
   model outcome=ed prestige salary year;
run;

proc logistic data=jobyrs2;
   where outcome ne 1;
   model outcome=ed prestige salary year;
run;
```

This procedure is justified as a form of conditional maximum likelihood. The resulting estimates are consistent and asymptotically normal, but there is some loss of precision, at least in principle. In practice, both the coefficients and their estimated standard errors usually differ only trivially from those produced by the simultaneous estimation procedure. We can see this by comparing the results in Output 7.6 with those in Output 7.5. The advantages of separating the estimation process are that you can

- focus only on those event types in which you are interested
- specify quite different models for different event types, with different covariates and different functional forms.

Output 7.6   *PROC LOGISTIC Results for Competing-Risks Analysis of Job Data*

Analysis of Maximum Likelihood Estimates

Variable	DF	Parameter Estimate	Standard Error	Wald Chi-Square	Pr > Chi-Square	Standardized Estimate	Odds Ratio
INTERCPT	1	0.3672	0.8254	0.1979	0.6564	.	.
ED	1	0.1895	0.0840	5.0911	0.0240	0.292760	1.209
PRESTIGE	1	-0.1125	0.0169	44.3193	0.0001	-1.283707	0.894
SALARY	1	-0.0255	0.0103	6.1688	0.0130	-0.331824	0.975
YEAR	1	0.7637	0.1742	19.2200	0.0001	0.541032	2.146

Analysis of Maximum Likelihood Estimates

Variable	DF	Parameter Estimate	Standard Error	Wald Chi-Square	Pr > Chi-Square	Standardized Estimate	Odds Ratio
INTERCPT	1	-1.5462	1.7055	0.8220	0.3646	.	.
ED	1	-0.7872	0.1999	15.5021	0.0001	-1.182506	0.455
PRESTIGE	1	0.1300	0.0274	22.5031	0.0001	1.391817	1.139
SALARY	1	0.0118	0.0155	0.5844	0.4446	0.157079	1.012
YEAR	1	-0.0296	0.2913	0.0103	0.9191	-0.021124	0.971

Now, what about competing risks for the complementary log-log model? Here, things are a little messier. It is possible to derive a multinomial model based on a continuous-time proportional hazards model, and this could be simultaneously estimated for all event types using maximum likelihood. This is not a standard problem, however, and no SAS procedure will do it without a major programming effort. Instead, we can use the same strategy for getting separate estimates for each event type that we just saw in the case of the logit model. That is, we delete all individual time units in which events other than the one of interest occurred. Then we estimate a dichotomous complementary log-log model for the event of interest versus no event. In effect, we are deliberately censoring the data at the beginning of any intervals in which other events occur. This should not be problematic because, even if we have continuous-time data, we have to assume that the different event types are noninformative for one another. Once we eliminate all extraneous events from the data, we reduce the problem to one for a single event type. Again, there will be some slight loss of information in doing this.

CONCLUSION

The maximum likelihood methods discussed in this chapter are attractive alternatives to partial likelihood when there are many ties and many time-dependent covariates. Not only are they much more computationally efficient, but they also give direct estimates of the effect of time on the hazard of an event. In my experience, novices often have difficulty with both the conceptualization and implementation of time-dependent covariates in PROC PHREG. They easily make mistakes that go unnoticed. By contrast, the methods discussed here have great intuitive appeal and are relatively straightforward to implement. Once the expanded data set is constructed, the analyst can proceed as in an ordinary logit regression analysis with no need to treat time-dependent covariates any differently than fixed covariates. This approach also has advantages whenever there is ambiguity about the time origin. Because time is treated just like any other covariate, there is great flexibility in specifying and testing alternative functional forms, and multiple time scales with different origins can be included in the model.

CHAPTER **8**
Heterogeneity, Repeated Events, and Other Topics

p.233 *Introduction*

p.233 *Unobserved Heterogeneity*

p.236 *Repeated Events*

p.247 *Generalized* R^2

p.249 *Sensitivity Analysis for Informative Censoring*

INTRODUCTION

This chapter deals with several issues that arise for all the methods we have previously discussed. The first two issues—heterogeneity and repeated events—are closely related. One problem with the models we have been considering is that biological and social entities usually differ in ways that are not fully captured by the model. This *unobserved heterogeneity* can produce misleading estimates of hazard functions and attenuated estimates of covariate effects. When individuals can experience more than one event, unobserved heterogeneity can also produce dependence among the observations, leading to biased standard errors and test statistics. We'll survey a variety of methods for dealing with these problems. Later in the chapter, we'll see how to compute a generalized R^2 and how to gauge the possible consequences of informative censoring.

UNOBSERVED HETEROGENEITY

An implicit assumption of all the hazard models we have considered so far is that if two individuals have identical values on the covariates, they also have identical hazard functions. If there are no covariates in the model, then the entire sample is presumed to have a single hazard function. Obviously, this is an unrealistic assumption. Individuals and their environments differ in so many respects that no set of measured covariates can possibly capture all the variation among them. In an ordinary linear regression model, this residual or unobserved heterogeneity is explicitly represented by a random disturbance term, for example,

$$y = \beta x + \varepsilon$$

where ε represents all unmeasured sources of variation in y. But in a Cox regression model, for example, there is no disturbance term:

$$\log h(t) = \alpha(t) + \beta x.$$

The absence of a random disturbance term does not mean that the model is deterministic. There is plenty of room for randomness in the relationship between the unobserved hazard $h(t)$ and the observed event time. Nevertheless, the presence of unobserved heterogeneity can cause some difficult problems in estimating the hazard function as well as the coefficients for the covariates.

The most serious problem is this: unobserved heterogeneity tends to produce estimated hazard functions that decline with time, *even when the true hazard is not declining for any individual in the sample* (Proschan 1963; Heckman and Singer 1985). This fact is most easily explained by an example. Suppose we have a sample of 100 people, all of whom have hazards that are constant over time. The sample is equally divided between two kinds of people: those with a high hazard of death (h=2.0) and those with a lower hazard of death (h=0.5). Unfortunately, we don't know which people have which hazard, so we must estimate a hazard function for the entire sample. Figure 8.1 shows what happens. The empirical hazard function starts out, as you might expect, midway between .5 and 2. But then it steadily declines until it approaches .5 as an asymptote. What's happening is that the high hazard people are dying more rapidly at all points in time. As a result, as time goes by, the remaining sample (the risk set) is increasingly made up of people with low hazards. Since we can only estimate the hazard function at time t with those who are still at risk at time t, the estimated hazard will be more and more like the smaller hazard.

Figure 8.1 *Empirical Hazard Function Produced by Mixing Two Constant Hazards*

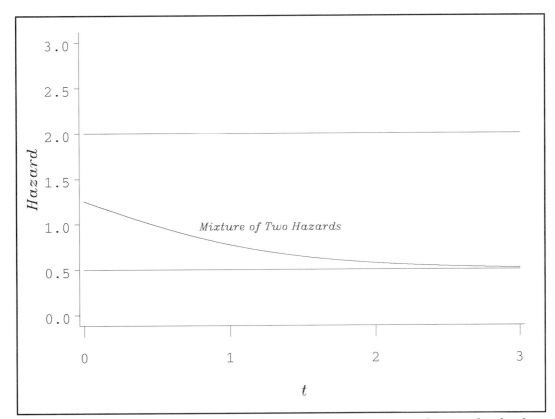

Of course, any real life situation will have more than two kinds of people, but the basic principle is the same. Those with higher hazards will tend to die (or experience whatever event is being studied) before those with lower hazards, leaving a risk set that is increasingly made up of low hazard people.

This problem has led to some potentially serious errors in interpreting research results. In the management literature, for example, there has been great interest in the hypothesis of the *liability of newness* (Hannan and Freeman 1984). This hypothesis says that when firms are just starting out, they are prone to failure because they lack capital, contacts, traditions, and so on. As firms get older and accumulate resources, they become more resistant to failure. Empirical studies invariably show that, in fact, younger firms do have higher rates of failure than older firms. But this fact does not necessarily prove the hypothesis. The results are equally consistent with the hypothesis that firms differ in their initial vulnerability to failure. Weaker firms go out of business quickly while stronger firms survive.

What can be done? As we'll see in the next section, when events are repeatable, it is quite feasible to separate the true hazard function from unobserved heterogeneity. But when events are not repeatable, as with both human and organizational death, the options are limited. If you find an empirical hazard function that is *increasing*, then you can validly conclude that the true hazard is increasing for at least some portion of the sample over some interval of time. But decreasing hazard functions are inherently ambiguous.

There have been numerous attempts to separate the hazard function from unobserved heterogeneity by formulating models that incorporate both. For example, we can insert a random disturbance term into a Weibull hazard model:

$$\log h(t) = \alpha \log t + \beta x + \varepsilon.$$

But models like this are highly sensitive to the choice of a distribution for ε or the form of the dependence on time. If such models are identified at all, it is only because of the imposition of a particular functional form. That situation is not conducive to drawing reliable conclusions.

What about estimates of the β coefficients? Are they affected by unobserved heterogeneity? Given what we know about linear models, it's a foregone conclusion that coefficients may be severely biased if the unobserved components are correlated with the measured covariates. The more interesting question is what happens when the unobserved disturbance is *independent* of the measured covariates. Early literature on this question seemed to suggest that coefficient estimates could be grossly biased in unexpected ways. But the work by Gail et al. (1984) is more persuasive. They showed that unobserved heterogeneity tends to attenuate the estimated coefficients toward 0. On the other hand, standard errors and test statistics are *not* biased. Therefore, a test of the hypothesis that a coefficient is 0 remains valid, even in the presence of unobserved heterogeneity. It's also important to realize that the attenuation of coefficients is not a problem unique to hazard models, but it occurs with a wide variety of nonlinear models, including logistic regression (Allison 1987).

REPEATED EVENTS

All the models and analyses in the preceding chapters presume that no individual experiences more than one event. That's a reasonable presumption if the event is a death. But most events in the social sciences are repeatable: births, marriages, job changes, promotions, arrests, residence changes, and so on. There are also many repeatable events that are of interest to biomedical scientists: tumor recurrences, seizures, urinary infections, and hospitalizations, to name only a few. Nevertheless, because so much of survival analysis has focused upon deaths, good methods for handling repeated events have been slow in coming. Several important developments have occurred in recent years, but little of that work has found its way into commercial software. In part, I suspect that's because a consensus on the best approach has yet to emerge. PROC PHREG does have some capabilities for handling repeated events, and I will describe those shortly. Before doing that, however, we need to consider what's wrong with conventional methods.

Problems with Conventional Methods

There are basically two approaches to analyzing repeated events with standard software. First, you can do a separate analysis for each successive event. Suppose, for example, that you have reproductive histories for a sample of ever-married women, and you want to estimate a model for birth intervals. You start with an analysis for the interval between marriage and the first birth. For all those women who had a first birth, you then do a second analysis for the interval between first birth and second birth. You continue in this fashion until the number of women gets too small to reliably estimate a model.

For a more detailed example, let's look at some simulated data on job changes. For 100 persons, I generated repeated job durations, from the point of entry into the labor market until 20 years had elapsed, at which time observation was terminated. Thus, people whose first job lasted more than 20 years were censored at year 20. Everyone else had exactly one censored job (the one still in progress in year 20) and at least one uncensored job. A total of 395 jobs were produced.

Each person was assigned a certain number of years of schooling (ED) that did not vary over jobs. Each job had a prestige score (ranging from 1 to 100), as well as a salary (in thousands of dollars) that remained constant during the job. The duration for each job was generated by a Weibull model that included ED, PRESTIGE, and the logarithm of SALARY as covariates. Coefficients were invariant across persons and across time.

Output 8.1 displays the first 20 cases out of the 395 jobs in the working data set. ID is a variable that distinguishes different persons. We see that these 20 jobs were held by four persons: 6 jobs for person 1, 1 job for person 2, 3 for person 3, and 10 for person 4. EVENT is the censoring indicator. The variable J simply keeps track of where each job is in a person's sequence of jobs. LOGSAL is the natural logarithm of salary.

Output 8.1 *First 20 Cases in Repeated Job Duration Data Set*

OBS	ID	EVENT	ED	J	DURATION	PRESTIGE	LOGSAL
1	1	1	7	1	2.3575	27	2.30259
2	1	1	7	2	4.5454	31	1.38629
3	1	1	7	3	1.0864	8	2.07944
4	1	1	7	4	3.5893	22	2.83321
5	1	1	7	5	4.6676	30	3.40120
6	1	0	7	6	3.7538	24	3.13549
7	2	0	14	1	20.0000	69	3.33220
8	3	1	16	1	7.3753	69	3.58352
9	3	1	16	2	11.2632	60	3.85015
10	3	0	16	3	1.3615	56	3.82864
11	4	1	12	1	1.1436	27	2.56495
12	4	1	12	2	0.7880	35	2.19722
13	4	1	12	3	1.0437	30	2.77259
14	4	1	12	4	0.2346	15	2.56495
15	4	1	12	5	0.7983	39	3.21888
16	4	1	12	6	1.2168	41	3.52636
17	4	1	12	7	0.9160	24	3.43399
18	4	1	12	8	0.3174	26	3.36730
19	4	1	12	9	0.6573	45	3.82864
20	4	1	12	10	1.7036	41	3.91202

The easiest way to run separate models for each job in the sequence is to sort the data by J and then include a BY statement in the PROC PHREG program:

```
proc sort data=jobmult;
   by j;
run;

proc phreg data=jobmult;
   model duration*event(0)=prestige logsal ed;
   by j;
run;
```

In Output 8.2, we see results for the first five job durations. As is typical of data like these, the number of observations declines substantially for each successive interval until, by the sixth job, it's really too small to support a credible analysis. The effect of PRESTIGE is fairly consistent over the five models, with more prestigious jobs having lower hazards of termination. The effect of ED is not significant in the second job, but it is clearly significant in the others. Its coefficient is much smaller for the first two jobs than for the later jobs. The salary effect varies greatly from job to job and hovers around the .05 level of significance, except for job 4, when it is far from significant.

Output 8.2 *PROC PHREG Coefficients for Successive Jobs (Selected Output)*

First Job (n=100)

Variable	DF	Parameter Estimate	Standard Error	Wald Chi-Square	Pr > Chi-Square	Risk Ratio
ED	1	0.172258	0.06597	6.81718	0.0090	1.188
PRESTIGE	1	-0.087139	0.01212	51.65374	0.0001	0.917
LOGSAL	1	-0.432494	0.21767	3.94785	0.0469	0.649

Second Job (n=72)

Variable	DF	Parameter Estimate	Standard Error	Wald Chi-Square	Pr > Chi-Square	Risk Ratio
ED	1	0.090441	0.06747	1.79675	0.1801	1.095
PRESTIGE	1	-0.071412	0.01555	21.08889	0.0001	0.931
LOGSAL	1	-0.770675	0.28446	7.33985	0.0067	0.463

Third Job (n=52)

Variable	DF	Parameter Estimate	Standard Error	Wald Chi-Square	Pr > Chi-Square	Risk Ratio
ED	1	0.433458	0.14648	8.75673	0.0031	1.543
PRESTIGE	1	-0.110485	0.02365	21.81831	0.0001	0.895
LOGSAL	1	-0.887060	0.41098	4.65871	0.0309	0.412

Fourth Job (n=34)

Variable	DF	Parameter Estimate	Standard Error	Wald Chi-Square	Pr > Chi-Square	Risk Ratio
ED	1	0.439562	0.12108	13.17837	0.0003	1.552
PRESTIGE	1	-0.101199	0.02613	14.99784	0.0001	0.904
LOGSAL	1	-0.194972	0.44619	0.19095	0.6621	0.823

Fifth Job (n=34)

Variable	DF	Parameter Estimate	Standard Error	Wald Chi-Square	Pr > Chi-Square	Risk Ratio
ED	1	0.349508	0.11327	9.52161	0.0020	1.418
PRESTIGE	1	-0.075922	0.02744	7.65587	0.0057	0.927
LOGSAL	1	-1.147650	0.58605	3.83492	0.0502	0.317

While this approach has some things going for it, it's inefficient in a couple of respects. It's tedious to do multiple analyses, and the more numbers you have to interpret, the more room there is for ambiguity and confusion. While it is tempting to interpret the job-to-job variations as real differences, I know for a fact that the underlying process is constant over time—after all, I generated the data! If the process is, in fact, invariant from one interval to the next, it's also statistically inefficient to produce several redundant estimates. That may not be much of a concern if you're working with census data and have 100,000 cases. But if you have only 100 cases, you want to use your limited information to the best advantage. An additional problem is that later jobs are a biased sample: the only people who had a fifth job are those who already had four jobs in the 20-year period. Of necessity, those four jobs were shorter than average, so it's likely that their fifth job will also be short.

There is a second general approach to repeated events that avoids these problems by treating each interval as a distinct observation, pooling all the intervals together, and estimating a single model. Output 8.3 shows the results of doing that for the 395 job durations. We now see that the effects of PRESTIGE and ED are highly significant, while the salary effect is far from significant.

Output 8.3   *PROC PHREG Results for Pooled Job Durations*

Variable	DF	Parameter Estimate	Standard Error	Wald Chi-Square	Pr > Chi-Square	Risk Ratio
LOGSAL	1	0.062486	0.11327	0.30431	0.5812	1.064
PRESTIGE	1	-0.092109	0.00597	237.80117	0.0001	0.912
ED	1	0.135422	0.02863	22.36942	0.0001	1.145

Unfortunately, this method introduces a new problem— dependence among the multiple observations. It's well known that whenever two or more observations come from the same unit (person, litter, organization), they tend to be more alike than two randomly chosen observations. In the birth interval example, we would expect that women who have short first intervals will also tend to have short second intervals, and so on. Pooling these observations without taking the dependence into account can lead to standard error estimates that are biased downward and test statistics that are biased upward. In essence, the estimation procedure is fooled into thinking it has more information than it actually does. Because observations are correlated, some of the apparent information in the sample is redundant.

Dependence among observations can be thought of as arising from unobserved heterogeneity. Second intervals tend to be like first intervals because there are unmeasured, stable factors affecting both intervals. If we could measure all of these factors and include them as covariates, the dependence problem would disappear. But, of course, that's not going to happen. As we saw in the preceding section, unobserved heterogeneity leads to artifactually declining hazard functions and coefficients that are attenuated toward 0. These two problems are still present with repeated events, but with the added problem of biased standard errors and test statistics. That's important to remember because some methods correct *only* the standard errors, while others can also correct biases in the coefficients and hazard functions.

Before we look at ways of correcting for dependence, let's first look at a simple way to *detect* it. Even though dependence is always likely to be present to some degree, it may be so small that it has trivial effects on the estimates. Hence, we need some way to judge just how substantial the problem is. Here's a simple ad-hoc way to do just that: Estimate a model for the *second* interval with length of the *first* interval as a covariate. You should also include the covariates you would otherwise put in the model since the important question is whether there is *residual* dependence after the effects of any covariates have been removed.

Output 8.4 shows the results of doing that for the 72 second jobs in the job duration data set. Two things are noteworthy here. First, the duration of the first job has a highly significant negative coefficient, indicating that long first jobs are associated with low hazards, implying long second jobs. Clearly, there is dependence here that ought to be corrected in some way. If the coefficient had *not* been significant, we could ignore the dependence without much fear of error. Second, the coefficients for the other covariates have changed substantially from the values in Output 8.2 for second jobs. While this is a further indication that dependence may be influencing the results in some way, these coefficients are not necessarily any better than those we have already estimated, and they may even be worse. In other words, this technique is only for diagnosing the problem, not for correcting it.

Output 8.4 *Model for Second Interval with First Interval as a Covariate*

Variable	DF	Parameter Estimate	Standard Error	Wald Chi-Square	Pr > Chi-Square	Risk Ratio
ED	1	0.036648	0.06953	0.27785	0.5981	1.037
PRESTIG2	1	−0.060441	0.01576	14.71353	0.0001	0.941
LOGSAL2	1	−0.283335	0.32508	0.75966	0.3834	0.753
DUR1	1	−0.269221	0.07639	12.42143	0.0004	0.764

Given the dependence in the job durations, we can't accept the pooled estimates in Output 8.3 at face value. At a minimum, the standard errors are likely to be too low and the chi-square statistics too high. The coefficients may also be attenuated toward 0, and there may be other biases if the unobserved heterogeneity is correlated with the measured covariates. (Note that these coefficient biases will also occur in the unpooled estimates in Output 8.2). What can we do about it? One approach is to ignore the possible biases and concentrate on getting better estimates of the standard errors and test statistics. The other approach is to formulate a model that incorporates unobserved heterogeneity and estimate that model by maximum likelihood or conditional likelihood. While this second approach can correct biases in the coefficients, it's more dependent on a correct specification of the model. For both approaches, there is at least one variant that we can implement with PROC PHREG.

The WLW Method

Wei, Lin, and Weissfeld (1989) proposed a method (WLW method) for getting robust variance estimates that allow for dependence among multiple event times. With these variance estimates, you can then get efficient pooled estimates of the coefficients and their standard errors, and you can also test a number of relevant hypotheses. The technique is sometimes described as a *marginal* or *population-averaged* method. The advantage of this method is that there is no need to make assumptions about the nature or structure of the dependence. On the other hand, there is no correction for biases in the coefficients that arise from unobserved heterogeneity. The WLW method can be implemented with Release 6.10, but it requires a PROC IML program (described in *SAS/STAT Software: Changes and Enhancements, Release 6.10*) to construct the new statistics. I've written a macro called WLW (described in Appendix 1, "Macro Programs") that makes it easy. For the job duration data, we can invoke the macro as follows:

```
%wlw(data=jobmult,dv=duration*event(0),cv=prestige logsal
    ed,evcnt=j,id=id,max=9,ties=efron)
```

DV is the usual specification of the dependent variable; CV is a list of covariates; EVCNT is the variable that records the number of the event in the individual's sequence; ID is a variable containing a unique identification number for each individual; and MAX is the maximum number of events recorded for any individual.

Here's an outline of what this macro does. First, it uses PROC PHREG to produce coefficient estimates for each event in the sequence, but it does so in such a way that all the coefficients show up in a single model. For some data sets, the number of cases at the higher levels of the event sequence may be so small that it's unreasonable to calculate coefficient estimates. In such cases, you can simply reduce the MAX= option to a lower number. For all the estimated coefficients, PROC PHREG outputs the DFBETA statistics described in the section **Residuals and Influence Statistics** in Chapter 5, "Estimating Cox Regression Models with PROC PHREG." PROC MEANS then sums those statistics for each individual. PROC IML uses these summed statistics to create the robust covariance matrix that is then used to produce test statistics and pooled coefficient estimates.

Here's a summary of the results from a WLW analysis of the job duration data. For testing the null hypothesis that all nine coefficients are equal for each covariate, we have

	Wald chi-square	df	p-value
PRESTIGE	14.78	8	.064
LOG-SALARY	12.01	8	.151
EDUCATION	19.31	8	.013

With the exception of education, the results seem reasonably consistent with equality of the coefficients. For the hypothesis that all coefficients are equal to 0, we have

	Wald chi-square	df	p-value
PRESTIGE	230.05	9	.0000
LOG-SALARY	44.51	9	.0000
EDUCATION	40.62	9	.0000

Clearly the hypothesis must be rejected in all three cases. Finally, the optimal, pooled coefficient estimates are

	Estimate	Standard error	Wald chi-square	p-value
PRESTIGE	-.0806	.0055	218.04	.0000
LOG-SALARY	-.674	.124	29.72	.0000
EDUCATION	.205	.044	21.32	.0000

These results should be compared with the naively pooled estimates in Output 8.3. The big difference is in the salary effect, which was positive and nonsignificant in Output 8.3 but is negative and highly significant here. For education, both the coefficient and the standard error are larger for the WLW analysis, with the chi-square statistic declining slightly. Finally, both the coefficient for prestige and its standard error remain about the same. Obviously the WLW method can produce different results than simple pooling. But, in this case at least, the changes were not quite as expected. In general, we expect the coefficients to remain about the same, with the standard errors increasing to correct for dependence.

The FEPL Method

A second approach to the problem of dependence not only corrects the standard errors and test statistics, but it also corrects for some or all of the bias in the coefficients caused by unobserved heterogeneity. The basic idea is to formulate a model that explicitly introduces a disturbance term representing unobserved heterogeneity. Models of this sort are sometimes described as *conditional* or *subject specific*.

Letting $h_{ij}(t)$ be the hazard for the jth event for individual i at time t, we can write

$$\log h_{ij}(t) = \alpha(t) + \beta x_{ij}(t) + \varepsilon_i$$

where ε_i represents unobserved heterogeneity. Notice that ε is subscripted by i but not by j, indicating that the unobserved component is constant from one job to the next. At this point, there are two ways to proceed. One way is to assume that ε_i is a random variable with a specified distribution, independent of x_{ij}. This leads to random-effects models or frailty models that can be estimated by maximum likelihood (Klein 1992; McGilchrist 1993). When events are repeated, such models are well identified and are not highly sensitive to choice of a distribution for ε. Unfortunately, SAS has no procedure for estimating models like this.

Alternatively, we can choose a fixed-effects model by assuming that ε_i is a set of fixed constants rather than a random variable. We can then absorb this constant into the baseline log-hazard function to yield

$$\log h_{ij}(t) = \alpha_i(t) + \beta x_{ij}(t).$$

This model allows for a separate baseline hazard function for each individual. We can easily estimate it with PROC PHREG by using the STRATA statement with an identification variable that distinguishes individuals. This is called the *fixed-effects partial likelihood* (FEPL) method. For the job duration data set, the SAS statements are as follows:

```
proc phreg data=jobmult nosummary;
   model duration*event(0)=prestige logsal;
   strata id;
run;
```

The NOSUMMARY option suppresses the information that is usually reported for each stratum. Otherwise, you get a line of output for every individual in the sample.

Notice that the variable ED is not included as a covariate. One drawback of the FEPL method is that it can only estimate coefficients for those covariates that vary across (or within) the successive spells for each individual. And since education does not vary over time for this sample, its effect cannot be estimated. On the other hand, the fixed-effect method implicitly controls not only for education *but for all constant covariates,* regardless of whether they are measurable and regardless of whether they are correlated with the measured covariates. In other words, this method controls for things like race, ethnicity, sex, religion, region of origin, personality—anything that's stable over time.

As Output 8.5 shows, a fixed-effects analysis for the job duration data yields results that are markedly different than those for the pooled, uncorrected analysis in Output 8.3, but they are not far off from the pooled WLW estimates in the preceding section. The estimates are also somewhat closer to the values used to generate the data.

Output 8.5 *Results of Fixed-Effects Partial Likelihood for Repeated Job Durations*

Variable	DF	Parameter Estimate	Standard Error	Wald Chi-Square	Pr > Chi-Square	Risk Ratio
LOGSAL	1	-0.810063	0.13817	34.37185	0.0001	0.445
PRESTIGE	1	-0.056451	0.00973	33.65095	0.0001	0.945

Fixed-effects partial likelihood was proposed by Chamberlain (1985) who expressed reservations about its use when the number of intervals varied across individuals and when the censoring time (time between start of an interval and the termination of observation) depended on the lengths of preceding intervals. Both of these conditions exist for the job duration data set and for most other applications to repeated events. Whatever the theoretical merit of these concerns, however, my own (1996) Monte Carlo simulations have convinced me that there is little or no problem in practice. There is one exception to that conclusion: the fixed-effects method does not perform well when the number of previous events is included as a covariate.

As noted, a major advantage of the FEPL method is that the unobserved disturbance term is allowed to be correlated with the measured covariates. However, when the disturbance term is *not* correlated with any of the covariates, the random-effects approach produces more efficient estimates (i.e., with smaller standard errors). This differential efficiency is especially great when the average number of events per individual is less than 2. The reason is that the FEPL method excludes two types of individuals from the partial likelihood function:

- those with no events, that is, those with only a single censored spell
- those with one uncensored spell and one censored spell, *if* the censored spell is shorter than the uncensored spell.

One circumstance in which the unobservable characteristics of individuals are not correlated with their measured characteristics is a randomized experiment. But with nonexperimental data, it's much safer to assume that they *are* correlated.

In sum, the FEPL method is the preferred technique for repeated events whenever

- the data do not come from a randomized experiment
- interest is centered on covariates that vary across intervals for each individual
- most individuals have at least two events
- there is a reasonable presumption that the process generating events is invariant over time.

If the data are produced by a randomized experiment or if the main interest is in covariates that are constant for each individual, a random-effects method is preferable. If a random-effects method is not available, the marginal method of Wei, Lin, and Weissfeld can correct the standard errors and test statistics, but it will not remove any biases due to unobserved heterogeneity.

Specifying a Common Origin for All Events

Another question that arises in the analysis of repeated events is whether the hazard varies as a function of time since the last event or time since the process began. All the analyses so far have made the former assumption, that the "clock" gets reset to 0 whenever an event occurs. But in many applications, it is reasonable to argue that the hazard depends on time since the individual first became at risk, regardless of how many intervening events have occurred. For example, the hazard for a job change may depend on time in the labor force rather than time in the current job.

PROC PHREG makes it easy to specify models in which the hazard depends on a single origin for all of an individual's events. As before, we create a separate record for each interval for each individual. But instead of a single variable containing the length of the interval, the record must contain a starting time (measured from the common origin) and a stopping time (also measured from the origin). Output 8.6 shows what the records look like for the job duration data set (omitting the covariates).

Output 8.6 *First 20 Cases for Job Duration Data with Start and Stop Times*

OBS	ID	EVENT	J	START	STOP
1	1	1	1	0.0000	2.3575
2	1	1	2	2.3575	6.9029
3	1	1	3	6.9029	7.9893
4	1	1	4	7.9893	11.5786
5	1	1	5	11.5786	16.2462
6	1	0	6	16.2462	20.0000
7	2	0	1	0.0000	20.0000
8	3	1	1	0.0000	7.3753
9	3	1	2	7.3753	18.6385
10	3	0	3	18.6385	20.0000
11	4	1	1	0.0000	1.1436
12	4	1	2	1.1436	1.9315
13	4	1	3	1.9315	2.9752
14	4	1	4	2.9752	3.2098
15	4	1	5	3.2098	4.0081
16	4	1	6	4.0081	5.2249
17	4	1	7	5.2249	6.1409
18	4	1	8	6.1409	6.4583
19	4	1	9	6.4583	7.1156
20	4	1	10	7.1156	8.8192

Letting START and STOP be variables containing the starting time and stopping time, the model is specified by the following program:

```
proc phreg data=strtstop;
    model (start,stop)*event(0)=prestige logsal ed;
run;
```

The results in Output 8.7 are quite similar to those in Output 8.3, which reset the origin for the hazard function at each job termination. Despite the fact that this method is billed as a technique for handling repeated events, it does nothing at all to solve the problem of dependence. It's possible, however, to combine it with the WLW method to get standard error estimates that *do* correct for dependence. On the other hand, you cannot use the FEPL method with the start-stop specification. The reason is that each individual is a separate stratum in FEPL. When events for an individual are arrayed on a common origin, the risk set for each event contains only one observation.

Output 8.7 *PROC PHREG Estimates with a Common Origin for Pooled Job Durations*

Variable	DF	Parameter Estimate	Standard Error	Wald Chi-Square	Pr > Chi-Square	Risk Ratio
PRESTIGE	1	-0.070950	0.00474	224.20460	0.0001	0.932
LOGSAL	1	-0.030983	0.11855	0.06831	0.7938	0.969
ED	1	0.113436	0.02935	14.93362	0.0001	1.120

GENERALIZED R^2

People who do a lot of linear regression tend to become attached to R^2 as a measure of how good their models are. When they switch to PROC LIFEREG or PROC PHREG, they often experience severe withdrawal symptoms because no similar statistic is reported. In this section, I show how a generalized R^2 can be easily calculated from statistics that *are* reported. Before doing that, I want to caution readers that R^2 is not all it's cracked up to be, regardless of whether it's calculated for a linear model or a proportional hazards model. In particular, R^2 does *not* tell you anything about how appropriate the model is for the data. You can obtain an R^2 of only .05 for a model whose assumptions are perfectly satisfied by the data and whose coefficients are precisely unbiased. Similarly, an R^2 of .95 does not protect you against severe violations of assumptions and grossly biased coefficients. All R^2 tells you is how well you can predict the dependent variable with the set of covariates. And even for prediction, some authorities argue that the standard error of the estimate is a more meaningful and useful measure.

Still, other things being equal, a high R^2 is definitely better than a low R^2, and I happen to be one of those who miss it if it's not there. With that in mind, let's see how we can calculate one for survival models. Unfortunately, there's no consensus on the best way to calculate an R^2 for non-linear models. In my opinion, many of the R^2s that are reported by some widely used packages are virtually worthless. The statistic that I describe here was proposed by Cox and Snell (1989) and was also one of three statistics endorsed by Magee (1990). It's the same statistic that is reported for PROC LOGISTIC in Release 6.10.

Let G^2 be the likelihood-ratio chi-square statistic for testing the null hypothesis that all covariates have coefficients of 0. This G^2 is reported directly by PROC PHREG and PROC LOGISTIC. For PROC LIFEREG and PROC PROBIT, you must calculate it yourself by fitting models both with and without the covariates and then taking twice the positive difference in the log-likelihoods. With that statistic in hand, you can calculate the R^2 as

$$R^2 = 1 - \exp\left\{-\frac{G^2}{n}\right\}$$

(8.1)

where n is the sample size. The justification for this formula is simple. For an ordinary linear regression model with normal error term, there is a likelihood-ratio chi-square statistic for the null hypothesis that all coefficients are 0. That chi-square statistic is related to the usual R^2 by the formula in equation (8.1). By analogy, we use the same formula for nonlinear models.

We can use this statistic for any regression model estimated by maximum likelihood or partial likelihood. Unlike the linear model, however, it cannot be interpreted as a proportion of variation in the dependent variable that is explained by the covariates. It's just a number between 0 and 1 that is larger when the covariates are more strongly associated with the dependent variable. Nevertheless, it seems to behave in similar ways to the usual R^2. In samples with no censored data, I have compared OLS linear regression models for the logarithm of time with various AFT models estimated by maximum likelihood and Cox models estimated by partial likelihood. In all cases that I have examined, the generalized R^2s from the likelihood-based procedures are similar in magnitude to the R^2 from the ordinary regression model.

Here are some examples. In Chapter 4, "Estimating Parametric Regression Models with PROC LIFEREG," we used PROC LIFEREG to estimate a Weibull model for the 432 cases in the recidivism data set, and we calculated a likelihood-ratio chi-square statistic of 33.48 for the test that all coefficients are 0. Applying the formula above, we get an R^2 of .0746. For the same data set, we used partial likelihood in Chapter 5 to estimate a proportional hazards model. As shown in Output 5.1, the likelihood-ratio chi-square statistic is 33.13, so the R^2 is virtually identical. For the 65 heart transplant cases, the PROC PHREG model in Output 5.6 had a likelihood-ratio chi-square statistic of 16.6, yielding an R^2 of .23.

SENSITIVITY ANALYSIS FOR INFORMATIVE CENSORING

In Chapters 2 and 6, we discussed the relatively intractable problem of informative censoring. Let's quickly review the problem. Suppose that just before some particular time t there are 50 individuals who are still at risk of an event. Of those 50 individuals, 5 are censored at time t. Suppose further that 20 of the 50 at risk have covariate values that are identical to those of the 5 who are censored. We say that censoring is *informative* if the 5 who are censored are a biased subsample of the 20 individuals with the same covariate values. That is, they have hazards that are systematically higher or lower than those who were not censored. Informative censoring can lead to parameter estimates that are seriously biased.

When censoring is random (that is, not under the control of the investigator), it's usually not difficult to imagine scenarios that would lead to informative censoring. Suppose, for example, that you're studying how long it takes rookie policemen to be promoted, and those who quit are treated as censored. It doesn't take much insight to suspect that those who quit before promotion have, on average, poorer prospects for promotion than those who stay. Unfortunately, there's no way to test this hypothesis. You can compare the performance records and personal characteristics of those who quit and those who stayed, but these are all things that would probably be included as covariates. Remember that what we're concerned about is what might be called *residual* informativeness, after the effects of covariates have been taken into account. And even if we could discriminate between informative and noninformative censoring, we have no standard methods for handling informative censoring. The best that can be done by way of correction is to include as covariates any factors that are believed to affect both event times and censoring times.

There is, however, a kind of sensitivity analysis that can give you some idea of the possible impact that informative censoring might have on your results. The basic idea is to redo the analysis under two extreme assumptions about censored cases. One assumption is that censored observations experience events immediately after they are censored. This corresponds to the hypothesis that censored cases are those that tend to be at high risk of an event. The opposite assumption is that censored cases have longer times to events than anyone else in the sample. Obviously, this corresponds to the hypothesis that censored cases are those that tend to be at low risk of an event.

This is the general strategy. Some care needs to be taken in implementation, however. Let's consider the leaders data that we analyzed extensively in Chapter 6. There were four outcomes, as coded in the variable LOST:

Code	Frequency	Reason
0	115	leader still in power at the end of the study
1	165	leader left office by constitutional means
2	27	leader died of natural causes
3	165	leader left office by nonconstitutional means

We saw that types 1 and 3 were similar in many respects. Output 6.11 displays estimates for a Cox model that combined types 1 and 3 but that treats types 0 and 2 as censoring. Now we want to see how sensitive those estimates in Output 6.11 are to possible informative censoring.

The censoring that occurred because the study ended is, in fact, random censoring because the leaders began their spells in power at varying points in time. It's possible that those who entered power later had higher or lower risks of exit than those who entered earlier. Nonetheless, we can control for this kind of random censoring by including START time as a covariate, which we did in Output 6.11. We can't do anything like that for deaths, however, so our sensitivity analysis will focus on the 27 cases that have a value of 2 for the LOST variable.

The first reanalysis assumes that if the 27 people had not died in a particular year, they would have *immediately* been removed from power by constitutional or nonconstitutional means. We can accomplish this reanalysis by removing the value 2 from the list of censored values in the MODEL statement, thereby treating it as if it were a 1 or a 3:

```
proc phreg data=leaders;
   model years*lost(0)=manner age start military conflict
         loginc literacy / ties=efron;
   strata region;
run;
```

The second reanalysis assumes that if those 27 leaders had not died of natural causes, they would have remained in power at least as long as anyone else in the sample. We still treat them as censored, but we change their censoring time to the largest event time in the sample, which, in this case, is 24 years. Since we're doing a partial likelihood analysis, we could change it to at any number greater than or equal to 24 and the result would be the same. If we were using PROC LIFEREG, which uses the exact times of all observations, we might want to change the censoring time to the longest observed time, either censored or uncensored. The longest censored time in this sample is 27 years.

Here's the SAS code for changing the censoring times to 24:

```
data leaders4;
   set leaders;
   if lost=2 then years=24;
run;

proc phreg data=leaders4;
   model years*lost(0,2)=manner age start military conflict
         loginc literacy / ties=efron;
   strata region;
run;
```

Compare the results for these two models, shown in Output 8.8, with those in Output 6.11. For each covariate, the two new estimates bracket the original estimate. The biggest difference is in the effect of age, which gets larger in the top panel, but much smaller in the bottom panel, to the point where it is no longer significant at the .05 level. This should not be surprising since AGE was the only variable of any importance in the model for deaths due to natural causes (Output 6.6). For the most part, however, the results in Output 8.8 are reassuring. We can be reasonably confident that treating natural deaths as noninformative censoring has no appreciable affect on the conclusions.

Output 8.8 *Sensitivity Analysis of Leaders Data for Informative Censoring*

Censored Cases Treated as Uncensored Cases

Variable	DF	Parameter Estimate	Standard Error	Wald Chi-Square	Pr > Chi-Square	Risk Ratio
MANNER	1	0.381453	0.15404	6.13230	0.0133	1.464
AGE	1	0.022885	0.00544	17.71749	0.0001	1.023
START	1	-0.017609	0.00813	4.69037	0.0303	0.983
MILITARY	1	-0.224045	0.15969	1.96845	0.1606	0.799
CONFLICT	1	0.129422	0.13029	0.98676	0.3205	1.138
LOGINC	1	-0.182036	0.08214	4.91121	0.0267	0.834
LITERACY	1	0.000670	0.00319	0.04409	0.8337	1.001

continued on next page

Output 8.8   continued

Censoring Times Recoded to 24

Variable	DF	Parameter Estimate	Standard Error	Wald Chi-Square	Pr > Chi-Square	Risk Ratio
MANNER	1	0.317252	0.15611	4.13008	0.0421	1.373
AGE	1	0.009960	0.00566	3.09478	0.0785	1.010
START	1	-0.013094	0.00824	2.52769	0.1119	0.987
MILITARY	1	-0.142010	0.16249	0.76381	0.3821	0.868
CONFLICT	1	0.208543	0.13673	2.32617	0.1272	1.232
LOGINC	1	-0.269625	0.08924	9.12811	0.0025	0.764
LITERACY	1	0.003772	0.00333	1.28110	0.2577	1.004

In interpreting output like this, you should remember that these are worst-case scenarios, and it's unlikely that either of the extremes is an accurate depiction of reality. The standard estimates are still the best guess of what's really going on. It's also worth noting that for many applications, one of these extremes may be much more plausible than the other. Naturally, you'll want to focus your attention on the extreme that is most sensible.

CHAPTER **9**
A Guide for the Perplexed

p.253 *How to Choose a Method*
p.256 *Conclusion*

HOW TO CHOOSE A METHOD

In this book we've examined many different approaches to the analysis of survival data: Kaplan-Meier estimation, log-rank tests, accelerated failure time models, piecewise exponential models, Cox regression models, logit models, and complementary log-log models. Each of these methods is worth using in some situations. Along the way I have tried to point out their relative advantages and disadvantages, but those discussions are scattered throughout the book. It's not easy to keep all the points in mind when designing a study or planning an analysis.

Many readers of early versions of this book urged me to provide a concluding road map for choosing a method of survival analysis. Although I give this kind of advice all the time, I do so here with some hesitation. While statisticians may have great consensus about the characteristics of various statistical methods, the choice among competing methods is often very personal, especially when dealing with methods as similar in spirit and results as those presented here. Five equally knowledgeable consultants could easily give you five different recommendations. I'm going to present some rules of thumb that I rely on myself in giving advice, but please don't take them as authoritative pronouncements. Use them only to the degree that you find their rationales persuasive.

Make Cox Regression Your Default Method

Given the relative length of Chapter 5, "Estimating Cox Regression Models with PROC PHREG," it will come as no surprise that I have a strong preference for Cox regression via PROC PHREG. This particular method

- is more robust than the accelerated failure time methods
- has excellent capabilities for time-dependent covariates
- handles both continuous-time and discrete-time data
- allows for late entry and temporary exit from the risk set
- has a facility for nonparametric adjustment of nuisance variables (stratification).

PROC PHREG can also do log-rank tests (using a single dichotomous covariate). With Release 6.10 (and later), PROC PHREG will even do Kaplan-Meier estimation (by fitting a model with no covariates and using the BASELINE statement to produce a table of survival probabilities).

Beyond these intrinsic advantages, Cox regression has the considerable attraction of being widely used, accepted, and understood. What's the point of choosing a marginally superior method if your audience is confused or skeptical and you have to waste valuable time and space with explanation and justification? For better or worse (mostly for better), Cox regression has become the standard, and it makes little sense to choose a different method unless you have a good reason for doing so. Having said that, I'll now suggest some possible good reasons. They are presented in the form of questions that you should ask yourself when deciding on a method.

Do You Have Many Time-Dependent Covariates?

Although PROC PHREG does a good job at handling time-dependent covariates, the programming necessary for creating and manipulating those covariates can often be complex and confusing. Furthermore, the complete code for creating the covariates must be a part of every PROC PHREG step. While this may be tolerable for a single time-dependent covariate, the task can easily become overwhelming when there are 15 or 20 such covariates. This is not uncommon in the social sciences where panel surveys with large numbers of questions are conducted at regular intervals of time.

In such situations, you may want to consider using one of the methods that produces multiple observations per individual: the piecewise exponential model described in Chapter 4, "Estimating Parametric Regression Models with PROC LIFEREG," or the logit and complementary log-log models of Chapter 7, "Analysis of Tied or Discrete Data with the LOGISTIC, PROBIT, and GENMOD procedures." With these methods, you need one DATA step to produce the multiple records, with all of the time-dependent covariates assigned the appropriate values for each record. Once the new data set is constructed, you can proceed to estimate as many models as you like with no additional data manipulation. In these models, the time-dependent covariates are treated just like the fixed covariates. This approach is particularly well suited to situations where an expert programmer is available to produce the data set, which is then passed to an analyst. The analyst can then fit relatively simple models without worrying about the complexities of the time-dependent covariates.

If you choose to go this route, then you must decide which of the three alternative methods is most appropriate. If the event times are measured with considerable precision, then the piecewise exponential method has the edge—there is no loss of precision in the estimation process. On the other hand, when event times are measured coarsely, the piecewise exponential method is inappropriate. In those cases, you should use the methods of Chapter 7. As we saw there, the complementary log-log model is preferable when there is an underlying continuous-time process, while the logit model is appropriate when the event times are truly discrete.

Is the Sample Large with Heavily Tied Event Times?

As we saw in Chapter 5, PROC PHREG *can* deal with situations in which there are many events occurring at the same recorded times using either the DISCRETE or the EXACT methods. Unfortunately, those options can take a great deal of computer time that increases rapidly with sample size. If you have a sample of 10,000 observations with only 10 distinct event times, you can expect to wait a long time before you see any output. Why wait when the alternatives are so attractive? The complementary log-log and logit methods of Chapter 7 estimate *exactly* the same models as the EXACT and DISCRETE methods with statistical efficiency that is at least as good as that provided by PROC PHREG. The only drawback is that you may have to reorganize the data to create multiple records per individual. If that's undesirable, another alternative is to fit accelerated failure time models with PROC LIFEREG using the interval censoring option. The disadvantage there is that you must choose one of the parametric models rather than leaving the hazard function unspecified. That brings us to the next question.

Do You Want to Study the Shape of the Hazard Function?

In some studies, one of the major aims is to investigate hypotheses about the dependence of the hazard on time. Cox regression is far from ideal in such situations because it treats the dependence on time as a nuisance function that cancels out of the estimating equations. You can still produce graphs of the baseline survival and hazard functions, but those graphs don't provide direct tests of hypotheses. And if you have any time-dependent covariates, you can't even produce the graphs.

With PROC LIFEREG, on the other hand, you can produce formal hypothesis tests that answer the following sorts of questions:

- Is the hazard constant over time?
- If not constant, is the hazard increasing, decreasing, or non-monotonic?
- If increasing (or decreasing), is the rate of change going up or down?

All of these questions are addressed within the context of smooth parametric functions. If that seems too restrictive, you can get much more flexibility with the piecewise exponential, logit, or complementary log-log models. With these models, the time scale is chopped into intervals, and the least restrictive models have a set of indicator variables to represent those intervals. Restrictions can easily be imposed to represent functions of almost any desired shape. A further advantage of these multiple-record methods is that two or more time axes can be readily introduced into a single model. A model for promotions, for example, could include time since last promotion, time since initial employment by the firm, time in the labor force, and time since completion of education.

So if you want to study the dependence of the hazard on time, there are good alternatives to Cox regression. But whatever method you use, I urge you to be cautious in interpreting the results. As we saw in Chapter 8, "Heterogeneity, Repeated Events, and Other Topics," the hazard function is strongly confounded with uncontrolled heterogeneity, which makes hazards look like they are declining with time even when they are constant or increasing. As a result, any declines in the hazard function may be purely artifactual, a possibility that you can never completely rule out.

Do You Want to Generate Predicted Event Times or Survival Probabilities?

As we saw in Chapter 5, you can use output from the BASELINE statement in PROC PHREG to get predicted median survival times or survival probabilities for any specified set of covariates. Because BASELINE produces a complete set of survivor function estimates, however, getting predicted values or five-year survival probabilities for a large number of observations can be rather cumbersome. Furthermore, predicted median survival times may be unavailable for many or all of the observations if a substantial fraction of the sample is censored. With PROC LIFEREG, on the other hand, you can easily generate predicted median survival times (or any other percentile) for all observations using the OUTPUT statement. Using my PREDICT macro, you can also produce estimated survival probabilities for a specified survival time.

Do You Have Left-Censored Data?

The only SAS procedure that allows for left censoring is PROC LIFEREG. In principle, it's possible to adapt Cox regression to handle left censoring, but I know of no commercial program that does this.

CONCLUSION

While it's good to consider these questions carefully, you shouldn't become obsessed with making the *right* choice. For most applications, a reasonable case can be made for two or more of these methods. Furthermore, the methods are so similar in their underlying philosophy that they *usually* give similar results. When they differ, it's typically in situations where the evidence is not strong for any conclusion. If you have the time, it's always worthwhile trying out two or more methods on the same data. If they lead you to the same conclusions, then your confidence is increased. If they are discrepant, your confidence is appropriately reduced. If they are widely discrepant, you should carefully investigate the reasons for the discrepancy. Perhaps you made an error in setting up one method or another. Maybe there's a serious peculiarity in the data. Search for outliers and examine residuals and influence diagnostics. Discrepancies are often a powerful indication that there is something important to be learned.

APPENDIX **1**

Macro Programs

p.259 *Introduction*

p.259 *The SMOOTH Macro*

p.261 *The LIFEHAZ Macro*

p.263 *The PREDICT Macro*

p.264 *The WLW Macro*

INTRODUCTION

In the main text, I introduced four macros for carrying out certain auxiliary analyses with PROC LIFETEST, PROC LIFEREG, and PROC PHREG. They are listed here with instructions and background information. They are also available on the World Wide Web at http://www.sas.com/.

All of the macro programs use keywords for the required and optional parameters. Default values (if any) are given after the equal sign in the parameter list. Thus, you only need to specify parameters that differ from the default value, and you can specify these parameters in any order in the macro call.

THE SMOOTH MACRO

The SMOOTH macro produces nonparametric plots of hazard functions using a kernel smoothing method (Ramlau-Hansen 1983). It works with either PROC LIFETEST or PROC PHREG. When used after PROC LIFETEST, the macro requires the data set produced by the OUTSURV option in the PROC LIFETEST statement. With PROC PHREG, the macro uses the data set produced by the BASELINE statement, and it specifically requires the survival probabilities. If there is more than one survival curve in the BASELINE or OUTSURV data set (e.g., if a STRATA statement is used in either procedure), SMOOTH produces multiple smoothed hazard curves on the same axes. The shape of the smoothed curve is heavily dependent on the WIDTH parameter that controls how much data on either side of a time point is used in estimating the hazard at that point. Narrower widths produce choppier graphs, while wider widths produce smooth graphs. The trick is to find a value that smooths over the random variation while preserving the major features. I recommend starting with the default (one-fifth of the range of event times) and adjusting from there. (It's easier than you might think. I find the process similar to focusing an overhead projector). SMOOTH requires SAS/GRAPH and SAS/IML software. It cannot be used with PROC PHREG if there are any time-dependent covariates because no BASELINE data set is produced.

For examples using SMOOTH, see the section **Log Survival and Smoothed Hazard Plots** in Chapter 3, "Estimating and Comparing Survival Curves with PROC LIFETEST," and the section **Estimating Survivor Functions** in Chapter 5, "Estimating Cox Regression Models with PROC PHREG."

Parameters

DATA=_LAST_	specifies the name of the data set containing survivor function estimates, produced by PROC LIFETEST or PROC PHREG. The default data set is the one most recently created.
TIME=	specifies the name of the variable containing event times.
SURVIVAL=SURVIVAL	specifies the name of the variable containing survivor function estimates (SURVIVAL is the automatic name in the OUTSURV data set produced by PROC LIFETEST).
WIDTH=	specifies the bandwidth of the smoothing function. The default bandwidth is one-fifth of the range of event times.

Program

```
%macro smooth (data=_last_, time=, width=, survival=survival);

data _inset_;
 set &data end=final;
 retain _grp_ _censor_ 0;
 t=&time;
 survival=&survival;
 if t=0 and survival=1 then _grp_=_grp_+1;
 keep _grp_ t survival;
 if final and _grp_ > 1 then call symput('nset','yes');
   else if final then call symput('nset','no');
 if _censor_=1 then delete;
 if survival in (0,1) then delete;
run;

proc iml;
use _inset_;
read all var {t _grp_};
%if &width ne %then %let w2=&width;
  %else %let w2=(max(t)-min(t))/5;
w=&w2;
```

```
z=char(w,8,2);
call symput('width',z);
numset=max(_grp_);
create _plt_ var{ lambda s group};
setin _inset_ ;
do m=1 to numset;
  read all var {t survival _grp_} where (_grp_=m);
  n=nrow(survival);
  lo=t[1] + w;
  hi=t[n] - w;
  npt=50;
  inc=(hi-lo)/npt;
  s=lo+(1:npt)`*inc;
  group=j(npt,1,m);
  slag=1//survival[1:n-1];
  h=1-survival/slag;
  x=(j(npt,1,1)*t` - s*j(1,n,1))/w;
  k=.75*(1-x#x)#(abs(x)<=1);
  lambda=k*h/w;
  append;
end;
quit;

%if &nset=yes %then %let c==group;
  %else %let c=;

proc gplot data=_plt_;
  plot lambda*s &c / vaxis=axis1 vzero haxis=axis2;
  axis1 label=(angle=90 f=titalic 'Hazard Function' ) minor=none ;
  axis2 label=(f=titalic "Time     (bandwidth=&width)") minor=none;
  symbol1 i=join color=black line=1;
  symbol2 i=join color=red line=2;
  symbol3 i=join color=green line=3;
  symbol4 i=join color=blue line=4;
run;
quit;

%mend smooth;
```

THE LIFEHAZ MACRO

The LIFEHAZ macro produces parametric plots of hazard functions based on models fitted by PROC LIFEREG. In the LIFEREG procedure, you must specify OUTEST=*name1* in the PROC LIFEREG statement. You must also use the OUTPUT statement with OUT=*name2* and XBETA=*name3*. By default, the hazard is plotted for the mean value of XBETA (the linear predictor). If you want a plot for a specific observation, you must specify the observation number (OBSNO) when you invoke the macro. This macro will not work if you use a CLASS statement in the LIFEREG procedure because no OUTEST data set is produced. This macro is also not intended for use when multiple

MODEL statements are used in a single PROC step. The macro requires SAS/GRAPH software.

For an example using LIFEHAZ, see the section **Generating Predictions and Hazard Functions** in Chapter 4, "Estimating Parametric Regression Models with PROC LIFEREG."

Parameters

OUTEST=   specifies the name of the data set produced by the OUTEST= option in PROC LIFEREG.

OUT=_LAST_   specifies the name of the data set produced by the OUT= option in PROC LIFEREG.

XBETA=   specifies the name used with the XBETA= option in the OUTPUT statement.

OBSNO=   specifies the sequence number of the observation for which you want plots of the hazard function. (The default method is to use the mean of the linear predictor to generate the hazards).

Program

```
%macro lifehaz(outest=,out=_last_,obsno=0,xbeta=lp);

data;
  set &outest;
  call symput('time',_NAME_);
run;

proc means data=&out noprint;
  var &time &xbeta;
  output out=_c_ min(&time)=min max(&time)=max mean(&xbeta)=mean;
run;

data;
  set &outest;
  call symput('model',_dist_);
  s=_scale_;
  d=_shape1_;
  _y_=&obsno;
  set _c_ (keep=min max mean);
  if _y_=0 then m=mean;
  else do;
    set &out (keep=&xbeta) point=_y_;
    m=&xbeta;
  end;
  inc=(max-min)/300;
  g=1/s;
  alph=exp(-m*g);
if _dist_='LNORMAL' then do;
  do t=min to max by inc;
  z=(log(t)-m)/s;
  f=exp(-z*z/2)/(t*s*sqrt(2*3.14159));
```

```
    Surv=1-probnorm(z);
    h=f/Surv;
    output;
    end;
end;
else if _dist_='GAMMA' then do;
  k=1/(d*d);
  do t=min to max by inc;
  u=(t*exp(-m))**(1/s);
  f=abs(d)*(k*u**d)**k*exp(-k*u**d)/(s*gamma(k)*t);
  Surv=1-probgam(k*u**d,k);
  if d lt 0 then Surv=1-Surv;
  h=f/Surv;
  output;
  end;
end;
else if _dist_='WEIBULL' or _dist_='EXPONENT' then do;
  do t=min to max by inc;
  h=g*alph*t**(g-1);
  output;
  end;
end;
else if _dist_='LLOGISTC' then do;
  do t=min to max by inc;
  h=g*alph*t**(g-1)/(1+alph*t**g);
  output;
  end;
end;
else put 'ERROR:DISTRIBUTION NOT FITTED BY LIFEREG';
run;

proc gplot;
  plot h*t / haxis=axis2 vaxis=axis1 vzero;
  symbol1 i=join v=none c=black;
  axis1 label=(f=titalic angle=90 'Hazard');
  axis2 label=(f=titalic justify=c 'time' f=titalic justify=c "&model");
run; quit;
%mend lifehaz;
```

THE PREDICT MACRO

The PREDICT macro produces predicted survival probabilities for specified survival times, based on models fitted by PROC LIFEREG. You must specify OUTEST=*name1* in the PROC LIFEREG statement. You must also use the OUTPUT statement with OUT=*name2* and XBETA=*name3*. This macro will not work if a CLASS statement is used in the LIFEREG procedure because no OUTEST= data set is produced. This macro is also not intended for use when multiple MODEL statements are used in a single PROC step. The macro requires SAS/GRAPH software.

For an example using PREDICT, see the section **Generating Predictions and Hazard Functions** in Chapter 4.

Parameters

OUTEST=	specifies the name of the data set produced by the OUTEST= option in PROC LIFEREG.
OUT=_LAST_	specifies the name of the data set produced by the OUT= option in PROC LIFEREG.
XBETA=	specifies the name used with XBETA= option in the OUTPUT statement.
TIME=	is the specified survival time to be evaluated. This time must be in the same metric as the event times.

Program

```
%macro predict (outest=, out=_last_,xbeta=,time=);

data _pred_;
_p_=1;
set &outest (keep=_dist_ _scale_ _shape1_ ) point=_p_;
set &out;
lp=&xbeta;
t=&time;
gamma=1/_scale_;
alpha=exp(-lp*gamma);
prob=0;
if _dist_='EXPONENT' or _dist_='WEIBULL' then prob=exp(-alpha*t**gamma);
if _dist_='LNORMAL' then prob=1-probnorm((log(t)-lp)/_scale_);
if _dist_='LLOGISTC' then prob=1/(1+alpha*t**gamma);
if _dist_='GAMMA' then do;
  d=_shape1_;
  k=1/(d*d);
  u=(t*exp(-lp))**gamma;
  prob=1-probgam(k*u**d,k);
  if d lt 0 then prob=1-prob;
  end;
drop lp gamma alpha _dist_ _scale_ _shape1_ d k u;
run;
proc print data=_pred_;
run;
%mend predict;
```

THE WLW MACRO

The WLW macro uses the method of Wei, Lin, and Weissfeld (1989) to produce tests and partial likelihood estimates for multivariate survival data, for example, repeated events. This method produces standard errors and test statistics that correct for possible dependence among the observations. The macro incorporates a SAS/IML program, written by Ying So, that appears in *SAS/STAT Software: Changes and Enhancements, Release 6.10.* The input data set must have one record for each spell (a time interval from origin to death or censoring). Multiple spells for a single individual must have a common identification number. Additional background is provided in **The WLW Method** in Chapter 8, "Heterogeneity, Repeated Events, and Other Topics," which also gives an example of usage. The WLW macro cannot be used with time dependent covariates, although the method could, in principle, be employed with such covariates. The macro will not work with SAS releases earlier than 6.10 because it uses the DFBETA statistics.

Parameters

DV=	specifies the two-part dependent variable, in the usual syntax for PROC PHREG.
CV=	specifies a list of covariates (the maximum number is 20).
EVCNT=	specifies the name of a variable that contains the number of the event in the individual's sequence.
ID=ID	specifies the name of a variable containing a unique identifier for each individual (either character or numeric).
MAX=	specifies the maximum number of events among all individuals. If you don't wish to analyze the higher order events (because of small subsample sizes), just enter a smaller number for MAX.
DATA=_LAST_	specifies the name of data set to be analyzed.
TIES=EFRON	specifies the method for handling ties (BRESLOW, EFRON, EXACT, or DISCRETE).

Program

```
/*Preliminary operations on parameter specifications*/
%do i=1 %to 20;
%let var&i=%scan(&cv,&i);
%if &&var&i=%then %goto out;
%if %length(&&var&i) > 6 %then %let vv&i=%substr(&&var&i,1,6);
%else %let vv&i=&&var&i;
%end;
%out: %let i=%eval(&i-1);
%let tot=%eval(&i*&max);
%do j=1 %to &i;
%let vdef&j=arr&j(_i_)=&&var&j*(evcnt=_i_);
%let cvd&j=&&vv&j..1-&&vv&j..&max;
%let ar&j=array arr&j(*) &&vv&j..1-&&vv&j..&max;
%end;

/*Create data set with covariate by time interactions*/
data expand;
ncv=&i;
set &data;
evcnt=&evcnt;
%do j=1 %to &i;
&&ar&j;
%end;
```

```
                    do _i_=1 to &max;
                      %do j=1 %to &i;
                        &&vdef&j;
                      %end;
                    end;
                    run;

                    /*Do PHREG model for all events*/
                    proc phreg data=expand outest=_a_ noprint;
                    model &dv=
                    %do j=1 %to &i;
                        &&cvd&j
                      %end;
                    /ties=&ties;
                    output out=_out1_ dfbeta=dt1-dt&tot/order=data;
                    id id;
                    strata &evcnt;
                    run;

                    /*Sum the DFBETA statistics*/
                    proc sort data=_out1_;
                    by id;
                    run;
                    proc means data=_out1_ noprint;
                    by id;
                    var dt1-dt&tot;
                    output out=_out2_(drop=id _type_ _freq_) sum=dt1-dt&tot;

                    /*Calculate the robust covariance matrix, perform tests*/
                    proc iml;
                    names={&cv};
                    nvar=ncol(names);
                    use _a_;
                    read all var _num_ into b;
                    b=b`;
                    use _out2_;
                    read all into x;
                    do i=1 to nvar;
                    stop=i*&max;
                    start=stop-&max+1;
                    bi=b[start:stop];
                    xi=x[,start:stop];
                    v=xi` * xi;
                    iv=inv(v);
                    se=sqrt(vecdiag(v));
                    reset noname;
                    cname={"Estimate", " Std Error"};
                    cname2={"Event"};
                    indx=(1:&max)`;
                    tmpprt=bi || se;
                    print / "Results For" (names[i]);
                    print indx[colname=cname2] tmpprt[colname=cname format=10.5];
                    print "Estimated Joint Covariance Matrix",, v;

                    /* H0: All coefficients equal to 0 */
                    chisq=bi` * iv * bi;
                    df=nrow(bi);
```

```
p=1-probchi(chisq,df);
print ,,"Testing H0: no treatment effects for" (names[i]), ,
"Wald Chi-Square = " chisq, "DF = " df,
"p-value = "p[format=5.4],;

/* H0: All coefficients equal to each other */
c=j(df-1,df,0);
do k=1 to df-1;
c[k,k]=1;
c[k,k+1]=-1;
end;
chisq= bi`*c`*inv(c*v*c`)*c * bi;
df=df-1;
p=1-probchi(chisq,df);
print ,,"Testing H0:Equal Coefficients for" (names[i]), ,
"Wald Chi-Square = " chisq, "DF = " df,
"p-value = "p[format=5.4],;

/* Assume coefficients equal. Estimate the common value */
nparm=nrow(bi);
e=j(nparm,1,1);
h=inv(e` * iv * e) * iv * e;
b1=h` * bi;
se=sqrt(h` * v * h);
zscore=b1 / se;
p=1- probchi( zscore * zscore, 1);
print ,,"Estimation of the Common Parameter for" (names[i]),,
"optimal weights = "h,
"Estimate = " b1,
"Standard Error = " se,
"z-score =" zscore,
"2-sided p-value = " p[format=5.4];
end;
quit;
run;

%mend wlw;
```

268

APPENDIX **2**
Data Sets

p.269 *Introduction*

p.269 *The MYEL Data Set: Myelomatosis Patients*

p.270 *The RECID Data Set: Arrest Times for Released Prisoners*

p.271 *The STAN Data Set: Stanford Heart Transplant Patients*

p.272 *The BREAST Data Set: Survival Data for Breast Cancer Patients*

p.272 *The JOBDUR Data Set: Durations of Jobs*

p.272 *The ALCO Data Set: Survival of Cirrhosis Patients*

p.273 *The LEADERS Data Set: Time in Power for Leaders of Countries*

p.274 *The RANK Data Set: Promotions in Rank for Biochemists*

p.275 *The JOBMULT Data Set: Repeated Job Changes*

INTRODUCTION

This appendix provides information about the data sets used as examples in this book. They are listed in the order in which they are discussed in the main text. All data are written in free format with the variables appearing in the order given in each of the following sections. These data sets are available via the Internet, as explained on the inside of the back cover.

THE MYEL DATA SET: MYELOMATOSIS PATIENTS

The MYEL data set contains survival times for 25 patients diagnosed with myelomatosis (Peto et al. 1977). The patients were randomly assigned to two drug treatments. The entire data set is listed in Output 2.1. These data are used extensively in Chapter 3 to illustrate the LIFETEST procedure and briefly in Chapter 5. The variables are as follows:

DUR	is time in days from the point of randomization to either death or censoring (which could occur either by loss to follow up or termination of the observation).
STATUS	has a value of 1 if dead; it has a value of 0 if censored
TREAT	specifies a value of 1 or 2 to correspond to the two treatments.
RENAL	has a value of 1 if renal functioning was normal at the time of randomization; it has a value of 0 for impaired functioning.

THE RECID DATA SET: ARREST TIMES FOR RELEASED PRISONERS

The RECID data set contains information on 432 inmates who were released from Maryland state prisons in the early 1970s. This data set is used briefly in Chapter 3 and extensively in Chapters 4 and 5. The first 20 cases are listed in Output 3.7. The data were kindly provided to me by Dr. Kenneth Lenihan who was one of the principal investigators. The aim of this research was to determine the efficacy of financial aid to released inmates as a means of reducing recidivism. Results from the study are described in Rossi, Berk, and Lenihan (1980). (This book also reports results from a much larger follow-up study done in Texas and Georgia.) Half the inmates were randomly assigned to receive financial aid (approximately the same amount as unemployment compensation). They were followed for one year after their release and were interviewed monthly during that period. Data on arrests were taken from police and court records. The data set used here contains the following variables:

WEEK   is the week of first arrest; WEEK has a value of 52 if not arrested.

ARREST   has a value of 1 if arrested; otherwise, ARREST has a value of 0.

FIN   has a value of 1 if the inmate received financial aid after release; otherwise, FIN has a value of 0. FIN is randomly assigned, with equal numbers in each category.

AGE   is the age in years at the time of release.

RACE   has a value of 1 if the inmate is black; otherwise, RACE has a value of 0.

WEXP   has a value of 1 if the inmate had full-time work experience before incarceration; otherwise, WEXP has a value of 0.

MAR   has a value of 1 if the inmate was married at the time of release; otherwise, MAR has a value of 0.

PARO   has a value of 1 if released on parole; otherwise, PARO has a value of 0.

PRIO   is the number of convictions prior to current incarceration.

EDUC	is the highest level of completed schooling, coded as
	2 = 6th grade or less
	3 = 7th to 9th grade
	4 = 10th to 11th grade
	5 = 12th grade
	6 = some college
EMP1-EMP52	represents the employment status in each of the first 52 weeks after release. These variables have values of 1 if the inmate was employed full time; otherwise, EMP1–EMP52 have values of 0. Data are missing for weeks after the first arrest.

THE STAN DATA SET: STANFORD HEART TRANSPLANT PATIENTS

Various versions of data from the Stanford Heart Transplant study have been reported in a number of publications. The data set used in Chapter 5, "Estimating Cox Regression Models with PROC PHREG," appeared in Crowley and Hu (1977). The sample consisted of 103 cardiac patients who were enrolled in the transplantation program between 1967 and 1974. After enrollment, patients waited varying lengths of time until a suitable donor heart was found. Patients were followed until death or until the termination date of April 1, 1974. Of the 69 transplant recipients, only 24 were still alive at termination. At the time of transplantation, all but four of the patients were tissue typed to determine the degree of similarity with the donor. The data set contains the following variables:

DOB	is the date of birth.
DOA	is the date of acceptance into the program.
DOT	is the date of transplant.
DLS	is the date last seen (death date or censoring date).
DEAD	has a value of 1 if the patient is dead at DLS; otherwise, DEAD has a value of 0.
SURG	has a value of 1 if the patient had open-heart surgery prior to DOA; otherwise, SURG has a value of 0.
M1	is the number of donor alleles with no match in the recipient (1 through 4).
M2	has a value of 1 if donor and recipient mismatch on the HLA-A2 antigen; otherwise, M2 has a value of 0.
M3	is the mismatch score.

All date variables are in the *mm*/*dd*/*yy* format.

THE BREAST DATA SET: SURVIVAL DATA FOR BREAST CANCER PATIENTS

The BREAST data set (displayed in Output 5.4) contains survival data for 45 breast cancer patients. The data are taken from Collett (1994) except that survival time for the eighth patient is changed from 26 to 25 to eliminate ties. The variables are as follows:

SURV   is survival time (or censoring time) in months, beginning with the month of surgery.

DEAD   1 = dead; 0=alive.

X   has a value of 1 if the tumor had a positive marker for metastatis; otherwise, X has a value of 0.

THE JOBDUR DATA SET: DURATIONS OF JOBS

The JOBDUR data set consists of 100 simulated observations of jobs and job holders. Results of analyzing these data were reported in Output 5.9 and 5.10. The variables are as follows:

DUR   is the length of the job in years (integer values only).

EVENT   1 = quit; 2 = fired; 0 = censored.

ED   is the number of years of completed schooling.

PRESTIGE   is a measure of the prestige of the job.

SALARY   is salary in thousands of dollars.

For the analyses in Chapter 5, firings were treated as censoring.

THE ALCO DATA SET: SURVIVAL OF CIRRHOSIS PATIENTS

The ALCO data set, displayed in Output 5.14, consists of simulated data for 29 alcoholic cirrhosis patients. The variables are as follows:

SURV   is the number of months from diagnosis until death or termination of study.

DEAD   has a value of 1 if the patient died; otherwise, DEAD has a value of 0.

TIME2-TIME10 represent the time of clinic visit in months since diagnosis.

PT1-PT10   is the blood coagulation measure at diagnosis and at subsequent clinic visits.

THE LEADERS DATA SET: TIME IN POWER FOR LEADERS OF COUNTRIES

The LEADERS data set, analyzed in Chapter 6, "Competing Risks," is described in detail by Henry Bienen and Nicolas van de Walle (1991), who generously provided me with the data. Each record in the data set corresponds to a spell in power for a primary leader of a country. I used a subset of the original data, restricting the spells to countries outside of Europe, North America, and Australia; spells that began in 1960 or later; and only the first leadership spell for those leaders with multiple spells. This left a total of 472 spells.

Each record includes the following variables:

YEARS	is the number of years in power, integer valued. Leaders in power less than one year have a value of 0.
LOST	0 = still in power in 1987; 1 = exit by constitutional means; 2 = death by natural causes; and 3 = nonconstitutional exit.
MANNER	specifies how the leader reached power: 0 = constitutional means; 1 = nonconstitutional means.
START	is the leader's year of entry into power.
MILITARY	is the background of the leader: 1 = military; 0 = civilian.
AGE	is the age of the leader, in years, at the time of entry into power.
CONFLICT	is the level of ethnic conflict: 1 = medium or high; 0 = low.
LOGINC	is the natural logarithm of GNP per capita (dollar equivalent) in 1973.
GROWTH	is the average annual rate of per capita GNP growth between 1965-1983.
POP	is population, in millions (year not indicated).
LAND	is land area, in thousands of square kilometers.
LITERACY	is literacy rate (year not indicated).
REGION	0 = Middle East; 1 = Africa; 2 = Asia; 3 = Latin America.

THE RANK DATA SET: PROMOTIONS IN RANK FOR BIOCHEMISTS

The RANK data, analyzed in Chapter 7, "Analysis of Tied or Discrete Data with the LOGISTIC, PROBIT, and GENMOD Procedures," contains records for 301 biochemists who at some point in their careers were assistant professors at graduate departments in the U.S. The event of interest is a promotion to associate professor. The data set includes the following variables:

DUR
is the number of years from the beginning of the job to promotion or censoring (ranges from 1 to 10, in integers).

EVENT
has a value of 1 if the person was promoted; otherwise, EVENT has a value of 0.

UNDGRAD
specifies the selectivity of undergraduate institution (ranges from 1 to 7).

PHDMED
has a value of 1 if the person received a Ph.D. from a medical school; otherwise, PHDMED has a value of 0.

PHDPREST
is a measure of the prestige of the Ph.D. institution (ranges from 0.92 to 4.62).

ART1-ART10
specify the cumulative number of articles published in each of the 10 years.

CIT1-CIT10
specify the number of citations in each of the 10 years to all previous articles.

PREST1
is a measure of the prestige of the first employing institution (ranges from 0.65 to 4.6).

PREST2
is the measure of the prestige of second employing institution (same as PREST1 for those who did not change employers). No one had more than two employers during the period of observation.

JOBTIME
is the year of employer change, measured from the start of the assistant professorship (coded as missing for those who did not change employers).

THE JOBMULT DATA SET: REPEATED JOB CHANGES

The JOBMULT data set contains simulated information for 395 jobs observed over a period of 20 years for 100 persons. The first 20 cases are displayed in Output 8.1, with analytic results in Output 8.2 through 8.7.

ID is a unique identification number for each *person*.

EVENT has a value of 1 if the job was terminated; EVENT has a value of 0 if censored.

ED is the number of years of schooling completed.

J is the number of the job in each person's sequence.

DURATION is the length of the job until termination or censoring.

PRESTIGE is a measure of the prestige of the job, ranging from 1 to 100.

LOGSAL is the natural logarithm of the annual salary at the beginning of the job.

276

REFERENCES

Aitkin, M.; Anderson, D. A.; Francis, B.; and Hinde, J. P. (1989), *Statistical Modelling in GLIM,* Oxford: Clarendon Press.

Allison, P. D. (1982), "Discrete-Time Methods for the Analysis of Event Histories," in *Sociological Methodology 1982*, ed. S. Leinhardt, San Francisco, CA: Jossey-Bass, 61-98.

Allison, P. D. (1984), *Event History Analysis*, Beverly Hills, CA: Sage Publications.

Allison, P. D. (1987), "Introducing a Disturbance Into Logit and Probit Regression Models," *Sociological Methods and Research,* 15, 355-374.

Allison, P. D. (1996), "Fixed Effects Partial Likelihood for Repeated Events." Forthcoming in *Sociological Methods and Research.*

Begg, C. B. and Gray, R. (1984), "Calculation of Polychotomous Logistic Regression Parameters Using Individualized Regressions," *Biometrika*, 71, 11-18.

Bienen, H. S. and van de Walle, N. (1991), *Of Time and Power*, Stanford, CA: Stanford University Press.

Breslow, N. E. (1974), "Covariance Analysis of Censored Survival Data," *Biometrics*, 30, 89-99.

Chamberlain, G. A. (1985), "Heterogeneity, Omitted Variable Bias, and Duration Dependence," in *Longitudinal Analysis of Labor Market Data*, eds. J. J. Heckman and B. Singer, New York: Cambridge University Press, 3-38.

Collett, D. (1994), *Modelling Survival Data in Medical Research*, London: Chapman & Hall.

Cox, D. R. (1972), "Regression Models and Life Tables" (with discussion), *Journal of the Royal Statistical Society*, B34, 187-220.

Cox, D. R. and Oakes, D. (1984), *Analysis of Survival Data*, London: Chapman & Hall.

Cox, D. R. and Snell, E. J. (1989), *The Analysis of Binary Data*, Second Edition, London: Chapman & Hall.

Crowley, J. and Hu, M. (1977), "Covariance Analysis of Heart Transplant Survival Data," *Journal of the American Statistical Association*, 72, 27-36.

DeLong, D. M.; Guirguis, G. H.; and So, Y. C. (1994), "Efficient Computation of Subset Selection Probabilities with Application to Cox Regression," *Biometrika*, 81, 607-611.

Efron, B. (1977), "The Efficiency of Cox's Likelihood Function for Censored Data," *Journal of the American Statistical Association*, 76, 312-319.

Elandt-Johnson, R. C. and Johnson, N. L. (1980), *Survival Models and Data Analysis*, New York: John Wiley & Sons, Inc.

Farewell, V. T. and Prentice, R. L. (1977), "A Study of Distributional Shape in Life Testing," *Technometrics*, 19, 69-75.

Farewell, V. T. and Prentice, R. L. (1980), "The Approximation of Partial Likelihood with Emphasis on Case-Control Studies," *Biometrika*, 67, 273-278.

Gail, M.H.; Lubin, J.H.; and Rubinstein, L.V. (1981), "Likelihood Calculations for Matched Case-Control Studies and Survival Studies with Tied Death Times," *Biometrika*, 68, 703-707.

Gail, M. H.; Wieand, S.; and Piantadosi, S. (1984), "Biased Estimates of Treatment Effect in Randomized Experiments with Nonlinear Regression and Omitted Covariates," *Biometrika*, 71, 431-444.

Garfield, E. (1990), "100 Most Cited Papers of All Time," *Current Contents*, February 12.

Gross, A. J. and Clark, V. A. (1975), *Survival Distributions: Reliability Applications in the Biomedical Sciences*, New York: John Wiley & Sons, Inc.

Hannan, M. T. and Freeman, J. (1984), "Structural Inertia and Organizational Change," *American Sociological Review*, 49, 149-164.

Harris, E. K. and Albert, A. (1991), *Survivorship Analysis for Clinical Studies*, New York: Marcel Dekker, Inc.

Heckman, J. J. and Honoré, B. E. (1989), "The Identifiability of the Competing Risks Model," *Biometrika*, 76, 325-330.

Heckman, J. J. and Singer, B. (1985), "Social Science Duration Analysis" in *Longitudinal Studies of Labor Market Data*, ed. J. J. Heckman and B. Singer, New York: Cambridge University Press, Chapter 2.

Hsieh, Frank Y. (1995), "A Cautionary Note on the Analysis of Extreme Data with Cox Regression," *The American Statistician*, 49, 226-228.

Institute for Scientific Information (1992), *Science Citation Index*, Philadelphia: Institute for Scientific Information.

Kalbfleisch, J.D. and Prentice, R.L. (1980), *The Statistical Analysis of Failure Time Data*. New York: John Wiley & Sons, Inc.

Kaplan, E. L. and Meier, P. (1958), "Nonparametric Estimation from Incomplete Observations," *Journal of the American Statistical Association*, 53, 457-481.

Klein, J.P. (1992), "Semiparametric Estimation of Random Effects Using the Cox Model Based on the EM Algorithm," *Biometrics*, 48, 795-806.

Lagakos, S. W. (1978), "A Covariate Model for Partially Censored Data Subject to Competing Causes of Failure," *Applied Statistics*, 27, 235-241.

Lawless, J. F. (1982), *Survival Models and Methods for Lifetime Data*, New York: John Wiley & Sons, Inc.

Lee, E. T. (1992), *Statistical Methods for Survival Data Analysis*, Second Edition, New York: John Wiley & Sons, Inc.

Long, J. S.; Allison, P. D.; and McGinnis, R. (1993), "Rank Advancement in Academic Careers: Sex Differences and the Effects of Productivity," *American Sociological Review*, 58, 703-722.

280

Magee, L. (1990), "R^2 Measures Based on Wald and Likelihood Ratio Joint Significance Tests," *The American Statistician*, 44, 250-253.

McGilchrist, C.A. (1993), "REML Estimation for Survival Models with Frailty," *Biometrics*, 49, 221-225.

Nakamura, T. (1992), "Proportional Hazards Model with Covariates Subject to Measurement Error," *Biometrics*, 48, 829-838.

Narendranathan, W. and Stewart, M. B. (1991), "Simple Methods for Testing for the Proportionality of Cause-Specific Hazards in Competing Risks Models," *Oxford Bulletin of Economics and Statistics*, 53, 331-340.

Petersen, T. (1991), "Time Aggregation Bias in Continuous-Time Hazard Rate Models," in *Sociological Methodology 1991*, ed. P. V. Marsden, Oxford: Basil Blackwell, 263-290.

Peto, R. (1972), Contribution to the discussion of paper by D. R. Cox." *Journal of the Royal Statistical Society*, B34, 205-207.

Peto, R.; Pike, M. C.; Armitage, P.; Breslow, N. E.; Cox, D. R.; Howard, S. V.; Mantel, N.; McPherson, K.; Peto, J.; and Smith, P. G. (1977), "Design and Analysis of Randomized Clinical Trials Requiring Prolonged Observation of Each Patient. II. Analysis and Examples," *British Journal of Cancer*, 35, 1-39.

Prentice, R. L. and Gloeckler, L A. (1978), "Regression Analysis of Grouped Survival Data with Application to Breast Cancer Data," *Biometrics*, 34, 57-67.

Proschan, F. (1963), "Theoretical Explanation of Observed Duration Dependence," *Technometrics*, 5, 375-383.

Prentice, R. L. and Pike, R. (1979), "Logistic Disease Incidence Models and Case-Control Studies," *Biometrika*, 66, 403-411.

Ramlau-Hansen, H. (1983), "Smoothing Counting Process Intensities by Means of Kernel Functions," *The Annals of Statistics*, 11, 453-466.

Rossi, P. H.; Berk, R. A.; and Lenihan, K. J. (1980), *Money, Work and Crime: Some Experimental Results*, New York: Academic Press, Inc.

Thompson, W. A. (1977), "On the Treatment of Grouped Observations in Life Studies," *Biometrics*, 33, 463-470.

Tuma, N. B. (1984), *Invoking RATE.* Unpublished program manual. Stanford, CA: Stanford University Press.

Wei, L. J.; Lin, D. Y.; and Weissfeld, L. (1989), "Regression Analysis of Multivariate Incomplete Failure Time Data by Modeling Marginal Distributions," *Journal of the American Statistical Association*, 84, 1065-1073.

282

Index

A

accelerated failure time (AFT) model
  competing risks analysis 200–206
  output from LIFEREG procedure, example
    64–66
  parametric regression models 62–66
actuarial method
  See life-table method
AFT method
  See accelerated failure time (AFT) model
age, as criterion for choosing time origin 22
ALPHA= option, LIFETEST procedure 35
alternative distributions for LIFEREG
    procedure 66
ARRAY statement 144

B

BASELINE statement, PHREG procedure
  combining with stratification 168
  effect of time-dependent covariates 173
  estimating survivor functions 165
  output, example 172–173
baseline survivor function 165, 171
BEST= option, PHREG procedure 184
bias, causes
  discarding censored data 4
  informative censoring 13–14
Bonferroni method 88
Breslow's approximation for tied data
  Breslow, Efron, and EXACT methods
    compared 133
  Breslow, Efron, and EXACT methods
    compared, example 133
  comparison of methods for handling
    136–137
  deterioration with large number of ties 132
  Efron approximation as alternative to 127,
    130

C

c.d.f.
  See cumulative distribution function
calendar time, as criterion for choosing time
    origin 23
categorical variables and CLASS statement
    78–79
CATMOD procedure
  DIRECT statement 194
  testing proportional hazards hypothesis for
    competing risks 193–194
CEIL function 106, 148
censored data 4–5

censoring 9–14
  See also interval censoring
  See also left censoring
  informative 13–14
  Kaplan-Meier estimation 30–31
  left versus right 9–10
  noninformative 13, 188, 208–209
  random 12–14
  right 10–14
  survival analysis for handling 4–5
changes
  determining when change occurs 2
  qualitative 2
  quantitative 3
chi-square statistic
  AFT model for competing risks analysis 201
  competing risks analysis 198–200
  log-rank test 39
  Wald test 85–88
  Wilcoxon test 39
CLASS statement, LIFEREG procedure 78–79,
    87
CLASS variables
  lack of hypothesis testing with LIFEREG
    procedure 86
  recidivism model, example 79
competing risks analysis 185–209
  accelerated failure time models 200–206
  alternative approach to multiple event types
    206–208
  alternative test for Weibull models 204–206
  constitutional exits, example PHREG
    procedure analysis 197
  covariate effects via Cox models 195–200
  Cox model for censoring deaths from natural
    causes 207–208
  deaths from natural causes, example PHREG
    procedure analysis 198
  estimates and tests without covariates
    190–194
  exits by any means, example PHREG
    procedure analysis 196
  exponential model for nonconstitutional exits,
    example 203
  global test for Cox model 198–200
  log-log survival plot for three types of leader
    exits, example 192
  log-log survivor functions for competing risk
    analysis 190–191
  logit model comparing constitutional and
    nonconstitutional exits 206
  nonconstitutional exits, example PHREG
    procedure analysis 197
  PHREG procedure analysis 195–198
  sample data for time in power example
    189–190

competing risks analysis *(continued)*
    separate estimation of models for each event
        type 187–188
    smoothed hazard plots 192–193
    smoothed hazard plots, example 193
    summary 208–209
    test of proportionality with CATMOD
        procedure, example 194
    type-specific hazards 186–188
    Weibull estimates for natural deaths,
        example 204
    Weibull model for nonconstitutional exits,
        example 202–203
conditional density 16
conditional probability theory 45
confidence intervals
    obtaining with LIFETEST procedure 34–36
    problems 36
confidence region 35
constant hazard function
    implying cumulative hazard function 167
    implying exponential distribution 19, 67
    interpreting 18
continuous probability distribution 16
continuous-time processes
    complementary log-log model for 216–219
CONVERGE= option, MODEL statement
    (LIFEREG procedure) 85
convergence
    See also nonconvergence
    forcing with MAXITER= and CONVERGE=
        options 85
    PHREG procedure's convergence criterion
        126
covariate-wise residuals 175–179
    graphs of Schoenfeld residuals versus time,
        example 178–179
covariates
    See also time-dependent covariates
    categorical variables and CLASS statement
        78–79
    lagged covariates 145–146
covariates, testing for effects
    competing risks analysis 195–200
    output from LIFETEST procedure, example
        52–54
    survival curves 52–55
COVB option, MODEL statement (LIFEREG
    procedure) 78
Cox, Sir David 111–112
Cox regression models 111–184
    ad-hoc estimates of time-dependent covariates
        147–150
    comparison of methods for handling tied
        data 136–137
    competing risks analysis 195–200
    competing risks analysis model for censoring
        207–208
    construction of partial likelihood with time-
        dependent covariates 140–142
    covariate-wise residuals 175–179
    covariates representing alternative time
        origins 142–143
    covariates that are undefined in some
        intervals 153–154

Cox models with nonproportional hazards
    154–155
    DISCRETE approximation method for tied
        data 134–136
    estimating survivor functions 165–173
    EXACT approximation method for tied data
        129–133
    individual residuals 173–175
    influence diagnostics 179–181
    interactions with time as time-dependent
        covariates 155–157
    left truncation and late entry into the risk set
        161–165
    nonproportionality via stratification 158–161
    partial likelihood 114–115
    partial likelihood, examples 115–122
    partial likelihood, mathematical and
        computational details 122–126
    proportional hazards model 113–114
    residuals 173–175
    summary 183–184
    testing linear hypotheses with TEST
        statement 181–183
    tied data 127–128
    time-dependent covariates 138
    time-dependent covariates with irregular
        intervals 150–152
    time-dependent covariates with regular
        intervals 143–147
    time-dependent covariates, heart transplant
        example 138–140
Cox-Snell residuals
    evaluating survival models 94
    obtaining in DATA step 96
    PHREG procedure 173
cumulated time-dependent variables 146–147
cumulative distribution function 14–15
cumulative hazard function 56, 166, 167

D

data
    See survival data
date variables 119
deviance residuals 173–175
    graph of deviance residuals, example 175
DFBETA statistic 179, 180
DIRECT statement, CATMOD procedure 194
DISCRETE approximation method for tied data
    134–136
    comparison of methods for handling
        136–137
    job duration results, example 136
discrete-time hazard 134
DIST= option, MODEL statement (LIFEREG
    procedure)
    EXPONENTIAL keyword 66
    GAMMA keyword 75
    LLOGISTIC keyword 73
    WEIBULL keyword 68
disturbance term
    lack of, in exponential model 67

DO loop
  time-dependent covariates measured at
      irregular intervals 150–152
double-exponential distribution 67
duration analysis 1

E

Efron approximation for tied data
  alternative to Breslow's approximation 127,
      130
  Breslow, Efron, and EXACT methods
      compared 133
  Breslow, Efron, and EXACT methods
      compared, example 133
  comparison of methods for handling
      136–137
  recidivism results, example 131–132
event history analysis 1
events
  See also competing risks analysis
  See also time origin
  See also time-dependent covariates
  definitions for survival analysis 1
  ranks of event times in partial likelihood
      estimates 115
  repeatable 3
EXACT approximation method for tied data
      129–133
  comparison of methods for handling 133,
      136–137
  comparison of methods for handling,
      example 133
  recidivism data results using Efron
      approximation, example 131–132
  recidivism data results using EXACT method,
      example 131
EXPAND procedure 149–150
exponential model 66–68
  applied to recidivism data, example 68
  competing risks analysis, example 203
  parametric regression 66–68
  piecewise exponential model 104–109

F

failure time analysis 1
forward inclusion procedure
  compared with univariate procedure 54
  testing for covariate effects, example 53
FREQ statement, LIFETEST procedure 49–50

G

gamma model 74–77
  goodness of fit 90
  interpretation of standard gamma model 76
  problems 74–75
  shape of hazard function 74
  standard model applied to recidivism data,
      example 76

survivor and hazard functions 77
  typical hazard functions, example 77
gamma model, generalized
  applied to recidivism data, example 75
  nesting of models 89
  restrictions implied by submodels 89
GENMOD procedure
  piecewise exponential model 108
  purpose 6
generalized R^2 247–249
Gompertz distribution
  typical hazard functions 20
  typical hazard functions, example 21
goodness-of-fit
  graphical methods for evaluating 91–97
  testing with likelihood-ratio statistic 88–90
gradient vector 84
graphics
  See plots
GRAPHICS option, LIFETEST procedure 34
Greenwood formula for standard error
      calculation 33, 45
Gumbel distributions 67

H

hazard function 15–19
  alternative distributions for LIFEREG
      procedure 66
  calculation for life-table method 46
  constant hazard function 167
  cumulative hazard function 56, 166, 167
  cumulative hazard function, example 168
  definition 15–16
  formulas 16
  gamma model 74, 77
  gamma model, example 77
  Gompertz distribution, example 21
  interpretation 17–19
  log-logistic model 72–73
  log-normal model 70–71
  log-survival and log-log survival plots 55–57
  log-survival and smoothed hazard plots
      55–59
  macro for graphing as function of time
      ˙103–104
  monotonic 90
  nonmonotonic 70, 90
  plot for grouped data, example 51
  plotting for life-table method 47–48
  proportional hazards models
  reciprocal of hazard 18
  relationship with p.d.f. and survivor
      function 16
  simple hazard models 19–21
  smoothed 170
  smoothed, example 170
  Weibull distribution, example 20
hazard models, proportional
  See proportional hazards models
hazards, type-specific
  See type-specific hazards
Hessian matrix 84

heterogeneity, unobserved
    See unobserved heterogeneity
hypothesis tests, LIFEREG procedure 85–88

I

ID statement, PHREG procedure 180
IF statement
    construction of partial likelihood with time-
        dependent covariates 141
    time-dependent covariates measured at
        irregular intervals 150–152
    time-dependent covariates, example 139
IML procedure 86
imputation of time-dependent covariates
    147–150
individual residuals 173–175
influence diagnostics 179–181
    statistics for myelomatosis data, example
        180
informative censoring 13–14
    lack of statistical test for 14
    sensitivity analysis 249–252
intensity function 16
    See also hazard function
intercept estimate, omitted in PHREG
    procedure output 117
interval censoring 99–100
    compared with left censoring 97
    definition 10
    managing with LIFEREG procedure 99–100
    recidivism data, example 100
intervals
    life-table method 43–44
INTERVALS= option, LIFETEST procedure
    43
ITPRINT option, MODEL statement (LIFEREF
    procedure) 84

K

Kaplan-Meier (KM) estimation 30–36
    censoring 30–31
    confidence intervals 34–36
    myelomatosis data estimates, example 32
    obtaining KM estimator using LIFETEST
        procedure 30
    output description 33
    plotting estimated survivor function 34
kernel smoothing 57
KM estimation
    See Kaplan-Meier (KM) estimation

L

lagged covariates 145–146
Lagrange multiplier test
    competing risks analysis 203
    LIFEREG procedure 85, 90
late entry into the risk set 161–165
left censoring 97–99
    See also censoring

AFT model for competing risks analysis 201
    compared with interval censoring 97
    definition 10
    left versus right censoring 9–10
    managing with LIFEREG procedure 97–99
    social science usage 10
    Weibull model, example 99
left truncation
    Cox regression models 161–165
life tables from grouped data 49–51
    hazard plot for grouped data, example 51
    output from LIFETEST procedure, example
        50–51
life-table method 41–48
    Conditional Probability of Failure statistic
        44–45
    Effective Sample Size statistic 44
    Failure statistic 45–46
    hazard function calculation 46
    Hazard statistic 46
    intervals 43–44
    Median Residual Lifetime statistic 45–46
    output from LIFETEST procedure, example
        43–44
    PDF statistic 46
    plots for survival and hazard estimates
        47–48
    plots for survival and hazard estimates,
        examples 47–48
    recidivism data, example 41–42
    standard errors of Survival probabilities 45
    Survival statistic 45
    total exposure time 47
LIFEHAZ macro
    plotting hazard as function of time 103–104
LIFEREG procedure
    accelerated failure time model 62–66
    AFT model for competing risks analysis 201
    alerting for convergence problems 85
    alternative distributions 66
    capabilities 62
    categorical variables and CLASS statement
        78–79
    CLASS statement 78–79, 87
    compared with PHREG procedure 61–62,
        109
    CONVERGE= option, MODEL statement 85
    COVB option, MODEL statement 78
    DIST=EXPONENTIAL option, MODEL
        statement 66
    DIST=GAMMA option, MODEL statement
        75
    DIST=LLOGISTIC option, MODEL
        statement 73
    DIST=WEIBULL option, MODEL
        statement 68
    estimating parametric regression models
        61–109
    exponential model 66–68
    fitting standard gamma model 75–76
    gamma model 74–77
    generating predictions and hazard functions
        101–104
    goodness-of-fit tests with likelihood-ratio
        statistic 88–90

graphical methods for evaluating model fit 91–97
hypothesis tests 85–88
ITPRINT option, MODEL statement 84
left censoring 10
left censoring and interval censoring 97–100
limitations 62, 109
log-logistic model 72–74
log-normal model 70–71
maximum likelihood estimation 79–81
maximum likelihood estimation, mathematics 81–84
maximum likelihood estimation, practical details 84–85
MAXITER= option, MODEL statement 85
MODEL statement 64, 97
ORDER option 78
OUTPUT statement 96, 101, 102
output, compared with PHREG procedure output 67, 116–118
OUTSURV option 93
piecewise exponential model 104–109
purpose 6
regression application example 64–66
residual plot for Weibull model 95
summary 109
Weibull model 68–70
LIFETEST procedure
ALPHA= option 35
compared with LIFEREG and PHREG procedures 52
default interval choice 43
FREQ statement 49–50
GRAPHICS option 34
INTERVALS= option 43
Kaplan-Meier estimation 30–36
Kaplan-Meier estimator as default 31
life tables from grouped data 49–51
life-table method 41–48
log survival and smoothed hazard plots 55–59
log-log survivor functions for competing risk analysis 190–191
methods for testing null hypothesis 29
obtaining KM estimator, example 31
OUTSURV= option 34
PLOTS= option 47, 55, 91
purpose 6
STRATA statement 36, 40–41, 54–55
summary 59–60
survival curve estimation and comparison 29–60
TEST statement 54–55, 59
testing for differences in survivor functions 36–41
testing for effects of covariates 52–55
WIDTH= option 43
likelihood displacement (LD) statistic 179
likelihood-ratio statistics
calculating with LIFEREG procedure 85–86, 88
competing risks analysis 199
goodness-of-fit tests 88–90
interpreting 90
LMAX statistic 179

log survivor function 56
log-log model
for continuous-time processes 216–219
log-log survival plots 55–57
myelomatosis data, example 57
recidivism data, example 92
specifying with PLOTS= option, LIFEREG procedure 55
log-log survivor functions, competing risk analysis 190–191
log-logistic model 72–74
applied to recidivism data, example 74
graphical method for evaluating 92–94
hazard function 72–73
plot for evaluating, example 93
survivor function 73
typical hazard functions, example 72
log-normal model 70–71
assumptions 63
choosing between log-normal and other models 88
compared with gamma distribution 75
fitting to recidivism data, example 65
graphical method for evaluating 92–94
plot for evaluating, example 94
residual plot for log-normal model, example 96
shape of hazard function 70–71
typical hazard function, example 71
log-rank test
compared with Wilcoxon test 38–39
computed from ungrouped data 41
formula 38
output from LIFETEST procedure, example 38
testing covariates for effects 52–54
log-survival plots 55–59
myelomatosis data, example 56
recidivism data, example 91
smoothed hazard plots 55–59
specifying with PLOTS= option, LIFEREG procedure 55
LOGISTIC procedure
purpose 6
LOGLOGS option, PHREG procedure 166
LOGSURV option, PHREG procedure 166
LOWER= option, PHREG procedure 172

M

macro programs
LIFEHAZ 103–104
PREDICT 102–103
SMOOTH 57–59, 192
Mantel-Haenszel test
See log-rank test
Martingale residuals 173
maximum likelihood estimation 79–81
capabilities 79–80
mathematics 81–84
practical details 84–85
principles 80–81
MAXITER= option, MODEL statement 85

methods for survival analysis
  criterion for choosing 233–256
ML estimation
  See maximum likelihood estimation
MMDDYY9. format 119
model fit
  See goodness-of-fit
MODEL statement, GENMOD procedure
  piecewise exponential model 108
MODEL statement, LIFEREG procedure
  CONVERGE= option 85
  COVB option 78
  DIST=EXPONENTIAL option 66
  DIST=GAMMA option 75
  DIST=LLOGISTIC option 73
  DIST=WEIBULL option 68
  ITPRINT option 84
  MAXITER= option 85
  syntax for censoring 97
  syntax, example 64
MODEL statement, PHREG procedure
  DISCRETE approximation method for tied
    data 134–136
  EXACT approximation method for tied data
    129–133
  removing individuals from and returning to
    risk set 165
  TIES=DISCRETE option 127
  TIES=EFRON option 131
  TIES=EXACT option 127, 208
monotonic hazard function 90
MULTIPASS option, PHREG procedure 142

N

nested models 88–89
Newton-Raphson algorithm
  Cox regression 125–126
  influence diagnostics 181
  maximum likelihood estimation 83–84
NOMEAN option, PHREG procedure 172
nonconvergence
  alerting by LIFEREG procedure 85
  gamma model 75
  maximum likelihood estimation 84
noninformative censoring
  competing risks analysis 188, 208–209
  lack of statistical test 14
nonmonotonic hazard function 70, 90
nonproportional hazard models
  Cox models with nonproportional hazards
    154–155
  nonproportionality via stratification 158–161

O

ORDER option, LIFEREG procedure 78
ordinary least squares (OLS) estimation 63
origin of time
  See time origin
OUT= option, PHREG procedure 166
OUTEST= option, OUTPUT statement 102

OUTPUT statement, LIFEREG procedure
  CONTROL= keyword 102
  defining output data set 96
  generating predictions 101–102
  OUTEST= option 102
  P= keyword 101
  QUANTILE= keyword 101
  STD= keyword 101
  XBETA= option 102
OUTPUT statement, PHREG procedure
  creating new data set 180
  diagnostic statistics 173
OUTSURV= option
  LIFEREG procedure 93
  LIFETEST procedure 34

P

p.d.f.
  See probability density function
parametric regression models, estimating
  61–109
  accelerated failure time model 62–66
  alternative distributions 66
  categorical variables and CLASS statement
    78–79
  exponential model 66–68
  gamma model 74–77
  generating predictions and hazard functions
    101–104
  goodness-of-fit tests with likelihood-ratio
    statistic 88–90
  graphical methods for evaluating model fit
    91–97
  hypothesis tests 85–88
  left censoring and interval censoring 97–100
  log-logistic model 72–74
  log-normal model 70–71
  maximum likelihood estimation 79–81
  maximum likelihood estimation, mathematics
    81–84
  maximum likelihood estimation, practical
    details 84–85
  piecewise exponential model 104–109
  Weibull model 68–70
partial likelihood 114–126
  basic principles 114–115
  construction of partial likelihood with time-
    dependent covariates 140–142
  examples 115–122
  Global Null Hypothesis statistics for breast
    cancer data, example 126
  heart transplant data, example 118–119
  left truncation and late entry into the risk set
    161–165
  mathematical and computational details
    122–126
  PHREG procedure output 116–118
  PHREG procedure output, example 116
  removing individuals from and returning to
    risk set 164–165

similarity with maximum likelihood
estimation 115
survival times for breast cancer patients,
example 123
percentiles, requesting with OUTPUT
statement 101
PHREG procedure
ad-hoc estimates of time-dependent covariates
147–150
advantages and disadvantages 183
approximation methods for tied data 127
BASELINE statement 165, 168, 172–173
BEST= option 184
compared with LIFEREG procedure 61–62,
109
comparison of methods for handling tied
data 136–137
competing risks analysis 195–198
construction of partial likelihood with time-
dependent covariates 140–142
convergence criterion 126
covariate-wise residuals 175–179
covariates representing alternative time
origins 142–143
covariates that are undefined in some
intervals 153–154
Cox model for censoring deaths from natural
causes 207–208
DISCRETE approximation method for tied
data 134–136
estimating Cox regression models 111–184
estimating survivor functions 165–173
EXACT approximation method for tied data
129–133
features 112
ID statement 180
individual residuals 173–175
influence diagnostics 179–181
interactions with time as time-dependent
covariates 155–157
left truncation and late entry into the risk set
161–165
limitations 112
LOGLOGS option 166
LOGSURV option 166
LOWER= option 172
MODEL statement 165
MULTIPASS option 142
NOMEAN option 172
nonproportionality via stratification 158–161
OUT= option 166
OUTPUT statement 173, 180
output, compared with LIFEREG procedure
output 67, 116–118
partial likelihood, examples 115–122
partial likelihood, mathematical and
computational details 122–126
purpose 6
SELECTION=SCORE option 184
summary 183–184
SURVIVAL= option 166
syntax 115
TEST statement for testing linear hypotheses
181–183
tied data 127–128

TIES=DISCRETE option, MODEL
statement 127
TIES=EFRON option, MODEL statement
131
TIES=EXACT option, MODEL statement
127, 208
time-dependent covariates with irregular
intervals 150–152
time-dependent covariates with regular
intervals 143–147
time-dependent covariates, heart transplant
example 138–140
UPPER= option 172
variable selection methods 183–184
piecewise exponential model 104–109
GENMOD procedure 108
increasing confidence 107
LIFEREG procedure 104–107
recidivism data, example 107
plots
cumulative hazard function for recidivism
data 167
cumulative hazard function for recidivism
data, example 168
evaluating log-logistic model, example 93
evaluating log-normal model, example 94
graph of deviance residuals, example 175
graphical methods for evaluating model fit
91–97
Kaplan-Meier (KM) estimation, example 34
life tables from grouped data, example
50–51
life-table method, examples 47–48
log survival and smoothed hazard plots
55–59
log-log survival plot for leader exits,
example 192
log-log survivor plot for recidivism data,
example 92
log-log survivor plots for recidivism data,
example 169
log-survival and log-log survival plots 55–57
log-survivor plot for recidivism data,
example 91
residual plot for log-normal model,
example 96
residual plot for Weibull model, example 95
PLOTS= option, LIFETEST procedure
obtaining plots of survival and hazard
estimates 47
specifying log-survival and log-log survival
plots 55, 91
PREDICT macro
predicting survival probability for specified
time 102–103
predicted survival times
generating 101–104
predicted median survival times for
recidivism data, example 101–102
recidivism data, example 103
probability density function 15
definition 15
formulas for expressing hazard function 16
relationship with hazard function and
survivor function 16

probability distribution, continuous 16
PROBIT procedure
  alternative test for Weibull models in
    competing risks analysis 205
  purpose 6
product-limit estimator
  See Kaplan-Meier (KM) estimation
proportional hazards models
  See also nonproportional hazard models
  competing risks analysis 193–194
  Cox regression 113–114
  equation for defining 39
  exponential, Gompertz, and Weibull models
    as members 21
  parallel hazard functions, example 114
proportional odds models
  Cox regression model 134
  log-logistic model 73
prospective versus retrospective survival data
  3–4

Q

qualitative changes 2
quantitative changes 3

R

R^2
  generalized 247–249
random censoring 12–14
  example 12
  informative censoring 13–14
  noninformative censoring 13
  precautions for studies with random
    censoring 14
ranks of event times in partial likelihood
  estimates 115
rate
  See hazard function
REG procedure 63
reliability analysis 1
repeated events 236–247
residual plots
  log-normal model, example 96
  Weibull model, example 95
residuals 173–179
  covariate-wise residuals 175–179
  deviance residuals 173–175
  graph of deviance residuals, example 175
  graphs of Schoenfeld residuals versus time,
    example 178–179
  individual residuals 173–175
  survival models 94–96
retrospective versus prospective survival data
  3–4
right censoring 10–14
  left versus right censoring 9–10
  random censoring 12–14
  singly Type I censored data 11–12
  Type II censoring 12
risk set
  definition 124

left truncation and late entry into risk set
  161–165
removing and returning individuals 164–165

S

SAS/STAT software
  capabilities for survival analysis 1–2
  procedures for survival analysis 6
Schoenfeld residuals 175–179
  graphs of Schoenfeld residuals versus time,
    example 178–179
  weighted 175
score residuals 175
score statistics
  competing risks analysis 199
  LIFEREG procedure 85
SELECTION=SCORE option, PHREG
  procedure 184
semiparametric method of Cox 112
sensitivity analysis
  for informative censoring 249–252
singly Type I censored data 11–12
SMOOTH macro 192
  calculating and graphing kernel estimates of
    hazard function 57–59
smoothed hazard plots
  competing risks analysis 192–193
  log survival and smoothed hazard plots
    57–59
standard error of medians, requesting with
  OUTPUT statement 101
standard error of Survival probabilities
  Kaplan-Meier (KM) method 33
  life-table method 45
STRATA statement, LIFETEST procedure
  defining groups 40–41
  defining groups by intervals for numeric
    variables 41
  relationship with TEST statement 54–55
  testing for differences 36
stratification
  advantages and disadvantages 160
  AFT model for competing risks analysis 201
  combining with BASELINE statement 168
  complications 160
  definition 158
  myelomatosis data with stratified Cox
    regression, example 159
  nonproportionality via stratification 158–161
survival analysis 1–7
  censoring 9–14
  computer performance notes
  definition 1
  describing probability distributions 14–17
  interpretation of hazard function 17–19
  knowledge requirements 6–7
  origin of time 22–25
  purpose and use 1–2
  reasons for using 4–5
  SAS/STAT procedures 5–6
  simple hazard models 19–21
survival analysis method, choosing 253–256
  SAS/STAT procedures overview 5–6

survival curve estimation and comparison
29–60
Kaplan-Meier method 30–36
life tables from grouped data 49–51
life-table method 41–48
log survival and smoothed hazard plots
55–59
testing for covariate effects 52–55
testing for differences in survivor functions
36–41
survival data
characteristics 2–4
prospective versus retrospective 3–4
structure of data 25–27
survival distributions 14–17
cumulative distribution function 14–15
differences across groups, example 39–40
hazard function 15–17
probability density function 15
SURVIVAL= option, PHREG procedure 166
survival probabilities
generating with PREDICT macro 102–103
survivor functions 36–41, 165–173
baseline 165, 171
calculation for life-table method 45
comparing for different subgroups 15
Cox regression with nonproportional effect,
example 171
definition 14–15
differences among three or more groups
40–41
differences between two groups, example
39–40
estimates for recidivism data at sample
means, example 166–167
estimating 165–173
formulas 16
gamma model 77
log-log survival plot for leader exits,
example 192
log-log survivor functions for competing risk
analysis 190–191
log-log survivor plots for recidivism data
168
log-log survivor plots for recidivism data,
example 169
log-logistic model 73
plotting for life-table method 47–48
portion of survivor function estimate for
recidivism data, example 172–173
relationship with p.d.f. and hazard function
16
survival curves for two treatment groups,
example 37
testing for differences 36–41
type-specific 187
SYMBOL1 statement, suppressing symbols in
graph 34

T

TEST statement, LIFETEST procedure
limitations 59
relationship with STRATA statement 54–55

TEST statement, PHREG procedure
results for recidivism data, example 183
testing linear hypotheses 181–183
tied data analysis, LOGISTIC, PROBIT and
GENMOD procedure 211–231
logit model for discrete time 212–216
tied data analysis, PHREG procedure 127–137
approximation methods 127
comparison of methods for handling
136–137
DISCRETE approximation method 134–136
EXACT approximation method 129–133
recidivism data, example 128
TIES=DISCRETE option, MODEL statement
127
TIES=EFRON option, MODEL statement 131
TIES=EXACT option, MODEL statement 127,
208
time origin 22–25
choice of origin 22
covariates representing alternative time
origins 142–143
criteria for choosing 22–25
time-dependent covariates 138–157
ad-hoc estimates 147–150
construction of partial likelihood 140–142
Cox models with nonproportional hazards
154–155
data requirements 3
definition 138
dichotomizing and trichotomizing 157
heart transplant example 138–140
including product of two variables 155–157
interactions with time 155–157
measured at irregular intervals 150–152
measured at regular intervals 143–147
representing alternative time origins
142–143
survival analysis for handling 4–5
transition analysis 1
Type I censored data 11–12
Type II censoring 12
type-specific hazards 186–188
formulating models for covariate
dependence 187
noninformative censoring 188
separate estimation of models for each event
type 187–188

U

univariate analysis
compared with forward inclusion
procedure 54
testing for covariate effects, example 53
unobserved heterogeneity 67, 233–237
UPPER= option, PHREG procedure 172

W

Wald test
competing risks analysis 199

Wald test *(continued)*
   LIFEREG procedure 85–88
   piecewise exponential model 107
Weibull distribution
   typical hazard functions 20
   typical hazard functions, example 20
Weibull model 68–70
   applied to recidivism data, example 70
   compared with gamma distribution 75, 77
   competing risks analysis 204
   competing risks analysis, example 202–203
   left censoring, example 99
   likelihood-ratio statistic 86
   parametric regression 68–70
   residual plot for Weibull model, example 95
WHERE statement 145
WIDTH= option, LIFETEST procedure 43
Wilcoxon test
   compared with log-rank test 38–39
   computed from ungrouped data 41
   output from LIFETEST procedure, example
     38
WLW macro 264–267

X

XBETA= option, OUTPUT statement 102

B O O K S
by
USERS

SAS Institute's
Author Service ®

Call your local SAS® office to order these other books and tapes available through the Books by Users℠ program:

Applied Multivariate Statistics with SAS® Software
by **Ravindra Khattree**
and **Dayanand N. Naik** ....Order #A55234

*Applied Statistics and the SAS®
Programming Language, Third Edition*
by **Ronald P. Cody**
and **Jeffrey K. Smith** ....Order #A56191

*Beyond the Obvious with SAS® Screen
Control Language*
by **Don Stanley**...................................Order #A55073

The Cartoon Guide to Statistics
by **Larry Gonick**
and **Woollcott Smith** ....Order #A55153

Categorical Data Analysis Using the SAS® System
by **Maura E. Stokes, Charles E. Davis,**
and **Gary G. Koch** ....Order #A55320

Essential Client/Server Survival Guide
by **Robert Orfali, Dan Harkey,**
and **Jeri Edwards** ....Order #A55305

The How-To Book for SAS/GRAPH® Software
by **Thomas Miron** ....Order #A55203

Learning SAS® in the Computer Lab
by **Rebecca J. Elliott** ....Order #A55273

The Little SAS® Book: A Primer
by **Lora D. Delwiche**
and **Susan J. Slaughter** ....Order #A55200

Mastering the SAS® System, Second Edition
by **Jay A. Jaffe** ....Order #A55123

*Professional SAS® Programmer's Pocket
Reference*
by **Rick Aster**......................................Order #A56198

Professional SAS® Programming Secrets
by **Rick Aster**
and **Rhena Seidman** ....Order #A56192

Professional SAS® User Interfaces
by **Rick Aster**......................................Order #A56197

Quick Results with SAS/GRAPH® Software
by **Arthur L. Carpenter**
and **Charles E. Shipp**..........................Order #A55127

*Reporting from the Field: SAS® Software
Experts Present Real-World Report-Writing
Applications* ....Order #A55135

*SAS® Applications Programming:
A Gentle Introduction*
by **Frank C. Di Iorio** ....Order #A56193

SAS® Foundations: From Installation to Operation
by **Rick Aster** ....Order #A55093

SAS® Programming by Example
by **Ron Cody**
and **Ray Pass** ....Order #A55126

*SAS® Programming for Researchers and
Social Scientists*
by **Paul E. Spector** ....Order #A56199

*SAS® Software Roadmaps: Your Guide to
Discovering the SAS® System*
by **Laurie Burch**
and **SherriJoyce King**..........................Order #A56195

SAS® Software Solutions
by **Thomas Miron** ....Order #A56196

SAS® System for Elementary Statistical Analysis
by **Sandra D. Schlotzhauer**
and **Ramon C. Littell** ....Order #A5619

SAS® System for Forecasting Time Series,
1986 Edition
by **John C. Brocklebank**
and **David A. Dickey** ....Order #A5612

SAS® System for Linear Models,
Third Edition
by **Ramon C. Littell, Rudolf J. Freund,**
and **Philip C. Spector**..Order #A56140

SAS® System for Regression,
Second Edition
by **Rudolf J. Freund**
and **Ramon C. Littell** ....Order #A56141

SAS® System for Statistical Graphics,
First Edition
by **Michael Friendly** ....Order #A56143

Statistical Quality Control Using the SAS® System
by **Dennis W. King** ....Order #A55232

A Step-by-Step Approach to Using the SAS®
System for Factor Analysis and Structural
Equation Modeling
by **Larry Hatcher** ....Order #A55129

A Step-by-Step Approach to Using the SAS®
System for Univariate and Multivariate Statistics
by **Larry Hatcher**
and **Edward Stepanski** ....Order #A55072

Table-Driven Strategies for Rapid SAS®
Applications Development
by **Tanya Kolosova**
and **Samuel Berestizhevsky** ....Order #A55198

Tuning SAS® Applications in the MVS Environment
by **Michael A. Raithel**..Order #A55231

Working with the SAS® System
by **Erik W. Tilanus**..Order #A55190

Audio Tapes

100 Essential SAS® Software Concepts (set of two)
by **Rick Aster** ....Order #A55309

A Look At SAS® Files (set of two)
by **Rick Aster** ....Order #A55207